W9-BTJ-812

GREEK HISTORICAL WRITING

GREEK HISTORICAL WRITING

A Historiographical Essay
Based on Xenophon's *Hellenica*

πάντων δὲ νεωτάτη σχεδόν ἐστι ἡ περὶ
τοῦ συγγράφειν τὰς ἱστορίας ἐπιμέλεια
—Josephus

by

W. P. Henry

ARGONAUT INC., PUBLISHERS
CHICAGO MCMLXVII

WINGATE COLLEGE LIBRARY
WINGATE, N. C.

LIBRARY OF CONGRESS CATALOGUE CARD NO. 65-26125

COPYRIGHT © 1966 ARGONAUT INC., PUBLISHERS
737 NORTH MICHIGAN AVENUE
CHICAGO, ILLINOIS 60611

MANUFACTURED IN THE UNITED STATES OF AMERICA

Hic Libellus

BENEDICTO SENECAE EINARSON

Magistro Longe Eruditissimo, Et Rerum
Copia Sententiarumque Varietate Praediviti,
At Praecipue
Viro Summae Gravitatis Comitate Conditae,
Amanter Dicatus Est

35273

CONTENTS

PREFACE

Our failure to understand ancient history is due mostly to our erroneous interpretation of ancient histories. Since we do not know what happened in the past but only what the historians say happened, our understanding of history is completely at the mercy of our evaluation of the records those historians have left us. The most important aspect of the study of history is therefore historiography. To set forth the proper approach to history within the compass of a limited essay, however, would be a formidable, if not impossible, undertaking, but a worthy preliminary objective to this end would be to refute the arguments of conventional interpretation and thus undermine confidence in the approach which they support.

Now, there are only three classical Greek histories from which to choose in selecting a subject for such an examination. To the study of one of these however, Xenophon's *Hellenica*, perhaps the most distinguished of modern authorities on ancient history particularly warned me against expecting to make any contribution, since a recent series of brilliant articles by leading scholars, he said, had all but laid the problems of the composition of this work to rest. It would be advisable, therefore, to select this one as the basis for our examination, since of the three it would appear to represent most successfully our modern approach to the historical writing of ancient Greece.

PART I

HELLENICA i-ii

INTRODUCTION

> First we should mention the faults of those
> who write history the wrong way.
> —Lucian (*How to Write History*, 6)

That the first two books of Xenophon's *Hellenica* compose a very insufficient history of the final period of the Peloponnesian War is a circumstance that has often been observed and as often deplored. The deficiencies in these parts are intolerable, the inclusions frequently irrelevant and trifling; the organization is negligent and the treatment rough and inconsistent throughout. Commentators, accordingly, have shown no hesitation in expressing their displeasure with such an inadequate account of the events of these critical years and in reproving the author who, feeling called to recount them, could yet be satisfied with so ineffectual a return on his efforts. Consequently, the history of the problem has been a long one, in the course of which, although almost every conceivable explanation has been advanced, agreement has been reached only on one point: a general dissatisfaction which writers never seem tired of expressing. Grosser,[1] who has taken as much interest in the problem as anyone else, speaks of the "pretty contemptible irregularity" he finds in this early section. Busolt[2] observes a "spotty and disproportionate treatment" of material that Campe[3] says consists only in "disconnected fragments, in unmotivated, defective notices" written in "a raw and awkward manner." Wilhelm Meyer,[4] although he is not convinced of Xenophon's full responsibility for the

---

[1] Richard Grosser, *Zur Charakteristik der Epitome von Xenophon's Hellenika* (Barmen, 1873), p. 6.

[2] Georg Busolt, *Griechische Geschichte* (2d ed.; Gotha, 1904), III, Part II, 696.

[3] J. Ch. F. Campe, "Die Kämpfe der Athener und der Peloponnesier im Hellespont (411-409)," *Jahrbücher für Classische Philologie* (hereafter cited as *JCP*), CV (1872), 709.

[4] Wilhelm Meyer, *De Xenophontis Hellenicorum auctoris in rebus scribendis fide et usu* (Halle, 1867), p. 21.

1

condition in which the *Hellenica* has come down to us, nevertheless reproves the "ridiculous brevity" of these early books. Vorrenhagen[5] adds that they were written in a "rather dry, enervated" style, and MacLaren[6] might well be elaborating that remark: "By and large, the first part of the *Hellenica* is written on a dead level of unrelieved dullness and monotony." In fact, De Sanctis[7] finds it difficult to conceive that Xenophon could have written the remaining books with the same intention as he did this "spare and hasty" collection of facts.

The deficiencies which have been lamented so eloquently above become all the more inexplicable when we consider the relation of the author to the times of which he became the historian. Whatever we may think about the date of composition and the author's purpose, there remains a fact that stands as an imposing obstacle in our search for a rational explanation for such unsatisfactory work. Xenophon in his youth, the impressionable time of one's life, was the contemporary[8] of one of the most stirring periods of Greek history, a time memorable for splendid victories, ferocious demagogues, and masterful personalities; a day of overwhelming defeats, of incalculable exuberation and confidence, and of savage and tyrannous oppression. Yet for all that we find ourselves before the appearance of indifference and inattention in the greater part of a narrative all too seldom relieved by an episode of major significance, wherein the author's interest awakens and the perfunctory chronicle quickens into a history. Otherwise there is seldom anything to indicate a lively concern on the author's part except the occasional incident that can be used to exemplify the heavy moral of self-reliance. And these shortcomings are even more disturbing when we realize that Xenophon has shown us his capabilities as a

---

[5] Elisabeth Vorrenhagen, *De orationibus quae sunt in Xenophontis Hellenics* (Elberfeld, 1926), p. 3.

[6] Malcolm MacLaren, "On the Composition of Xenophon's *Hellenica*," *American Journal of Philology* (hereafter cited as *AJP*), LV (1934), 123.

[7] Gaetano De Sanctis, Review of *Xénophon: Helléniques*, I, by J. Hatzfeld, *Rivista di Filologia* (hereafter cited as *RF*), n.s. XVI (1938), 71.

[8] By almost any calculation Xenophon would have been of age by 411.

historian in the remaining portion of the *Hellenica,* where he reveals himself, if not as a first-rate historian, as a writer who is able to comprehend the events of an age in something of their relation to one another and to set them forth with recognizable proportion and organization. This it is, in fact, which constitutes the "problem" of these first two books; for if he had given us no reason to believe that the peculiarities of this section were owing to anything but his own inability, we might rest satisfied that we had pursued the matter as far as the idiosyncrasies of the author's personality, and beyond that we could not go. The contrast between this section and the rest of the *Hellenica,* however, compels us to search for some explanation for this difference.

First we must describe the difference. Our knowledge of the period in general alone would be enough to suggest that more of importance happened during the years in question than we meet with in Xenophon. In addition, however, there are in our possession other accounts of the period, and these often differ markedly from that of Xenophon's in fact and content. Foremost among them is Diodorus Siculus, judging by whose history we find that Xenophon is guilty of some remarkable omissions. For example, we find no mention of the disastrous shipwreck off Mt. Athos, where Diodorus (xiii. 41. 1-3), following Ephorus, relates that an entire squadron of fifty ships, proceeding from Euboea to the scene of the major naval activities in the Hellespont, was lost together with all the crews except twelve survivors. Of this we learn nothing from Xenophon, though it would appear to fall within his province; and if it does, it is surprising that a catastrophe of this magnitude should be omitted. Again, Xenophon else-where[9] gives great attention to the matter of diplomatic nego-tiations, as did his predecessor Thucydides. It is to Diodorus (xiii. 52-53), however, that we must turn to learn of the mis-sion led by Endius which the Spartans dispatched to Athens after the Battle of Cyzicus to treat for peace and an end to the war, while Xenophon, although dwelling on the despera-

---

[9] In the first two books alone: i. 3. 8-13, 4. 1-7, ii. 2. 12-13, 17-23.

tion of the Peloponnesians after the battle,[10] passes over the Spartan offer in silence. Moreover, Xenophon makes no mention of Alcibiades' raid on the territory of Cyme, in Lydia, which Diodorus, who narrates those operations, informs us was one of the major reasons for Alcibiades' loss of favor at Athens (xiii. 73-74. 1). Xenophon even discusses Alcibiades' dismissal and touches on the causes, but he makes no reference to the Cymeans' complaint about the violation of their territory (i. 5. 16-17). Finally, we might note the section[11] Diodorus devotes to the campaign of Pausanias against the Eleians in 402, which seems to have no counterpart in the *Hellenica*.

Other accounts independent of Diodorus also tend to confirm our suspicion that an appreciable number of significant happenings during the closing years of the century has been ignored in the *Hellenica*. The orator Lysias is another of those who supply us with information which we could expect to appear in Xenophon, but which is wanting there. It is puzzling, for example, that the decree of the Lacedaemonians prohibiting sanctuary in states of the Peloponnesian alliance to exiles from the oppression of the Thirty in Athens should not find mention in Xenophon;[12] yet it does not. Lysias[13] refers to it, though, and we have no reason to challenge what he says. Another surprising omission is that of the recovery of Nisea by the Megarians and the ensuing Battle of Mount Cerata, which must have taken place in 409. We have a remarkable testimony of these events in the new (Florentine) fragment of the *Hellenica Oxyrhynchia*,[14] which, in the opinion of most, is the source of the account of Diodorus (xiii. 65. 1-2) for these operations.

Other examples could, of course, be added to those men-

---

[10] Xenophon quotes the message sent by the forces in the Hellespont (i. 1. 23). It was undoubtedly the receipt of this alarming dispatch that occasioned the proposals offered by Endius.

[11] xiv. 17. 4-12, 34. 1. Cf. *Hell.* iii. 2. 23-31?

[12] Cf. ii. 4. 2.

[13] xii (Against Eratosthenes). 95, 97; cf. Diodorus xiv. 6.

[14] Fragment A, col. 1. See Marcello Gigante, *Le Elleniche di Ossirinco* (Rome, 1949), pp. 1x-1xii.

tioned above, but enough have been adduced to establish our
first point: that there is a disturbing number of important
events which go altogether unrecognized in the opening portion of our history. Turning to those which Xenophon has
seen fit to include, we are again surprised at the irregularities
which everywhere meet the eye. Transitions between events
are frequently awkward and loose; reference is notoriously
poor, with characters appearing suddenly or vanishing without reason. Even when operations are described in detail the
picture is too often curiously incoherent and difficult to
reconstruct and follow exactly. Examples which could be
produced to illustrate this "frequent sketchiness and incompleteness in exposition and form"[15] offer themselves abun-
dantly from all sides and can be had by turning to the account
of almost any incident. In the narrative of the exploits of
Callicratidas and Conon (i. 6. 15-18), for example, we are
required to conceive a situation wherein Callicratidas could
espy Conon departing to Samos from somewhere around
Lesbos—we are not really told where—and wherein Callicratidas would be between Conon and that destination. Yet
Conon must not be able to keep ahead of Callicratidas who,
it turns out, is pursuing him, although Conon has the speedier
fleet; in fact, he has the best rowers of the best navy of his
day: Xenophon stresses this point. Now attempts have been
made, and some not unconvincingly, to divine Xenophon's
meaning and form a plausible reconstruction of the operations
he is trying to describe, but in every case it has been found
necessary to supply some fact or element which is essential
to the understanding but which Xenophon has failed to
include.

This same carelessness of internal consistency is also seen
in the transitions between episodes, so that we often have
difficulty in determining connections. In i. 1. 31, for example,
we learn that the successors of the Syracusan generals arrive
at Miletus, where they assume command of the fleet. Yet the

---

[15] Ludwig Breitenbach, *Xenophon's Hellenika*, I (2d ed. rev.; Berlin,
1884), 10.

last time the fleet was mentioned it was still abuilding at Antandrus, and we are thus left to assume that in the meanwhile, its construction completed, it had proceeded to Miletus. As Xenophon says that the former generals remained until their successors arrived, and since the Syracusan fleet and its leaders are kept in full view until that arrival, the transfer to Miletus must have occurred during the period covered by the continuous narrative of secs. 29-31; yet not a word about it is said.

Again, in i. 6. 29 we are apprised of the presence of Erasinides as one of the generals in command of the Athenian fleet at the Battle of the Arginusae. This is natural enough in itself; he had been chosen as one of the ten new generals who were elected (i. 5. 16) after the dismissal of Alcibiades following the Battle of Notium. We have learned in the meantime (i. 6. 16), however, that Erasinides had accompanied Conon in the flight from Callicratidas which we have discussed above, and that these commanders had been blockaded together in Mytilene. One may, to be sure, point to sec. 26, where we are told that the force of the blockaders was reduced, and suggest that a thinner line might have permitted Erasinides' escape, which would after all require but a single vessel. In that case, however, he would have had to outstrip Callicratidas (it was his departure that weakened the blockade), who came directly from Mytilene and arrived off the Arginusae the evening before the battle. Since such a feat would have been impossible, we are compelled to think that Erasinides escaped during the full blockade; after all, blockades, even tight ones, have been "run" before. Turning to our history, however, we learn of only one vessel that managed to pass the blockade, and that too with the greatest difficulty (i. 6. 19-22). Even a rescue expedition sent from Samos was unable to get through. There remains, then, only one answer and it is a surprising conclusion. The one vessel which found its way through the blockade apparently had the general Erasinides aboard. And, although Xenophon describes this exciting exploit with careful attention, he is content to say nothing of the presence of the important official who commanded the fleeing ship and who brought the desperate tidings to Athens. Xenophon leaves him in Mytilene and has him simply reappear in the line off the Arginusae with nothing said of his actions in between, even though he seems to be describing those very actions.

Further examination serves only to disclose numerous such discrepancies and vexing omissions. Why does Xenophon not inform us of the Athenian acquisition of Chalcedon? He is clearly required to do so as he has told us of the disposition the Athenians made of the city in i. 3. 8, where they broke off their siege of the place, and of the capitulation of its Athenian garrison to Lysander in ii. 2. 1. At some time in between, then, the Athenians came into possession of the city, though Xenophon seems in no way anxious to tell us how or when. Again, in ii. 4. 19 we read of a Board of Ten which had charge of the Piraeus; it is referred to as though it were familiar to the reader, though no mention of it has been made before. "The embassy" returning from the Persian captial makes a sudden appearance in i. 4. 2 without our having heard of any such embassy before. Nor has anyone been able to establish what connection the statement that the Lacedaemonians took Delphinium and Eion has with the context in which it is introduced in i. 5. 15. It seems to be an extraneous notice inserted at this point capriciously and bearing no formal relation to the story being told.

Perhaps Xenophon's disjointed style of narration proves most annoying of all when he falls into it in the midst of a scene he is following closely in which each element succeeds directly on what went before and in turn explains what is to come. This is what happens, for example, in the course of the siege of Byzantium, described in i. 3. 14-22. After the Athenians had effected their entrance, the commanders of the Peloponnesian garrison, "who knew nothing of what was going on," hurried to the market place with all their troops. It immediately occurs to one to ask why the garrison, if they knew nothing of the introduction of the Athenians, hurried to the rescue. Yet perhaps we should be content, seeing that Xenophon has at least taken the defenders' presence into account, even though their presence proved useless; for in the case of the Battle of Cyzicus we are wanting even that. The encampment at Cyzicus of the satrap Pharnabazus and his army, which had just proved of advantage to the Peloponnesians during the Battle of Abydos, is specifically mentioned by Xenophon in i. 1. 12-14 as one of the factors which deterred Alcibiades from attacking the city immediately upon his arrival. When he does attack the following day, however, a battle ensues which is of the same character as that of Abydos, with ships drawn up ashore and fighting along the strand—yet we hear not one word this time of Pharnabazus and his army. We learn that by the day after the battle he had withdrawn along with the defeated Peloponnesians and had left the city to Alcibiades, but we search in vain to discover why the satrap was so obliging to Athenian interests the previous day during the annihilation of his friends.

So it is that we observe the uncertain movement of Xenophon's style. Never altogether hurried, he obliges us with a certain accommodation of detail so that we incline to expect the promised consistency, only to be presently unsettled from our hopes as we come on some unsightly omission or are suddenly acquainted with an extraneous particular pulled in whole from some strange setting with the loose ends of its former attachment still about it. Nor upon turning away from the confusion of the single episodes to consider the organization of the whole do we find relief from our difficulties, for there again we meet with the same willful exposition selecting now only this and now that incident to distinguish with suitable fullness. It is this characteristic, in fact, together with the one we have previously observed, Xenophon's fitful habit of omitting events of considerable moment, that imparts the distinctive "ununiformity" *(Ungleichmässigkeit)* so often observed in this portion of the *Hellenica*. The term is Breitenbach's[16] but there is a great variety of synonyms to choose from, as each student of Xenophon, not content with that used by another, has sought out some expression of his own. "Dis-

---

[16] I, 10.

proportion,"[17] "unevenness,"[18] "curious inequalities of treatment"[19] are still other ways of putting it. As a test of the accuracy of these observations we might consider the case of Xenophon's account of the Battle of Abydos (i. 1. 2-7). It was a momentous encounter involving one hundred and fifty-one triremes and over thirty thousand men.[20] It was an important battle; the victory lay with the Athenians who weakened the fleet of their enemy sufficiently to enable Alcibiades to defeat them later at Cyzicus, where the entire remaining portion of the Peloponnesian navy was lost. The Battle of Abydos, then, was a major factor in assuring to Athens the supremacy of the Hellespont and in prolonging the war for another five years. The little scene (i. 1. 27-31) depicting Hermocrates' farewell to his men is not important. He leaves the scene of the war and never returns.[21] Much of the talk is of Hermocrates' plans to return to Syracuse, and yet history[22] tells us that all these preparations came to nothing as he died in the attempt. Thus the passage in question is given over to a person and an incident which have no further relation to the war. Yet for all that there is more space by half[23] allotted to this pleasant adieu than to the great engagement referred to above. Nor is that all, for the account of the battle is somewhat incoherent and offers problems that vex us. Was it by chance that Alcibiades made his sudden entrance on the scene or was he coming intentionally to the rescue? In view of the considerable amount of activity which had already taken place, how is it possible for the battle which followed to have begun "early" that same day? Furthermore we would simply like to know about the battle, how it went, the

[17] Bernard Büchsenschütz, *Xenophons Griechische Geschichte* (7th ed.; Leipzig, 1908), I. 11.

[18] Busolt, III, Part II, 696.

[19] E. C. Marchant and G. E. Underhill, *Xenophon: Hellenica* (Oxford, 1906), p. xi.

[20] Assuming a complement of approximately two hundred men for each trireme. See A. W. Gomme, *A Historical Commentary on Thucydides* (Oxford, 1945), I, 19.

[21] With the exception of i. 3. 13.

[22] Diodorus xiii. 75. 8.

[23] There are 22 (Oxford) lines given to Abydos, 36 to Hermocrates.

moments of excitement and danger. But these matters are denied us, and their space is given over instead to the popularity of Hermocrates. Or again, we might turn to the account —"notice" would be a better word—of Agis' demonstration beneath the walls of Athens and Thrasyllus' sally which turned him back (i. 1. 33-34). It must have been a dramatic moment; all indications are at hand. The words, "Thrasyllus led forth the Athenians and all others who were in the city," bespeak a desperation which sought every available means to thwart the danger. Xenophon returns to a comparable incident at i. 6. 24-25, when in like distress the Athenians rushed all in the city aboard the ships for the rescue of Conon at Mytilene. There the temper of the occasion is expressed with commensurate feeling; with Agis and Thrasyllus, however, all the makings of a similar story are forgone, and the affair is passed over in a few lines. And one is increasingly troubled at this indifference when he notices how space better spent on such matters is devoted to ineffectual doings about which we would as soon know less: compare the protracted narrative in i. 3. 8-13, 4. 1-7, about some negotiation and an embassy, which could have been gotten off in a few lines or omitted altogether. And so on.

Before turning away finally from the question of proportion, it might be well to note a curious tendency throughout this first part of the *Hellenica* for the work to grow in fullness as it progresses, *cum incalescat scriptor*. An effective means of illustration would be to notice the location of the very passages we have been using as examples. The Battle of Cyzicus, the Battle of Abydos, and the raid of Agis to the walls were cited as examples of important episodes treated briefly; these three events all occur within the first chapter of Book One and together account for 54 (Oxford) lines. To the Battle of the Arginusae alone, occurring toward the end of that book, 39 lines are given. But this increasing amplitude is only a tendency: Hermocrates' 35 lines also fall in that first book; and the storming of Lampsacus, the "wealthy city, full of wine and grain and all other kinds of supplies," the important acquisition in the Hellespont which compelled the Athenians to defend their interests in that region at Aegospotami—this merits only 7 lines of the narrative of Book Two (1. 18-19).

Speaking generally (and remembering that our divisions into books are not always of equal length), we observe that Books One and Two together relate the events of approximately nine years; the remaining five books cover about thirty-eight years; or some seven to eight years each. This carries us further: virtually all[24] the events of the first part take place in the eastern Aegean and in Attica; whereas those in the following books stretch out over all the eastern Greek world: Asia Minor, the Peloponnese, Macedonia, Corcyra. Each part also employs a different method of grouping the events in narration. In the first books, except for a few fleeting allusions occasioned by some matter presently in hand, the events are grouped together with all the others which occur during the same year, in the way they would be found in a chronicle. In the remaining portions of the *Hellenica,* however, Xenophon allows himself a freer hand in the matter and groups events more according to unity of development, often throwing the happenings of a common episode together and pursuing the story uninterruptedly over the space of two or more years if need be. Then he returns to events in other quarters, taking them up where he left off several years back. The Lacedaemonian invasion of Elis occurred in 399, for example; but as Xenophon, at the beginning of Book Three, takes up the thread of the narrative of the Lacedaemonian campaign of 400 in Asia Minor, he carries the exposition in continuous sequence down to the truce concluded by Dercylidas and the satraps in 397 (iii. 2. 21). Then shifting attention to mainland Greece, he relates the expedition against Elis and other matters which had meanwhile occurred. Again, in Book Four (chap. 8) we find a similar retrogression which recapitulates the events of the previous seven years. In the first two books, however, Xenophon adheres to an annalistic exposition.

The question of chronology suggests in turn another that

---

[24] If we make exception of the "synchronistic" notices referring to events in Persia and Sicily. See below, p. 42.

touches on a large issue. The circumstance that Xenophon's history begins *in medias res* at almost if not exactly the point where that of Thucydides so abortively terminates, cannot fail to suggest to all an intentional connection between the two works. There are in fact numerous characteristics of the first part of the *Hellenica* which strengthen this assumption. One remembers Thucydides' habit of organizing his narrative in terms of the seasons of the year during which military operations could or could not conveniently take place.[25] Comparable statements throughout Xenophon's first books seem to be reminiscences of his practice, as do also statements identifying certain years as respective years of the war.[26] Then there is also a series of notices, given in the manner of chronicles, which refer to events of a distinctive character or to important events in other parts of the world which occur during each year of the war. They are given along with the statements about the passing of the years and seem to serve the purpose of identifying each year with reference to other systems of chronology. In any case, some see in these notices a suggestion of the comprehensive outlook of Thucydides' history, which likewise makes reference to occurrences in other parts of the world. The argument for a formal connection with the history of Thucydides receives its strongest support, however, from the condition of the opening section of our *Hellenica*. There is no introduction; the narrative begins in a manner which seems to assume the reader's familiarity with the location and antecedents of the story that is so summarily introduced. It is a puzzling start, and even with the help of Thucydides we are unable to find a place for all of the elements that confront us, although there is a general correspondence. But the "abrupt and summary element,"[27] which is so greatly in evidence in this unceremonious beginning, assumes a dependence on some preceding account; and, of course, there is none other but that of Thucydides, which apparently ends in the very year the *Hellenica* begins.

[25] Thuc. v. 26. 1.
[26] As at i. 3. 1, 6. 1.
[27] Breitenbach, I, 11.

Nevertheless, even when we remember the difference in the scope of the two works and consider, accordingly, that all the elements of Thucydides' account could not be continued in the briefer sequel, might we not feel justified in demanding that at least those that are continued should be taken up where they were left and given an even continuity? Yet this is not so. Thucydides leaves the Athenian armament at Cyzicus, for example, whereas in the opening scene of the *Hellenica* it is discovered in the Hellespont, and Xenophon does not say how it happened to arrive there. Again, in i. 1, 2, we find Dorieus coming into the Hellespont from Rhodes, whereas in Thucydides (viii. 84. 2) we met him last in Miletus. Although such differences do not necessarily constitute contradictions, it might nevertheless be fair to say that there is no direct connection between the two works.

To the reader of the *Anabasis* or the latter books of the *Hellenica,* Xenophon's style in these first two books, particularly in the early parts, is not easy to recognize. Enough has been said of style in the broader sense of arrangement and treatment to illustrate the truth of that statement, but it applies as well to the more particular features that have to do with the choice of words and the formation of sentences. The sentences tend to be short and the diction terse and restrained; accordingly, there is a remarkably sparing use of particles, which serve as a transition between thoughts, connecting them and explaining the relation of each to the others with which it is grouped. An author is naturally less solicitous of the continuity between clauses when his presentation is overt and ingenuous, and he is inclined to employ particles of transition when the thoughts become subtler and when it is necessary to establish more precisely their relation to the context. In any case, a few observations given in the form of statistics will illustrate this striking difference. One precaution must be observed, however; in view of the tendency for the narrative to become more and more spacious in the opening books, our results will be more indicative if we set ii. 3. 10, about the point the war ends, as a limit and consider the portion prior to it as more representative of the severer diction. So

WINGATE COLLEGE LIBRARY
WINGATE, N. C.

limited, then, we find that in this opening part the particle μήν does not appear at all, whereas its use is common enough (73 times) thereafter. Or again, δή: in this beginning portion it occurs only 7 times, whereas in the remainder of the *Hellenica* it appears 211 times, although the former division is one-fifth the size of the latter. Γέ also occurs but 7 times in the narrative of the war, 130 times thereafter. Finally, the use of the suffix, -περ, "adding force or positiveness to the word to which it is added," might be taken as an indication of style. Up to ii. 3. 10 it is used 11 times; thereafter 151 times.[28] But the reader is less convinced by the witness of these statistics than by his own observation as he turns from these early pages of the *Hellenica* to the passages in subsequent parts and is impressed with the noticeable difference. The statistics serve only to confirm, not form, the impression.

In fine, we might say that the characteristics which constitute the "problem" of the first two books of the *Hellenica* are twofold: the internal incongruities, and the contrast that the section as a whole makes with the remaining parts of the work. As a problem it may be classified as historiographical and thus claims our attention, since the circumstances under which an account of history is written affect our interpretation of that account. It is because of our interest in history, then, that we turn to the discussion before us.

CHAPTER I

THUCYDIDES, BOOK NINE

> Of the historians, Thucydides ended his history, having included a period of twenty-two years in eight books, although some divide it into nine.
>
> —Diodorus (xiii. 42. 5.)

Someone long ago noted that the basis for the belief that the first two books of the *Hellenica* were written as a completion of the history of Thucydides is hardly more than the simple observation that Xenophon begins approximately at

---

[28] Adalbert Roquette, *De Xenophontis Vita* (Königsberg, 1884), p. 39.

the point where Thucydides so abruptly ends. The conviction
which this observation supports is perhaps the most fundamental of all the assumptions made about the *Hellenica;* so
basic is it, in fact, that it might appear surprising that it should
be referred to as an assumption and even more surprising that
the assumption should be called into question. However firm
and however prevalent the belief may be, it nevertheless rests
on evidence so slight and is opposed by objections so strong
and leads to conclusions so important that we cannot afford
to pass it over without challenge. One would think it inevitable
that the opening of the *Hellenica,* coming as it does at almost
the very point where the former work ends, was chosen with
reference to the close of Thucydides, and certainly the question of the relation between the two works can never be
finally settled without our dealing with this issue. We shall
leave the full discussion of this problem for another occasion,
however, and for present purposes we shall simply state that
the possibility exists that the *Hellenica* was originally begun
with no reference to the ending of any preceding work, and
that this possibility is strong enough to warrant our raising
the question of whether Xenophon was intending to complete
the history of Thucydides. That problem, moreover, is twofold: whether Xenophon, in writing the first part of the *Hellenica,* merely recognized the existence of the work of Thucydides and perhaps came to some extent under his influence;
or whether Xenophon's account of the final years of the
Peloponnesian War constitutes a formal attempt to continue
and complete the unfinished history of Thucydides in style
and in conception.

Although, as was said above, we do not intend in this discussion to make a thorough investigation of the many problems encountered in the opening of the *Hellenica,* some allusions to those difficulties will be in order. "Thereafter a
few days later" (μετὰ δὲ ταῦτα οὐ πολλαῖς ἡμέραις ὕστερον)
would not be so unusual a fashion for a work purporting to be
the continuation of another to take its beginning, if it were
at all clear to what the "thereafter" and the "later" were
meant to refer. The last event mentioned by Thucydides is the

arrival of Tissaphernes in Ephesus and his sacrifice there to
Artemis. As this, however, would appear to be a strange point
of reference for fixing the time of a battle and particularly
of one which stands in no direct relation to the activities
of the satrap, it has been suggested that Xenophon is attempting to make connection with Thucydides in a more
general way, so that the events that Xenophon is referring to
are in fact the last naval engagements related by Thucydides.[29]
This solution, however, seems to entail as many difficulties
as it eludes, in view of the fact that the scene of those naval
operations was the Hellespont, for there, we learn from Thucydides (viii. 85. 1), Mindarus was in command of the Peloponnesian fleet. In subsequent sections of this opening portion
of the *Hellenica* Mindarus is still in charge, and it is nowhere
stated that authority over the forces had been returned to him
from Agesandridas, who is the commander in the battle of
i. 1. 1. Ludwig wonders, too, why Thymochares would have
now been invested with the command of the Athenian forces,
seeing that Alcibiades, Thrasybulus, and Theramenes had
been commanding the fleet up to this point (Thuc. viii.
105); nor do we learn of their regaining the leadership when,
as before, they appear as the commanders.[30] Moreover, in
secs. 5 and 12, where the place of action is still the Helles-

---

[29] Breitenbach, I, 32f.; Busolt, III, Part II, 695 and n. 2; J. S. Watson and
Henry Dale, *The Cyropaedia and the Hellenics* (London, 1861), p. 287,
n. 1. Hatzfeld's concurrence in this position, expressed on p. 29 of his
edition of the *Hellenica*, is to be disregarded, as he later renounced this
view in the article mentioned below, p. 17, n. 2.

[30] Alfred Ludwig, "Ueber den Anfang von Xenophons Hellenika," *JCP*,
XCV (1867), 153. Actually, Xenophon does not say outright that Thymochares was in command during the battle of i. 1, but it is difficult to see
otherwise just what purpose mention of his arrival has to do with the
account of the battle. It could not be that he was bringing reinforcements
and his arrival, strengthening the Athenians to the point of confidence,
precipitated the fight, since Xenophon specifies that he brought with him
only a "few" ships, and, in an area where the hostile armaments counted
in the hundreds of vessels, this tiny increment would have meant nothing.
Nor would the victorious Athenians have needed the supplement to their
number to encourage them to engage the enemy. In all, Ludwig is probably
right in making the inference that the author is describing a battle between
Thymochares and Agesandridas.

pont, it is not found necessary to specify the location when parties arrive on the scene. In sec. 8, however, our attention is directed away from that region as the Athenians depart in all directions to collect money and Thrasyllus sets off to Athens. Accordingly, when in the next sentence Tissaphernes sails into the Hellespont, Xenophon is required to specify that region, since the scene has changed. Now in sec. 2, immediately after the description of the battle between Thymochares and Agesandridas, when Dorieus comes on the scene of action, we are told where it is that he arrives—the Hellespont —as though the scene were herewith changing.[31] To these considerations Hatzfeld[32] adds the observation that the term, "Peloponnesians," is reserved for the fleet of the Peloponnesian alliance in these sections of the *Hellenica,* whereas "Lacedaemonian" (as in i. 1. 1) is used only of the Spartan contingent.[33]

[31] *Ibid.* It is also noteworthy that arrivals on a scene already in view (in secs. 5 and 12) are described with ἐπεισπλέω, whereas Dorieus (in sec. 2), whose arrival seems to be setting the scene, is brought in with εἰσπλέω.

[32] Jean Hatzfeld, "Le début des 'Helléniques'," *Mélanges Desrousseaux* (Paris, 1937), p. 212.

[33] Is this strictly true? Hatzfeld also says that Thucydides observes this distinction, but what are we to do with viii. 95. 1, where a Lacedaemonian (according to Hatzfeld, p. 215, n. 6) fleet is referred to as "Peloponnesian"? As to Xenophon, for whom Hatzfeld says that, beginning with i. 1. 6, "dans la suite des *Helléniques,* le mot de Λακεδαιμόνιοι désigne, soit l'État lacédémonien, soit l'armée lacédémonienne" (p. 212, n. 3), in *Hellenica* i. 6. 31, "Lacedaemonian" is used to refer to the entire Peloponnesian fleet, of which only ten ships were Spartan (6. 34). It might be safer to say that Xenophon and Thucydides as well are careful to make a distinction in places where confusion would otherwise result. In viii. 103-109, Thucydides makes many references to the fleet under Mindarus, and in every case he refers to it as "Peloponnesian" except once. That is in viii. 106. 3, where the Spartan contingent is mentioned, and this one time alone is "Lacedaemonians" used. Likewise, when Xenophon in i. 6. 31 uses "Lacedaemonian" of the Peloponnesian fleet, he is careful to use another term, "Laconian" (i. 6. 34), to refer to the Spartan contingent alone. There is no confusion produced in i. 6. 31, because there it is obvious to whom "Lacedaemonian" refers. When that term appears suddenly in i. 1. 1, however, with no context to make it clear to whom the designation is being applied, the safer and more probable course is to take it to refer to the party it strictly designates.

The solution to these difficulties that is usually adopted, as we have said above, is to look upon the phrase, "thereafter," with which the *Hellenica* begins, as referring to no particular event in the previous work but rather relating generally to the situation of the war as we last find it in Thucydides. This relieves us, to be sure, of the difficulty of making a connection between the arrival of Tissaphernes in Ephesus and the battle of *Hellenica* i. 1. 1; and, as that battle is supposedly fought in the Hellespont, it would succeed the last operations that took place in that region. Thus we are not given the location of the opening scene, which is supposed to be the Hellespont, as though it were the same as the last scene described in Thucydides. That, however, is Ephesus, the one previous is Aspendus, the one before that Antandrus, the one before that Samos, and the one before that is Elaeus for the Peloponnesians and Cyzicus for the Athenians. It is difficult to believe, therefore, that Xenophon could have expected the reader's attention to revert to a scene so remote in his mind as the Hellespont would have been after so many confusing changes, or that the effect of these intervening distractions could have been removed merely by the author's beginning vaguely, "after these things." This suspicion is confirmed, moreover, when we examine the beginning phrase closely, for it is apparently not meant to be vague nor refer to matters in general but rather to some specific event. This is evident from the words that follow: "a few days later"; for it would be illogical to combine an expression meant to have only an indefinite signification with one whose force is relatively exact and particular. The second expression could have no meaning, in fact, if the one before it, which conditions its meaning, is to be construed in an indefinite sense.[34]

Another difficulty that is encountered when we accept the thesis that we are not to look for a close connection between the two works nor to expect that the last event in Thucydides be taken up in the beginning of Xenophon is that there *is* a

[34] Might we compare a sentence beginning, "Somewhere in the orchard a few inches from the first tree"?

close connection and the last event *is* continued in the *Hellenica*. In Thuc. viii. 109, Tissaphernes sets out for the Hellespont; as he is passing through Ephesus the story is broken off. It is resumed in *Hellenica* i. 1. 9, where his arrival in the Hellespont is recorded. Of course we could maintain that Thucydides meant to bring Tissaphernes only to Ephesus for the time being, to resume matters in the Hellespont, and to return later to the satrap and his journey to the Hellespont; and that, accordingly, Thucydides was not on the point of relating the satrap's advent on the scene of action when the narrative was abruptly ended. It would appear rather strange, however, for the historian to break the story of the journey into parts when all of it could have been reserved for one relation in one place. His practice in these sections, besides, is to group events in long episodes, giving ample treatment to the development of things and bringing each sequence to some meaningful point before turning from it to treat in similar fashion a series of happenings that occurred elsewhere; and not jerkily leaping off to another theme after a few sentences and leaving a story fragmentary and in suspension. It is much more logical to assume that Thucydides was about to relate the journey of Tissaphernes, just as he set out to do, all at once, and we should therefore expect that in a work purporting to be a continuation of Thucydides the narrative would be arranged in such a way as to continue the exposition in the manner in which it had been begun in the previous work.

Nor can any convincing explanations be put forward in Xenophon's defense at this point. For when we argue that Xenophon's account conflicts with that of Thucydides in such a way that the former could not begin where the latter ended, we are making a strong argument against the theory that the *Hellenica* is a continuation of Thucydides. Nor need we concede anything to those[35] who claim that Xenophon was being careless here and that with characteristic laziness he neglected to establish a precise connection with Thucydides. It is of course true, as we have mentioned before, that one of the

[35] E.g., MacLaren, *AJP*, LV, 122.

faults of these first two books is the awkwardness of transition between events. When a work is written, however, primarily for the purpose of completing another work, the most important of all connections is that which occurs at the point where the succeeding work takes up the thread of narrative laid down by the account which it is completing. Yet in the case of the connection with Thucydides, at this most sensitive continuity in the entire work we find the most abrupt transition of all. If we are to say that Xenophon is in general careless, we would expect him to be merely less careless here. How are we to explain the fact that he has reserved his greatest show of negligence for the very point where we would expect it the least? Besides, the opening phrase is such as to suggest that it was worded through care and not indolence, for the simplest and most effortless way to begin would be to omit any connecting phrase whatsoever. To have done so, moreover, would have effected a smoother continuity and would have avoided the perplexing reference that refers, we are told, to something other than it appears to. In adding this unnecessary and misleading transitional phrase, Xenophon evinces concern to produce a continuity, and a close one at that, with something that has gone before; and thus, though there may be a case for thinking that Xenophon was in error, there is little room for thinking that he was negligent.

There is in the beginning of the *Hellenica* a singular repetition of the occurrences that are related toward the end of Thucydides, yet no notice is taken by Xenophon of this curious similarity. In the former work the Athenians and the Peloponnesians fight a battle between Sestos and Abydos, the Athenians emerging victorious. Thereafter the Athenians set sail for Cyzicus, which has revolted. Sighting an enemy squadron, they do battle with the crews on land. The Athenians win the struggle, capture the enemy ships, and seize Cyzicus without a fight. Thereupon, they levy money from the citizens. Sometime before these operations and shortly after an unsuccessful raid of Agis from Decelea to the walls of Athens, when the King was repulsed with the loss of a few of his soldiers,[36] Clearchus the son of Ramphias and Helixus the Megarian were dispatched by the Peloponnesians to Byzantium in a move that opened the final, Hellespontine, phase of the war.[37]

Now when this same course of events unfolds itself again in the beginning of the *Hellenica,* no more inviting opportunity is anywhere offered for one historian's taking recognition of the work of another, and particularly of the very author he is supposedly completing. Elsewhere,[38] moreover, Xenophon shows himself not averse to making references to the writings of others, often when the connection is much looser than in our present instance. Yet when the Athenians go to Cyzicus, for example, they are not said by Xenophon (in i. 1. 18) to "return" thither, but simply to arrive. They do not "retake" Cyzicus, nor have the Cyzicenes "again" revolted, nor do the Athenians levy "more" money from them. Nor is Agis said[39] to make "another" unsuccessful raid to the walls, nor are a few of his troops "again" lost to the Athenians. Moreover, when Clearchus the son of Ramphias and Helixus the Megarian are again sent on the identical mission to Byzantium, although under the same circumstances and for the very purpose as before,[40] not the remotest intimation is given of the remarkable repetition that this course of developments forms of a series of events related in the closing pages of Thucydides. To say nothing of direct references to Thucydides, there are not even found any indirect allusions to that work in the *Hellenica,* in places, moreover, where the temptation to make such references would have been almost irresistible.[41]

---

[36] Thuc. viii. 71.   [37] Thuc. viii. 80.
[38] Cf. *Hell.* iii. 1. 2; *De re equestri* i. 1; *Anab.* i. 8. 27, ii. 6. 4.
[39] In *Hell.* i. 1. 33-34.   [40] *Hell.* i. 1. 35-36.
[41] Some place should probably be found for mention of a solution often proposed to satisfy difficulties when other methods seem to fail. Underhill, p. xvii, suggests that something has fallen away from the end of Thucydides; whereas O. Riemann, *Qua rei criticae tranctandae ratione Hellenicon Xenophontis textus constituendus sit* (Paris, 1879), p. 52; Büchsenschütz, I, 5ff.; Wilhelm Nitsche, *Ueber die Abfassung von Xenophons Hellenika,*

We should make a final remark about Xenophon's supposed carelessness in the opening portion of the *Hellenica*. We have seen how he takes little notice of the particulars of the situation as they were last described by Thucydides; when these same elements are taken up by Xenophon for treatment in his own narrative, however, each is ushered in and properly accounted for. That is to say, although Xenophon, as we have seen, ignores the fact that Thucydides left Dorieus in Miletus (viii. 84) or Theramenes in Athens (viii. 92), when these figures first appear in the *Hellenica* their immediate place of origin (Rhodes, i. 1. 2; Macedonia, i. 1. 12), which is all that is important for Xenophon's narrative, is duly designated.[42] For his own purposes, then, the notoriously negligent Xenophon is here careful of effecting continuities and avoiding abrupt introductions, but he manifests no comparable solicitude for the same particulars as they were last described by Thucydides. How or why the Athenians returned to Sestus from Cyzicus, where Thucydides left them, or even that they

(Berlin, 1871), p. 36; and G. R. Sievers, *Commentationes de Xenophontis Hellenicis: Pars prior (I-II)* (Berlin, 1833), pp. 8ff., think that a portion of the *Hellenica* has vanished. These solutions (both are, of course, possible) rest merely on inference, and as no real evidence can be cited in their support, none can be urged in refutation; thus we can merely record their existence and pass on. It is to be noted, however, that the necessity for these solutions arises from the assumption that Xenophon must be completing Thucydides, and this is based in turn on the observation that the one work begins generally where the other ends. As the connection is a poor one, however, the theory of the lost portion is called upon to supply the deficiency created by the former assumption. Consider the reasoning of Breitenbach, for example: μετὰ δὲ ταῦτα shows that Xenophon professed to be continuing Thucydides (p. 36); that the *Hellenica* bears little resemblance to Thucydides, therefore, means that the similarity had not yet been elaborated (pp. 49-50). This allows us to ascribe any elements in the *Hellenica* reminiscent of Thucydides to the attempt to imitate that work (p. 48), whereas the points in which there is no similarity where it would be expected do not count against the thesis, since the *Hellenica* is unfinished and these matters had not yet been brought into conformity with the model (pp. 50-51). When, however, we turn back to the starting point of the thesis, the opening words of i. 1. 1, and impugn their efficacy for establishing a conceptual identity between the two works, the objection is not allowed, since we are told, the beginning is unfinished, too (p. 53).

[42] Excepting the controversial battle of i. 1. 1, of course, where the narrative opens *in medias res*.

returned at all, Xenophon, as we mentioned above, nowhere says. Yet, when in his own account the Athenians return to Cyzicus from Sestus, their motivation for doing so and a full account of their voyage thither is given (i. 1. 11-13). Xenophon in this opening portion of the *Hellenica,* then, shows a carelessness, to be sure; but the indifference is less toward his own exposition than to completing the account of his predecessor, and the deference he shows toward his own narrative is not accorded that of Thucydides.

Accuracy is supposed to be another respect in which Xenophon in the first two books is following the manner of Thucydides. Elsewhere, we are told, he is satisfied with approximations of quantities, numbers, and distances, whereas in the part of his work written in imitation of Thucydides' style Xenophon makes an effort to be careful and precise.[43] Delebecque elaborates this point further; he finds that certain characteristic passages of the opening part of the *Hellenica* seem to affect this exactitude, whereas in others the precision gives way to estimation.[44]

In evaluating this thesis we must draw a distinction. It may be stated as the difference between accuracy and specification. Those who find these qualities to be identical will have little difficulty in accepting the position stated above; one, however, who may not always be willing to see in precision a sign of reliability will be receptive to the argument about to be made. For in fact the tendency (which does indeed exist) toward precision evident in Xenophon's history of the war is perhaps of just the opposite significance to that attributed to it by those scholars whose theory we are discussing. When, for example, we read in i. 1. 5 that Alcibiades sails up with eighteen ships to precipitate the Athenian victory off Abydos, are we to assume that the figure is more credible than, let us say, the

<hr>

[43] E. H. O. Müller, *De Xenophontis Historiae Graecae parte priori* (Leipzig, 1856), p. 5; Marta Sordi, "I caratteri dell'opera storiografica di Senofonte nelle Elleniche," *Athenaeum,* n. s. XXVIII (1950), 49; Vorrenhagen, p. 2.

[44] Édouard Delebecque, *Essai sur la vie de Xénophon* (Paris, 1957), p. 43, and below pp. 80-81.

distance of "six or seven stades" that Xenophon records (ii.
4. 6) the men of Phyle pursued the cavalry of the Thirty in
404, merely because the one figure is specific and the other
somewhat indefinite? Would the reliability of the latter figure
be increased if it instead had been reported as "seven stades"?
If so, are we prepared to hold that Diodorus' account (xiii.
100. 3) of the losses of the Peloponnesians off the Arginusae
is more accurate than that of Xenophon? For Xenophon hesitates to specify and ventures (i. 6. 34) only that the losses
amounted to "more than" sixty-nine, whereas Diodorus confidently asserts that they were precisely seventy-seven. Exactness, therefore, must never be taken outright as a sign of
correctness; in fact, in brief and general accounts where the
author does not otherwise betray any great familiarity with
the details of his subject, it might be well to view a pretense
at precision with some measure of distrust.

Besides, there is a suspicious character to the precision of
this part that is said to be written in the manner of Thucydides. Let us consider the first chapter, wherein the precision is
supposedly extreme.[45] There we meet with twenty-two cases
where an attempt is made to convey an impression of size
or amount. Two of these are approximations.[46] Fourteen of
the remaining are round numbers,[47] of which two are divisible
by 5 alone and twelve are evenly divisible by 10. Now we
would of course expect that some figures would be round by
nature: it would be surprising, for example, to find the Athenians (in sec. 34) alloting to Thrasyllus a force of, let us say,
nine hundred and ninety-nine instead of the one thousand men
they sent him. But is it not a bit questionable that exactly
thirty Peloponnesian ships should be captured at the Battle
of Abydos; or that Mindarus was able to fit out no more than
exactly sixty ships immediately thereafter; or that Alcibiades

---

[45] See Delebecque, pp. 43-44, who spends more time over the problem
than anyone else. We shall not consider such phrases as "a while later,"
or "shortly thereafter"; and, of course, we disregard sec. 37, generally
agreed to be interpolated.

[46] Secs. 1, 34.

[47] Secs. 2 (14), 5 (18), 11 (1), 13 (86), 36 (3,9).

effected his escape to Sardis and arrived back on the scene precisely thirty days after his capture; or that he should remain in Cyzicus an even twenty days after its seizure before departing? Even in cases where we are given figures that are convincingly unrounded we cannot be certain whether the author was making use of exact documentation from detailed sources or whether his precision was obtained by simple inference from the limited information at hand. The seemingly accurate figure of eight-six for the number of Athenian ships gathered at Proconnesus (sec. 13), for example, is not necessarily independently derived but appears to be the author's simple addition of the few figures before him. The forty ships of sec. 8, the twenty of sec. 12, the other twenty of sec. 12, the five from Clazomene of sec. 11; together, these (all round numbers) amount to eighty-five; and adding to that the dispatch ship of sec. 11, we have our eighty-six.[48] However that may be, let us turn to Thucydides' own account of these same operations, which he was relating when his history was so suddenly broken off, and which account Xenophon is said to be continuing in the former's style. In Thucydides' description,[49] then, we find twenty-seven notices of amounts and quantities, a few more than in the account of Xenophon in just over the same number of pages.[50] Of these, three[51] are

---

[48] By contrast, in the equivalent account in Thucydides viii. 99ff. (discussed below), the totals cannot be justified by simple calculation of the figures mentioned in individual instances, but seem to constitute separate particulars of information. That is to say, by adding to the sixty-seven ships of viii. 100. 5 the eighteen of 102. 1, and the two of 103. 3, and subtracting the four of 102. 2, we do not arrive at the figure of seventy-six, which Thucydides says, in 104. 2, was the number of Athenian ships that participated at Cynossema. Nor by adding to the seventy-three of viii. 99. 1 the sixteen of 99. 1 and 102. 1, and the three of 102. 3, and subtracting the two of 103. 3 do we come up with the sum of eighty-six Peloponnesian ships that are reported in 104.2 to have fought in that same battle. Thucydides therefore appears more concerned with reporting exactly what he knows than in presenting a speciously consistent account in which all the elements seem to balance neatly and agree, and his method represents a reliability that we should credit more highly than the confidence of those historians who profess an accurate knowledge of all details.

[49] The Hellespontine phase opens in viii. 99.

[50] Seven (Oxford) pages to six in Xenophon.

[51] viii. 99 once; 100, twice.

approximations, which Thucydides is not supposed to be guilty of. And of the remaining twenty-four figures, only five are divisible by 5 alone,[52] and not one is evenly divisible by 10.

Thus to whatever cause any peculiarities in numbers are attributable in the opening portion of the *Hellenica*, they can hardly be seen as a token of greater accuracy and above all can in no way whatsoever be related to the great critical method of Thucydides.[53] No less is this the case with the objectivity that Xenophon is said to observe in this section of his history. "Austerity" might actually be a better description of the manner he adopts in which some have found a reminiscence of Thucydides' style. Müller[54] finds that Xenophon does not employ the means of characterization here that he makes use of in the rest of the *Hellenica:* we get none of the informal

---

[52] In viii. 100. 1, 4, 103. 3, 106. 3 (twice).

[53] Much the same argument must be made against Sordi, *Athenaeum,* XXVIII, 49, who contends that the wealth of particulars found in the first part of the *Hellenica* betrays Thucydidean influence. The difficulty, however, is that, far more than in the remainder, it is just in these first two books that inconsistencies and irreconcilable details occur with the greatest frequency. The reader has already been introduced to this aspect of the problem above (pp. 5ff.), but we shall cite another example as an illustration. Sordi includes among the types of information characteristic of the first part "the exact time of day when a certain event takes place." In i. 1. 2-3, Dorieus is said to have sailed into the Hellespont "at daybreak." Thereupon he is sighted by the Athenian watch, the Athenians (presumably at Madytus) learn of the approach of Dorieus, they send out a squadron to meet him, they engage him at sea, they chase him to land and carry on the fight on the beach, and finally depart. Mindarus, meanwhile, sacrificing on a height at Ilium, descries the battle, descends (presumably to Abydos), launches his ships, proceeds to the place where the ships of Dorieus are still beached to pick them up. The Athenians, in turn, spy Mindarus, and they set out, now in full force, to encounter him; when they arrive, the battle begins, "and they fought," records Xenophon, following his unusually well documented sources, "from early morning." This is typical of the great number of inconsistencies everywhere met with in this curious first part of the *Hellenica*. Granting (questionably) that the narrative here is especially replete in particulars, is it not evident that to be more circumstantial is not necessarily to be more accurate? In other parts of the *Hellenica,* Xenophon produces fewer inconsistencies by recording only those particulars he can be certain of, and for this, in effect, he is called "non-Thucydidean."

[54] Müller, p. 6; also cf. Sordi, *Athenaeum,* XXVIII, 10-11, 42.

conversations, anecdotal gestures, and *bons mots* that are
found later on,[55] just as are also wanting those instances where
the author intervenes to pass judgment on the conduct or
character of some figure he is describing.[56]

Here we are conveniently spared a discussion of whether
such a style of writing is any indication of objectivity or is
characteristic of the manner of Thucydides. Such a consideration would lead to interesting results, but we need not be led
as far as raising the issue at all, since Müller's description of
Xenophon's style is simply not true. There are several passages
in the opening section which could qualify as having been
inserted to characterize rather than to advance the narrative,
but none are more distinctive than those found in i. 1. 27ff.
and in i. 5. 1ff. The first concerns the replacement of Hermocrates, the Syracusan general. Now there is a striking parallel
in Book Five to the scene Xenophon depicts of the departure
of this popular leader. In that passage another inspiring commander, Teleutias, bids farewell to the troops, and in fact
Müller[57] singles out this very scene as an example of the
method that Xenophon is supposed to be using in the latter
books, in contrast to the first ones, of characterizing a figure
by portraying his spirit and bearing.[58] The two passages are
herewith given (in Brownson's translation):

Hell. v. 1. 3, 13ff.	*Hell.* i. 1. 27ff.
For when [he] was going down to the sea as he set out for home, there was no one among the soldiers who did not grasp his hand and one decked him with a garland, another with a fillet. . . . And he called them together and spoke as follows: ". . . I am more desirous of your being supplied than of be- ing supplied myself; indeed, by	[He] urged the soldiers to con- tinue zealous in the future, as they had been in the past, and to be true men in obeying every order. . . . The men, however, and particularly the captains and marines and steersmen, set up a shout at this and bade the generals remain in command. . . . Those who had associated with [him] felt exceedingly the

[55] Müller, p. 6, "Desunt narratiunculae illae et colloquia lepidissima
quibus in altera parte historiam tam egregie illustrare solet ut et rerum
gestarum et morum indolisque hominum saepe quasi imaginem oculis
lectorum subjecisse videatur."

[56] *Ibid.*   [57] *Ibid.*, n. 8.

[58] *Hellenica* v. 1. 3; it is continued in secs. 14ff.

the gods, I should prefer to go without food myself for two days than to have you go without for one. And just as my door was open in days past, as you know, for him to enter who had any request to make of me, so likewise it shall be open now. . . . Now you in like manner were in former days, as I know, good men; but you must strive to prove yourselves even better men. . . ." Thus he spoke, and they all set up a shout, bidding him give whatever order was needful, in the assurance that they would obey.

loss of his care and enthusiasm and democratic spirit. For the best of those whose acquaintance he made, both captains and steersmen and marines, he used to gather every day in the morning and evening to his own tent, where he communicated to them whatever he was planning to say or do; he instructed them also, sometimes directing them to speak *ex tempore* and sometimes after deliberation. As a result of this, [he] enjoyed the greatest reputation in the general council, and was thought superior to all others as speaker and adviser.

Both of these passages are descriptive and characterizing; they constitute parentheses in the narration, wherein the author pauses to report words and actions of little significance in themselves and important only indirectly. Each admirably qualifies as an attempt to provide an impression "rerum gestarum et morum indolisque hominum," that Müller so curiously asserts is absent from the opening part of the *Hellenica*. Without being specially apprised as to which of the passages quoted above is found in the first part and which is that of Book Five, and judging alone from the spirit of each, the reader would be at a loss, it is submitted, to decide the provenience of either.

Our other example requires even less attention, since there are few passages in the entire *Hellenica* that satisfy Müller's requisites so superbly as the charming little "after-dinner" scene, where Lysander inveigles a promise of money from Cyrus the Persian (i. 5. 1ff.). It is in fact unnecessary to dwell on this example par excellence of a "narratiuncula et colloquium lepidissimum," to which the reader's attention is herewith invited.[59]

A few words are in order, however, concerning the other

[59] For yet another fine "imago rerum gestarum et morum indolisque hominum" in the first part of the *Hellenica,* see i. 6. 5ff.

features of the objectivity that Xenophon is supposedly observing in his history of the end of the war. The fact that he does not intervene anywhere in the first person is taken as an indication that he is imitating Thucydides.[60] Bruns[61] in fact finds Thucydides' influence prevailing on Xenophon in this respect throughout the entire *Hellenica*. We shall not concern ourselves at present with the explanations Bruns offers to account for the numerous exceptions to his proposition that are found after ii. 3. 10;[62] we are more interested here in the refutation of his view offered by Römpler,[63] who points out that there is no such Thucydidean law against subjective appraisals. Thucydides himself, in fact, indulges in praise, censure, and evaluation on numerous occasions.[64]

---

[60] Müller, p. 6.

[61] Ivo Bruns, *Das literarische Porträt der Griechen, im fünften und vierten Jahrhundert* (Berlin, 1896), pp. 35ff.

[62] Bruns contends that Thucydides bequeathed certain stylistic principles to Xenophon to be observed in his historiography. Among these was a prohibition against expressing personal opinions, as irrelevant to the objective narration of the facts. Bruns uses such statements of Xenophon's as that of ii. 3. 56 to prove his point, contending that in these instances Xenophon cannot resist the impulse to deliver himself of his opinion about the deeds in question. But of course Xenophon is "apologizing," not for recording his *opinion* about the behavior of Theramenes, but rather for recording that behavior. In any case, this characterizing by revealing mannerisms and little traits of personality occurs frequently throughout the *Hellenica*, so Bruns has to say that Xenophon transgressed Thucydides' stylistic laws on every page because Xenophon's nature was not receptive to Thucydidean objectivity and wilfully resisted its domination. Testimony for the existence of any such laws in Xenophon's composition, thus, seldom occurs, whereas there are many indications of the opposite tendency. (And so the exceptions prove the rule.)

[63] Römpler, *Studie über die Darstellung der Persönlichkeit* (1893), pp. 33ff. I am acquainted with this work only through MacLaren, *AJP*, LV, 125.

[64] It remains to review Müller's argument that Xenophon sticks to the facts in i-ii. 3. 10, never interrupting the narrative to approve or disapprove as he does elsewhere. The discussion above has sufficed to show that even if this were so there is nothing Thucydidean in it, but I cannot let the matter simply pass lest it be inferred that Müller's observation is true (whereas it is not). He says (p. 6): "Nusquam, ut saepe in parte altera, intermisit simplicem et aequabilem historiae tenorem ut ex narratore existeret aut accusator aut eorum quos accusaverant defensor," and he cites the following passages (n. 9): iii. 2. 21-23. iv. 2. 18, 4. 1-3, 6. 15, and a few others. It is hard to see just what the subjective element is in most

It is frequently said[65] that in the first two books Xenophon imitates Thucydides' "annalistic" exposition,[66] which we have described above, whereas in the following books this method is abandoned in favor of a sequential organization. The difficulty, however, is that there seems to be no occasion in the first part for employing the latter system. For in order to use a successive presentation, it is necessary that there be (at least) two separate regions of activity in (at least) one of which there is enacted a continuous succession of events unrelated to those taking place elsewhere and to the understanding of which knowledge of none of those other events is necessary; so that the account can be pursued over several years without interruption, as is done in iii and iv, before resuming the narrative of occurrences elsewhere. In i-ii. 3. 10 there are, indeed, two quarters in which activities take place: the scene of the war itself in Asia and the Hellespont; and Athens. There are only four[67] scenes that take place in Athens: the

of these, but I think he assumes that there is a kind of implication present that betrays Xenophon's own position. When, for example, he records in iv. 2. 18 that the Thebans waited until they were transferred to a position in the line other than that opposite the Spartans to declare the time propitious for battle, Müller, I think, takes Xenophon to imply that he disapproves of their conduct. In any case, there are a number of passages in the first part that qualify as well as constituting indirect suggestions of the author's view, but the one I wish especially to call attention to is that of i. 4. 13-17. Bruns, p. 36, claims that, because Xenophon (he says) is presenting both sides of the issue (the character of Alcibiades) here, he is working under the influence of the objective method he inherited from Thucydides. This is objectivity, however, of a strange sort indeed. The author delivers a eulogistic vindication of Alcibiades the like of which he accords to few characters throughout the entire history—this constitutes the one side of the issue, and the other "side" is compressed into one sentence, in which it is simply stated, in effect, that Alcibiades is certainly a very bad fellow. But it is enough to show in the eyes of Bruns that Xenophon is here "objective" and "Thucydidean."

[65] Müller, pp. 1-2; Vorrenhagen, pp. 2-3; Rudolph Müller, *Quaestionum Xenophontearum capita duo* (Halle, 1907), p. 67; Sordi,*Athenaeum*, XXVIII, 37-38; J. Hatzfeld, *Xénophon: Helléniques*, I (Paris, 1936), 6; MacLaren, *AJP*, LV, 124.

[66] τοῖς χρόνοις ἀκολουθῶν that is, instead of ταῖς περιοχαῖς τῶν πραγμάτων (Dion. of Hal., *To Pompey*, 773).

[67] Disregarding momentary references incidental to activities elsewhere, as in i. 6. 24-25, 3. 22, 4. 10.

mission of Thrasyllus and the repulse of Agis (i. 1. 33-35); the return of Alcibiades (i. 4. 8ff.); the trial of the generals (i. 7. 1ff.); and the siege of Athens (ii. 2. 10ff.).

Now which of these events is unrelated to the war in Asia? Thrasyllus was one of the generals who were conducting the war; he received the armament, which he led on the raid to Asia, at Athens, whence he set out on the expedition. So Athens is here really a base of operations in the war, just as Sparta was in iii. 4. 1 when the expedition of Agesilaus was dispatched to Asia. For this event, too, where he is employing the sequential method, Xenophon shifts the scene to Sparta. The mission of Thrasyllus to Athens and the departure of his expedition to Asia is therefore closely related to—indeed, a part of—the war in the East. And how much more is this so of the return of Alcibiades, who was not merely one of the generals, but the leading figure of the war and who upon his return (sec. 2) "was proclaimed general-in-chief with absolute authority, the people thinking that he was the man to recover for the state its former power"? Thereupon he and all the generals with him, leading the force of one hundred ships that had been given them, depart for Asia to re-open hostilities.

From the mere circumstance alone that we learn almost as much about the Battle of the Arginusae from the narrative of the trial of the generals as we do from the account of the fighting itself, we might reasonably wonder how this scene could be omitted without depriving the reader of a clear impression of the battle.

The fourth episode, the siege of Athens, does not constitute a case in point, for then all parties converge on Athens and it becomes the *Kriegsschauplatz* itself.

Another approach to our problem would be to consider whether the account of any of the events that take place in Athens interrupts the narrative of events elsewhere. Thrasyllus departs to Athens (i. 1. 8) just after the Battle of Abydos and just before that of Cyzicus. These two battles are part of the same operation, they are fought by the same forces, and they occur in close succession. To have continued, therefore, with the fortunes of Thrasyllus at the point where his departure is mentioned, would have broken the exposition of a series of related events, and Xenophon, accordingly, reserves the description of Thrasyllus' mission for a later time. When he reverts to it he is able to follow Thrasyllus continuously without interrupting and without interruption until the completion of the entire matter in i. 2. 13. When the narrative returns from the scene of warfare to the doings of Thrasyllus, moreover, the Athenians are left in the Hellespont (i. 1. 22), the Peloponnesians in Chios (i. 1. 32), and the Syracusans in Miletus (i. 1. 31). During the course of the next year, dominated by Thrasyllus' raid, no mention is made of the main Athenian armament nor of that of the Peloponnesians. Only the ships of the Syracusans are reported to have engaged in warfare, and that was with Thrasyllus. Thus the mission of Thrasyllus leads directly into the expedition to Asia, and that it does not interfere with the narrative of events elsewhere is shown by the fact that no events are recorded as having taken place elsewhere, even during the expedition. And when the main Athenian force is again mentioned, it is the occasion of its being joined by that under Thrasyllus (i. 2. 13).

In the same way the reader may investigate the other two episodes in question, whereby he will again discover that Xenophon is here no more arranging his narrative in a peculiarly annalistic manner than in a distinctively sequential one. The influence to be sought, in fact, is not so much that of Thucydides as of simple logic; Xenophon lays out the history in the way he does because it is the most convenient way of doing it. Could one imagine, for example, his reserving the story of Thrasyllus' mission for a later time, let us say three or four years after its occurrence, when it could have been suitably related in the context in which it happened without disturbing any other sequence of narration?

Perhaps one is surprised to find that it was possible that events occurring in different quarters could be related in direct connection with one another, so that the narrative of each scene, rather than interfering with the others, actually appears complementary to them. It is a disputed question whether Xenophon participated in any of the military or naval operations he narrates in the part of his history given to the Peloponnesian War. Noting only that the majority of writers thinks it fairly likely that he did take part in some operations, we may pass on to a point about which there is no dispute whatsoever; namely, that during the latter years of the war Xenophon lived in Athens. For one who professes to be continuing the history of Thucydides, however, this is an arresting fact. As a resident of Athens Xenophon must have been hard put to it at times to gather information from both sides about the battles and negotiations that occurred at the scene of warfare in Asia, matters that he could seldom have personally witnessed. No such impediment existed, however, as to the happenings in the capital, where the citizens themselves participated in council and where activities were on public display. Indeed, we have a token of what opportunity was afforded an observer of Athenian affairs in Xenophon's fully detailed account of the trial of the generals after the Battle of the Arginusae. Thucydides, as is very well known, gave great attention to political vicissitudes and to the constitutional controversies that went on in Athens, yet about these matters from Xenophon, who was eminently situated for observing them, we learn nothing. It is only when an event in Athens bears some immediate relation to the combat itself and is very nearly a part of it that Xenophon will bring it to us, and thus it is that the activities in Athens are so well integrated with those of Asia in his pages. In Xenophon's conception of his work, occurrences that do not arise directly out of the hostilities on the scene of warfare, however important those political matters may be to the war indirectly, are not, unlike with Thucydides, to be included. It is well enough to say that Xenophon was not interested in such things and ignored them. This would justify his neglect of these issues in a history independently conceived and executed in its own spirit, to be sure, but it militates strongly against the notion that Xenophon was at all concerned about continuing the account of Thucydides.[68] And more remarkable yet is the circumstance that no sooner has Xenophon supposedly satisfied his obligation to complete the work of his predecessor than he turns to the factional controversy during the reign of the Thirty Tyrants and manifests the greatest interest in the constitutional issues that led to the downfall of that regime.

Xenophon's history of the Thirty Tyrants, in fact, presents several interesting contrasts with the account that precedes it. We are told[69] that the oration[70] of Euryptolemus (i. 7. 16-33), delivered in defense of the generals who fought the Battle of the Arginusae, is reminiscent of the speeches of Thucydides, and this in turn is taken to indicate that Xenophon was attempting to write in the style of his predecessor.[71] It is well known that the distinctive feature of Thucydides' speeches is the function they serve of interpreting events: as the narrative apprises us of the particulars of a situation, so the speeches are meant to develop its significance and convey the author's interpretation of facts and personalities. For all that, however, the speech Xenophon inserts in his account of the war measures up to these requirements perhaps less than any other speech in his history—yet it is introduced at what is probably the most inviting point in the entire *Hellenica* for summarizing a situation and appraising a course of events, and for expressing an author's own evaluation of men and manners. The raging of demagogues, the passion of a mob, the manipulations of the wily Theramenes, the weak submission of the Prytanes, the philosopher's resolute refusal: here we have the full reversal of the democracy whose ideal we met in Pericles' noble oration in Thucydides. All the lofty aspirations signalled

[68] Cratippus, however, who was also said to have written a continuation of Thucydides' history, seems to have paid attention to political matters (Plutarch *Bellone an pace* . . . *Athenienses*, 345[d].

[69] Marta Sordi, "I caratteri dell'opera storiografica di Senofonte nelle Elleniche," *Athenaeum*, n. s. XXIX (1951), 347; E. Müller, p. 7.

[70] There is only one set speech in i-ii. 3. 10; the others (i. 1. 28, i. 6. 5, 8-11) are short, extempore exhortations.

[71] Vorrenhagen, p. 138, says that Xenophon's conception of the use of orations in a history is identical with that expressed by Thucydides in i. 22.

in that great address at the beginning of the war now find their dreadful sequel in this one scene of wild ochlocracy, and if ever there were two answering passages in separate works these they are. And what oration does Xenophon choose to introduce at this point to exploit this most accommodating of opportunities? Just the one we would least expect from one emulating the style of Thucydides. Euryptolemus' speech is informative, for it clarifies a few points of Athenian legal procedure, and we are thankful for that. It is also graceful, and contributes to our knowledge of the oratory of the period.[72] It is even an honest speech and it shows the speaker's sincerity. But Thucydidean? Not one whit. No enduring thought, no searching interpretations, no revelation of meaning and character. That Xenophon could not fully measure up to his great predecessor simply shows that he was no Thucydides; that he did not try to do so, however, argues that there is no connection between their works.

Turning to the speeches of Critias and Theramenes, however, our expectations, so greatly deceived in what has gone before, are all suddenly fulfilled, and here at last it may be said that Xenophon becomes no unworthy imitator of Thucydides.[73]

Everyone[74] agrees that the style of i-ii. 3. 10, at least in certain of its features, differs conspicuously from that of the rest of the *Hellenica,* but there is little concurrence about what interpretation we should place on this disparity. Some[75] would forbid our drawing any significance from it whatsoever and would lay it to the inexplicable caprice of the author. Among those who acknowledge a significance, some such as Ditten-

---

[72] See Vorrenhagen, pp. 16ff.

[73] See George Grote, *A History of Greece* (2d ed.; London, 1888), VI, 468ff. Grote refers to them as speeches "so full of instructive evidence as to Greek political feeling" that he gives a three-page abstract of their contents.

[74] With probably the single exception of De Sanctis. For his position, see below, pp. 137-38, 165ff.

[75] Such as J. J. Hartman, *Analecta Xenophontea* (Leipzig, 1887), pp. 36ff.

berger[76] account for the difference by saying that the first part
of the *Hellenica* was the first written and thus exhibits the
traces of an earlier style. And still others,[77] though recognizing the early character of the style in the beginning section,
incline rather to attribute this difference to a more remarkable
cause: Xenophon wrote his opening pages in imitation of the
style of Thucydides. For the present little can be made of this
last position, since its support is derived from arguments the
discussion of which must be reserved for a later occasion.[78]
They seek to show, however, that the subsequent portions of
the *Hellenica* were the first written, and thus the "early" style
of the first part must be a conscious reversion. In any event,
so far as internal considerations go, and they are our only
present concern, there is no evidence for thinking that Xenophon wrote this section in an earlier style for any reason other
than that he wrote it at an earlier period. And there exists
moreover, a strong internal indication that the stylistic peculiarities of Books One and Two are in no way related to an
attempt by the author to duplicate the hand of Thucydides.
It is this: if Xenophon had made a great effort to copy the
style of Thucydides by using words and forms employed by
his predecessor, by the same token he would have abstained
from other words and forms foreign to Thucydidean practice.
It is a well-known fact that Xenophon departs from Attic
usage in many particulars in his writings. Tycho Mommsen,[79]
studied the relation between the use of the preposition σύν
and that of μετά with the genitive, and in the course of his
investigations he discovered that, although the meaning of
these prepositions is identical, in the best times the former
was employed only in the poets and in Xenophon whereas

[76] W. Dittenberger, "Sprachliche Kriterien für die Chronologie der
Platonischen Dialoge," *Hermes,* XVI (1881), 330ff.

[77] Such as R. Müller, pp. 67, 69.

[78] See below, pp. 38 n. 87; 146.

[79] Tycho Mommsen, *Beiträge zu der Lehre von den griechischen Prae-
positionen* (Berlin, 1895).

Thucydides conformed to normal prosaic idiom.[80] Or again, from the studies of Weber[81] it is known that Xenophon is practically alone among Attic prose writers, including Thucydides, in his peculiar use of ὡς in final clauses and in his choice of introductory particles for object clauses.[82] And even in antiquity Xenophon's reputation as a writer with a strong penchant for distinctly non-Attic words was well established,[83] and this same tendency has become the subject of modern investigation as well.[84]

It was Richards,[85] however, who set himself the task of determining to what extent the style of the first part of the *Hellenica* (i-ii. 3. 10) differs from that (of at least the beginning: ii. 3. 11-end) of the remaining portion, and he discovered in just this opening part the presence of a considerable number of these distinctive traits that mark Xenophon's style

[80] *Ibid.*, pp. 1, 356, 361-68, 383. The thesis of his study (of 660 pages) is stated on the first page, and begins: "Σύν gehört in guter Zeit fast nur der edlen Dichtersprache und dem Xenophon an."

[81] Philipp Weber, *Entwickelungsgeschichte der Absichtssätze*, Vol. II, Part II of the *Beiträge zur historischen Syntax der griechischen Sprache*, ed. M. Schanz (Würzburg, 1885), p. 89.

[82] Cf. the statement, too, made by J. M. Stahl, Review of *De Xenophontis vita*, by A. Roquette, *Philologischer Anzeiger*, XVI (1886), 34-43, concerning the use of the future optative in Xenophon (p. 35): "Derselbe kommt bei ihm öfter vor als in der gesammten übrigen classischen Litteratur von Pindar an, bei welchem sich das erste Beispiel desselben findet, bis Deinarchos einschliesslich, und zwar ungefähr von 14:11."

[83] Cf. the remarks of Helladius, the Alexandrian grammarian under Theodosius the Younger, as reported by Photius *Bibl. Cod.* 279, p. 533, b, 25.

[84] Gustav Sauppe, *Xenophontis opera*. Vol. IV: *Historia graeca* (Leipzig, 1866), pp. 289-301. Sauppe notes forty-four Ionic, Doric, and poetic words occurring in the *Hellenica*, and fifty-nine more words there "a consuetudine optimorum scriptorum recedentia vel recentioribus communia." Alfred Rausch, *Quaestiones Xenophonteae* (Halle, 1881). (Part One is on Xenophon's use of poetic words.) W. Th. Jungclaussen, *De Campio et Büchsenschützio Xenophontis Hellenicorum interpretibus* (Meldorf, 1862). Jungclaussen cites numerous words that the *Hellenica* has in common only with Hellenistic and κοινή writers, such as Polybius, the authors of the Septuagint, and those of the New Testament.

[85] Herbert Richards, "The Hellenics of Xenophon," *The Classical Review*, XV (1901), 197ff.

38   GREEK HISTORICAL WRITING

off from that of Thucydides and all other Attic writers.[86] He
concludes:

What light, if any, on the origin and history of Xn's departures from
ordinary Attic idiom do we gain from the study of a composition [i.e., i-ii.
3. 10] generally and reasonably agreed to be early? We find him already
using such words and forms, notable in various ways, as (1)σύν, ὡς, μέχρι:
(2)ἔλεξεν, ἀντίος, μείων: (3)φάμενος, δυνασθείς. Touching only the fringe
of a somewhat extensive enquiry, we may therefore say that in an early
work he is already using a diction that distinguishes him from all other
Attic prose-writers without exception. . . .[87]

---

[86] The following are typical of Richards' remarks concerning stylistic
phenomena of i-ii. 3. 10 (pp. 198-99): "X's characteristic use of σύν
instead of μετά appears about ten times" (Mommsen, p. 356, finds that
Xenophon prefers the poetic σύν to the prosaic μετά with the genitive
at a rate of two to one, whereas in Thucydides we find the former only
once to every twelve occurrences of the latter; and on p. 365 he states
that there is no significant difference in this respect between the individual
books of the *Hellenica*.); "ἅμα used as a preposition, with the dative
of a person, rare and Xenophontean, is found . . ."; "the characteristic
uses of ὡς = ὥστε and ὡς final are represented by at least one instance
apiece"; "μέχρι used as a conjunction, decidedly rare in Attic, is found
half a dozen times in Book i"; "δυνασθείς is a form of the aorist used
by X. alone of Attic prose-writers"; "προνομή *foraging*, a very Xn. word
not in Herodotus or Thucydides"; "a very unusual use of πρός (usually
εἰς), for which L. and S. refer only to Polybius"; "κατηγορεῖν κατά τινος
(1. 7. 9) is not quoted from any other place."

[87] Richards, *The Classical Review*, XV, 200. A more promising way of
handling the question has been pointed out by Eduard Schwartz, "Quellenuntersuchungen zur griechischen Geschichte," *Rheinisches Museum für
Philologie* (hereafter cited as *RMP*), XLIV (1889), 177 and n. 1, who seeks
to discover "stilistische Nachahmungen" of Thucydides' style in Xenophon.
He detects a similarity of phrasing between *Hell*. iii. 2. 25 and Thuc. i.
30. 3, and between *Hell*. ii. 4. 31 and Thuc. viii. 92. 9; and he cites five
examples (i. 3. 18, 4. 13, ii. 3. 15, iv. 8. 28, v. 1. 28) of what he calls
Thucydidean anacolutha and participial constructions in the *Hellenica*.
Aside from the possibility that these imitations, if such they be, could be
owing merely to an attempt (conscious or otherwise) on Xenophon's part
to emulate Thucydides' style with no profession of completing him, and
aside, too, from the fact that only two of the examples given above fall
under our present consideration, the number of instances Schwartz cites
is too small to be meaningful. In two works written in the same age, and
on the same subject, and of such an extent as these, we would expect to
find at least this number of similarities occurring out of coincidence alone.
But the method itself is sound and invites further exploration. It would
be interesting to know at what point in the composition of the *Hellenica*
Xenophon read Thucydides (assuming, with probability, that he at some
time did) and whether he came under Thucydides' influence.

The chronological system that is employed in the opening books of the *Hellenica* poses a dilemma for those maintaining that this portion was written as a completion of Thucydides. The notices of dates and times we find here are notoriously confused, and the difficulties are immense and appear beyond hope of reconciliation. But this does not in itself constitute the embarrassment, for those who wish to establish the connection with Thucydides, against which this disordered chronology so strongly tells, have free recourse to expunging all that they may find difficult or offensive to their thesis, since pratically no one who has studied the problem will begrudge them the removal of sizeable portions, if indeed not all, of what stands in our text as a temporal outline for a history. It is just this removal, however, that creates the problem, since there is no part of this chronological apparatus that is not indispensable for establishing the relation with Thucydides.

Thucydides makes an issue of chronology. He regards it an important matter, and his close adherence throughout his history to the method he adopts gives point to his conviction. Since Greek states did not follow the same calendar, no one system could be adopted that would be universally meaningful nor was there any assurance that a given month within any one system would recur at exactly the same time the following year, since accurate annual intercalations were not employed. Abandoning the usual methods of dating, then, he chose simply to indicate the order of each year of the war in relation to the others and then to fix the completed system as a whole in terms of more general chronologies by indicating its relation to them at some point.[88] Moreover, if he had taken as his basis some such cycle as the Athenian archon-year, according to which Hellanicus grouped the events of his *Attic Chronicle,* the narrative would have been broken by divisions occurring in the middle of the periods into which a history of military operations naturally falls. These periods are of course the seasons, which regulate the activities of war by land and sea,

---

[88] Gomme, I, 5ff.

are common to all of Greece and are capable of subdivision for greater specification.[89]

These are the prominent characteristics of Thucydides' chronological arrangement, therefore, and ones which an account posing as a continuation is bound to follow.[90] To the extent to which this system is ignored in the *Hellenica,* that history cannot be the continuation of Thucydides. Turning to the *Hellenica,* however, we do find that all of these elements are represented, and this in itself would constitute strong evidence for a connection between the two works. The difficulty arises, however, when we begin to examine the particulars conveyed to us through this apparatus, and the problems which then confront us are so great that, if we may anticipate somewhat in saying so, Xenophon could not have been responsible for such an erroneous store of information. In fact we need not conduct a full examination of the problem, since practically all of those who hold to the "continuation" theory acknowledge, with good reason, that most of these notices introduced in imitation of Thucydides' scheme have been inserted by a later hand. They contain references to Olympiads,[91] for instance, whereas Polybius[92] informs us that Timaeus was the first to use them regularly as a means of dating events. Besides, commentators have found that at least one (i. 2. 1) of these is in error in equating the twenty-third year of the war with the ninety-third Olympiad, whereas it was really the last year of the ninety-second. Another (ii. 3. 1)

---

[89] *Ibid.* and Busolt, III, Part II, 675.

[90] E. Müller, p. 8, concedes this point in the strongest terms: "Expectaverit aliquis, in supplemento Xenophontis, ut quod secundum annorum sit, certe temporum descriptionem, quod quasi primum est historiae elementum, planam esse et dilucidam, similemque Thucydidae; quae quidem tam accurata est ut non modo quo anno sed etiam qua anni parte singula gesta sint perspicue cognoscatur. Atqui hoc postremum non ubique a Xenophonte indicari antea jam diximus; verum etiam ipsam annorum rationem apud eum adeo confusam et turbatam esse constat, ut nisi ex Thucydide eam corrigere liceret, vix quidquam certi de septem postremis belli Peloponnesiaci annis statui posset," although he allows for textual corruption.

[91] i. 2. 1, ii. 3. 1.

[92] xii. 12. 1. The information given above, as it stands, and this reference to Polybius were adopted by me from many modern authorities (such as Marchant and Underhill, p. xxxvii; Hatzfeld, *Helléniques,* I, 154, n. 1; Wm.

does not even designate the number of the Olympiad, although
the victor is named. Again, although Thucydides makes scat-
tered references to the Athenian archons in office at a particular time, these notices never constitute any systematic method
of dating nor do they so much serve the function of connecting
the events within his narrative to one another as that of relating the narrative as a whole to general history.[93] Besides, we
may recall that he specifically rejects archon lists as appropriate for accurate historical chronology.[94] In Xenophon, however, the archon-year is made the basis of dating, as are, too,
the terms of office of Spartan ephors. The two are, moreover,
equated as though they marked the same period of time, and
the system is imperfectly followed so that error is again in
evidence.[95] Then, there is a series of notices of contemporary

Smith, *A Dictionary of Greek and Roman Biography and Mythology*, III,
1130; Lionel Pearson, *Early Ionian Historians*, p. 115; J. H. Krause, Olym-
pia, p. ix; and perhaps Richard Laqueur, *R. E.*, VI A 1, col. 1199;
"epoch-making"), and thus along with them I joined the ranks of those
who credulously take the word of others about the contents of ancient
citations. In this way, through mimeographic error, there comes into being
a body of ancient literature purely modern in origin. All that Polybius
says is that Timaeus compared various chronological lists, including the
register of Olympic victors, with one-another, and he does not even say
that Timaeus was the first to do that. Even the reference is wrong. Older
editions (as Schweighäuser, 1790) used a system which numbered the
passage in question as xii. 12. But by the time most of the learned
authorities themselves were copying the reference from others before them,
the editions more generally in use (as Dindorf, Teubner, 1867) had already
begun numbering it as xii. 11. But it is especially interesting to note that,
not only does the ancient author (Polybius; or Diodorus, v. 1) adduced in
attestation of Timaeus' "innovation" not bear out the claim, but other
scholars (as A. Böckh, *C. I. G.*, II, 304; F. Goeller, *De situ et origine
Syracusarum*, p. 197; H. F. Clinton, *Fasti Hellenici*, III, 490) cited by the
learned authorities as supporting their version, also fail to confirm any
such thing, but simply interpret the passage correctly instead. But, nothing
daunted, the authorities persist: "Polybius expressly states"; "well established
on the word of Polybius"; etc., etc.

[93] Thucydides seems to be employing Olympiads in iii. 8. 1 and v. 49. 1;
but in both cases the references are made to date, not the other events of
the history, but the particular Olympic festivals themselves.

[94] v. 20.

[95] Twice the officials are not even inserted, to begin with, and in one
case where they are (i. 6. 1; cf. ii. 3. 10), the names are inserted in the
wrong place.

events in Sicily and Persia introduced by the formula, καὶ ὁ ἐνιαυτὸς ἔληγεν [96] a formula, moreover, which is reserved exclusively for presentations of these notices. Again we meet with error. To pass over other instances, we may single out that of ii. 3. 5, where the Battle of Gela is related after the fall of Athens, whereas that encounter actually occurred the previous year;[97] and the notice of ii. 1. 8-9, where Darius' "sister" (the interpolator does not even know her name) is mentioned as the daughter of Xerxes, whereas her father was in reality Artaxerxes. Besides, the forms, Δαρειαῖος and κόρη [98] are not those Xenophon would have used. The other formulae by which chronological data are introduced, τῷ ἐπιόντι (or ἄλλῳ) ἔτει and τοῦ ἐπιόντος ἔτους are always accompanied by the achon and ephor for the year; are accompanied by the Olympiad [99] when it is given; and are sometimes given along with notices of portentous phenomena (eclipses, temples burnt) occurring within the year, and with the number of the year of the war. The phenomena and the numbers of the years of the war, however, also occur in the text independently of this formula; the names of the archons and ephors, however, never occur except in connection with the formula. The notices containing the numbering of the years of the war

[96] In ii. 1. 8 the case of the expression is dative. ii. 3. 5 constitutes an exception, for ἐνιαυτός is not used; nor, however, is the notice inserted at the end of the year.

[97] Marchant and Underhill, pp. xxxviiif.

[98] Cf. Cyrop. viii. 3. 10.

[99] I wonder how useful the following consideration is in determining the genuineness of these Olympiad notices. In De Thuc. 826 Dionysius of Halicarnassus seems to imply that Thucydides rejected Olympiads as a system of dating. The Oxyrhynchus Commentator of Thucydides (Grenfell and Hunt, VI, #853, pp. 115-16, 137; Hude, Scolia in Thuc., 1927, p. 108) objects that by Thucydides' time Olympiads had not come into general use for chronological purposes. Now the question I would like to ask is this: Is it very likely that the commentator could have been sufficiently confident, that during Thucydides' day Olympiads were not yet so used, to take exception to the word of Dionysius, if Thucydides' younger contemporary was already so employing them in apparently and probably the earliest part of his history? If it is not likely, and I do not see how it could be, it is also not very likely that by the end of the second century A. D. (the terminus ad quem of the papyrus: G&H, p. 109) these Olympiad entries had yet been made in Xenophon's account.

cannot possibly be genuine: at least two, it is agreed, are wrong, while another states that the war lasted twenty-eight and one-half years. And even if we should believe this calculation correct, we could not believe that its author was writing under the influence of Thucydides, whose explicit statement (v. 26. 1) it directly contradicts.

There are also occasional instances where reference is made to the season of the year. Almost everyone concedes that the greater part of this matter was added to the text by an interpolator, but an attempt is usually made to justify the «ἔτος» formula and the several references to the seasons. This formula, it is said, although always associated with the spurious notices of ephor and archon, could simply have served as the occasion for the insertion of the foreign material, and thus we need not think the two are inseparable.[99a] The case for even the formula, however, rests on decidedly unsure grounds. To save that of i. 6. 1 it must be contended that the election of Alcibiades' successors took place before the regular elections the next year and that those successors were re-elected in that regular election, and this argument many find altogether unacceptable.[100] Still more difficult to comprehend, however, is the outright omission of two of these notices. As Thucydides' account ends during the events of 411, the twenty-first year of the war, we expect to find indication in the *Hellenica* of the beginnings of seven years, in order for the war to have lasted the specified twenty-seven years, whereas in reality we get but five. And more surprising still is the fact that one of those that are wanting seems to be the very first one of all.[101]

Turning to the occasional references to the seasons of the year, we find no evidence that they were inserted in recognition of the «ἔτος» notices, nor the reverse. Each in fact goes its own way, now coinciding with the other, now not,

[99a] Georg Busolt, "Zur Chronologie Xenophons," *Hermes,* XXXIII (1898), 661ff.

[100] Karl Julius Beloch, *Griechische Geschichte* (2d. ed.; Strassburg, 1912-27), II, Part II, 250ff.

[101] *Ibid.,* pp. 245ff, 392.

as though each constituted a separate system of notation, and as though they had not, therefore, all been supplied to the text at the same time. Most of the references to the season of the year seem to be more or less intimately connected with the narrative, to grow out of it logically, and do not appear to have been added for the sake of form alone. For all that, however, the advent or close of only seven seasons, out of a required total of fourteen, is indicated. And even the value for the thesis that this apparent attention to the seasons in which events occur is reminiscent of the practice of Thucydides is partially vitiated by the circumstance that some references to the passage of seasons are contained in the remaining five books, as well.

Breitenbach[102] claims that there are seven examples in i-ii. 3. 10 of the practice also employed by Thucydides of relegating to the end of the season events that could not be included in the account of the major happenings during those periods. But he must include all of i. 1 after sec. 11 as being still in the year 411, and this is a much disputed point. As he himself notes six other instances that constitute exceptions, however, it is evident that we have not to do here with any copying of Thucydidean devices. To make that perfectly clear, however, is the fact that Thucydides specifies the time of the year; he very seldom is content with the "about that time" so frequently employed in the *Hellenica* where we suspect that the author does not really know the temporal relation between events. Thucydides' formula is almost invariably "during that same summer" or "winter."

In fine, we have very little reason to believe, judging from the chronology of the first two books of the *Hellenica,* that they were written as a continuation of Thucydides. It is ironical, too, that much of the chronological apparatus introduced by later editors is in the manner of Thucydides. They had to supply, erroneously at so great a remove of time,[103] what the

---

[102] Breitenbach, I, 41.
[103] There is some remarkable evidence provided by Dionysius of Halicarnassus which seems to have been overlooked in connection with the spuriousness of this chronological apparatus which produces an apparent

contemporary continuator neglected. Why was it left to interpolators to insert the numbers of the years of the war, in imitation of Thucydides, or to make the references to contemporary affairs in Sicily? Necessary to a formal connection with Thucydides is the chronological plan, as we have seen; yet for this critical point Xenophon shows a wanton indifference and gives only the slightest evidence that he was concerned about a matter by which Thucydides set so great store—the very matter in fact to which we would expect one to turn his attention first in laying out a history along Thucydidean lines. Breitenbach, who believes that Xenophon is continuing Thucydides, on the head of chronology must nevertheless conclude that, of the external apparatus employed by Thucydides for organizing events in terms of the seasons of the year, Xenophon retains only the barest essentials.[104]

We have concluded from a previous discussion that in the beginning of his narrative of the close of the war Xenophon takes no recognition of the history of Thucydides. The argument is sometimes advanced, however, that elsewhere Xeno-

similarity between the chronological organization of *Hell.* i-ii and the annalistic system of Thucydides. The critic identifies Xenophon with Herodotus in outlook, method, and style, just as he classifies Philistus with Thucydides in this same way (*To Pompey* 777-82; *De vett. scrip. censura*, 426-28). One of the chief points of difference between Herodotus and Thucydides is the chronological system (sequential, annalistic) each employs, and it is easy to see that he thought that the method each followed produced a profound difference in the character of each of these historians' account (*To Pompey* 773-74; *De Thuc.* 825-30). Now, how could Dionysius have allowed himself to indulge in the neat comparison he makes between Xenophon and Herodotus, in contrast to Thucydides, if the opening books (which he has special reference to in the comparison with Hdt.: *To Pompey* 778) of the *Hell.* had been caparisoned with the elaborate chronological apparatus with which our texts are now fitted out and which effects so strong an outward identity with the system of Thucydides? Moreover, we have Dionysius' direct testimony (*De Thuc.* 830) that no subsequent historian adopted Thucydides' chronological system. So not only does this show that the chronological apparatus of *Hell.* i and ii is supposititious but that it was introduced into the text sometime after the beginning of the first century of our era.

[104] *Ibid.*, pp. 39-40.

phon does evince a desire to relate his history to that of Thucydides, and this contention is supported by citations from the *Hellenica* that are said to be reminiscent of matter in Thucydides. The "answering" passages in the *Hellenica* are of two kinds: those that recapitulate thoughts previously expressed by Thucydides, and those that allude to specific episodes related in his work. Insofar as it is supposed that the narrative of these events in the *Hellenica* was intended to recall Thucydides, however, it seems to be assumed that had it not been for that historian the events of 431 to 411 would not have been publicly known. Before we can establish that an allusion in the *Hellenica* to some particular also touched on in Thucydides was intended as a reference to Thucydides' account of the matter, we must show that Xenophon's remark is directed, not so much to the mere occurrence of the event, but to Thucydides' distinctive treatment of it. The destruction of Melos did not happen in Thucydides; it happened on Melos, and all the Greek world would have known about it. For Xenophon merely to make reference (in ii. 2. 3) to this calamity, therefore, does not necessarily mean that he is alluding to the account of that event in Thucydides. On these grounds, then, most of those so-called allusions can be dismissed, such as the reference to the cities that the Athenians had destroyed (ii. 2. 3) or the account of the dismissal of Hermocrates (i. 1. 27-31). Sordi says[105] that the latter incident obviously derives from Thucydides' account in viii. 85, where mention is made of Hermocrates' opposition to Tissaphernes and to his eventual replacement, but few are likely to agree with that. The account in Xenophon, in the first place, is entirely after his own manner, with great emphasis on the personal and anecdotal element so characteristic of his writings and not distinctively Thucydidean. Moreover, Xenophon includes many particulars not given in Thucydides even though they could well have been mentioned there: the full identity of Hermocrates' successors (sec. 29; cf. Thuc. viii. 85. 3), Hermocrates' demeanor before his men (sec. 30), the

---

[105] *Athenaeum*, **XXIX**, 345.

favorable issue of Hermocrates' and Astyochus' plea (sec. 31; cf. Thuc. viii. 85. 4), and the patronage of Pharnabazus (sec. 31), about which Thucydides is silent although he mentions the hostility of Tissaphernes (viii. 85. 3), which Xenophon says was the reason why Pharnabazus gave Hermocrates his support. Then of course there is the departure scene itself, with the speech of Hermocrates and the response of the men, which Thucydides had no occasion to, and did not, report. Xenophon, therefore, gives no indication that he was depending on Thucydides for his account of the dismissal of Hermocrates.

The case is somewhat stronger, however, for two passages concerning Alcibiades. Xenophon takes the occasion of Alcibiades' return (i. 4. 13ff.) in 407 to deliver an opinion about that controversial figure which agrees with the evaluation made by Thucydides (vi. 28) upon the occasion of Alcibiades' banishment in 416. According to both historians, Alcibiades' downfall was encompassed by jealous rivals who wished to succeed to his position of prominence and favor with the people. It is difficult to say how distinctive this view of things was at the time; certainly it was shared by some, seeing the majority of the people so heartily welcomed the exile's return (sec. 20). And we must remember that, unlike Thucydides who delivers his opinion in the first person, Xenophon is actually representing the judgment here presented as that voiced by the bystanders (sec. 13). Hence one might reasonably question the originality of the analysis, said to be Thucydidean, of the Alcibiades affair and wonder whether Xenophon is so much repeating the interpretation of Thucydides as concurring in one that he shared. Nevertheless it must be admitted that in places the similarity in thought between the two accounts is arresting[106] and we cannot at all dismiss the likelihood of a connection between them. Such a conviction, however, is not as strongly justified in the second instance: that of Alcibiades' famous counsel to the satrap Tissaphernes of favoring neither party too strongly in the war but of wearing

---

[106] Notably Thuc. vi. 28. 2 and *Hell*. i. 4. 13.

out both through feigned and ineffectual support.[107] Certainly
Thucydides was not alone in suspecting this motivation for
the dilatory and equivocal behavior of Tissaphernes. No one[108]
failed to see that the subtle barbarian was insincere in his pro-
fessions to the Peloponnesians and that his inaction was bene-
ficial to the Athenians. And, as no one was unaware that
Tissaphernes had made Alcibiades his advisor, the origin of
this policy would have been evident enough to all. It would
be difficult to maintain, therefore, that there is anything
peculiarly Thucydidean in Xenophon's observation on the
policy of Tissaphernes.

Sordi[109] also calls our attention to a similarity between a
statement of Archidamus', in Thucydides i. 81. 4, and one
made by Agis recorded in *Hellenica* i. 1. 35 and suggests that
the former remark may have served as the inspiration for the
latter. In each case the observation is made that, since the
Athenians are sustained from the sea, military operations by
land against the city are of no avail, and that, accordingly,
the efforts of the Lacedaemonians should be directed at disrupting the maritime communication of Athens with the
sources of her maintenance. In fact the two are not quite
parallel; Archidamus envisions an actual rivalry by sea,
whereas Agis adopts the less advanced, though more truly
Spartan, policy of another campaign by land against "the
country from which the grain was coming in by sea." It is
enough, however, that in each instance the speaker is made
to perceive the true foundation of Athenian power in her
access by sea to the ports and markets of the world. It is the
speech of Archidamus in which the thought is developed
fully, and many issues relating to this central point are raised:
the Spartan superiority in heavy infantry gives no advantage
against a people whose power and possessions lie across the
sea (81. 1-2); as the states of the Athenian alliance are composed of islands, it is difficult for them to unite for an insur-
rection (81. 3); the great disadvantage that faces a landed

---

[107] Thuc. viii. 46. 4; cf. *Hell.* i. 5. 9.
[108] Including Hermocrates; see Thuc. viii. 85. 2; cf. Plut *Alc.* xxvi. 7.
[109] *Athenaeum*, XXIX, 344.

power in a struggle against a maritime state is immobility (80. 3); for all of Athens' resources abroad, however, the Attic hinterland is a matter of concern to her and will be a factor of some moment to the Spartan cause (82. 3-4; cf. 81. 1-2). Now if we turn to the *Athenian Constitution* of the so-called Old Oligarch, we can find a striking counterpart to each of these four points made in the address of Archidamus,[110] and we then find ourselves before the problem of whether Thucydides copied from the *Athenian Constitution* or whether the "Old Oligarch" derived his ideas from Thucydides. The answer is of course obvious: that, whereas the possibility of a connection exists, it is altogether unnecessary to limit our choice to such a simple alternative. The ideas we are dealing with, both the general one to which Sordi has called attention and the more special ones that we have just noticed, must have formed the subject of much discussion at the time. These and many similar observations on matters pertinent to the war were probably shared by many, and it is in vain that we search among them for origins and derivations and lines of influence. There is nothing any more uniquely characteristic of Thucydides about the observations he shares with Xenophon than there is something peculiar to the "Old Oligarch" in the ideas he has in common with Thucydides.

With that we have exhausted the major arguments urged in support of the thesis that in the first two books of the *Hellenica* Xenophon was intending to write the formal continuation and conclusion of Thucydides. So far from finding any conceptual relation between the two works, however, we are at a loss to discover much evidence that Xenophon was even acquainted with Thucydides' history or came under its influence in any respect. And besides we have adduced many, it is hoped, strong indications to the contrary. These have been derived from a study of the beginning chapters of the *Hellenica* as well as from examination of some passages further along in the opening section. The same result, moreover, is obtained as we turn to the end of that part. Our study must

---

[110] (1) ii. 1, (2) ii. 2, (3) ii. 4-5, (4) ii. 14, 16. Cf. also *Hell.* vii. 1, 3-10.

be directed, of course, by the well-known statement made by Thucydides himself in v. 26. 1, where he determines for us the precise moment at which he intended to terminate his history of the Peloponnesian War. There he says (Crawley's translation):

> The history of this period has been also written by the same Thucydides, an Athenian, in the chronological order of events by summers and winters, to the time when the Lacedaemonians and their allies put an end to the Athenian empire, and took the Long Walls and Piraeus. The war had then lasted for twenty-seven years in all . . . with the difference of a few days.

The ending that Xenophon has given to his narrative of the war has always proved a vexing annoyance for those who hold that he was completing Thucydides. There are several reasons why this is so; the one ordinarily alleged, however, is that, ending the history of the war where we will, Xenophon at no point gives any indication that he intends us to distinguish a break between the narrative of the war and that of the Thirty which follows. Even if we are to think that the history of the Thirty was appended later, the fact remains that it is made to follow on that of the war with no discernible change or interruption.[111] As this is obviously so, those who uphold the "completion" theory are forced to impugn—not Xenophon's method: to do so would weaken their hypothesis—but Thucydides' conception of his own history of the Peloponnesian War and his famous declaration in v. 26. 1.[112] It is a perplexing thesis to deal with, and it has a logic all its own that is somewhat difficult to understand. Schambach's statement[113]

[111] See Büchsenschütz, I, 5.

[112] Breitenbach, I, 51-52, argues that, since Thucydides gave a prologue in which he traced the causes of the war, he would have had to add an epilogue in which he described the effects of the war. And just as the prologue (which reviewed Greek history from the earliest times) dwelt on remote as well as immediate causes, the epilogue—"ohne Zweifel"—would have shown the immediate as well as ultimate effects of the war. (The fall of Rome? The War of Jenkins Ear?) The reason for this lies in considerations of artistic symmetry: if we have something at the beginning, we must have another just like it at the end for balance and proportion. (Shame on Thucydides for not reading his Emerson: "A foolish consistency is the hobgoblin of little minds!")

[113] Otfried Schambach, *Untersuchungen über Xenophon's Hellenica* (Jena, 1871), pp. 11-12.

of this unusual approach, however, is perhaps the most concise. This scholar finds it certainly doubtful whether Thucydides would not have incorporated the account of the Thirty into his history after all, had time for completion of his work been granted him, "und so von dem ausgesprochene Plane doch noch abgewichen sein würde," in proof of which he cites the authority of Krüger and Breitenbach, and he makes a reference to French history, which is taken to show that we have a right to extend Thucydides' history beyond the point at which in his mistaken judgment he thought it ought to end.

A lost play of Shakespeare's is discovered. We had known about it from references, but until now it had never been seen. It is intact, except for the very last scene, which, owing to the considerable weathering the MS has undergone, did not, unfortunately, survive. The Argument, however, from the Master's own hand is recovered along with the play, and in that summary the plot, together with the development of the missing scene, is revealed. We are surprised to find, however, that upon appearance of the published edition the final scene, which has been restored for us by the editor, departs radically from the version in the Argument. To our indignant remonstrations Dr. Wissenschaft, the scholarly editor to whose learned efforts the novel termination is accountable, gravely replies that, whatever Shakespeare may have *said* about the way he closed the piece, when he in fact did arrive at the end he could have concluded in no other way than that given in the present version, "und so von dem ausgesprochene Plane doch noch abgewichen sein würde." Thereby settling that.

In the beginning of this discussion the observation was made that the most critical part of a work purporting to be a completion of another is the point at which the successor takes up the unfinished task of the work that went before. If that is true, the next most important moment is that where the supplement comes to a close. In concluding the first part of the *Hellenica,* Xenophon is not merely ending his own history of the war but as the continuator of Thucydides he is putting the conclusion to the whole design, embracing not only the latter years but the entire history of the war from its outset.

We should therefore expect that the manner in which Xenophon brings the narrative to a close would indicate the desire to render an effective consummation to the grand history of his predecessor. Although the ending that we do find is indeed not an unworthy one, relative to its importance as the termination to the history of the war as conceived by Thucydides, it altogether fails to meet our expectations.

We have said that Xenophon's ending is appropriate, and it fittingly, if briefly, captures the spirit of the moment in a way that recalls in one survey the entire course of the war. All the crimes that Athens so vengefully committed against smaller states that dared to resist her arrogant intentions are to be visited now upon her in one great calamity of terrible retribution. This is an effective way to end a history of the war, but as yet we have met with no means of determining whether it was Thucydides' distinctive conception of the war that Xenophon was attempting thereby to conclude. It is not until the actual moment arrives (ii. 2. 23) that Thucydides specified as his goal that we get the indication we are seeking (ii. 2. 22-23 in Brownson's translation):

Theramenes acted as spokesman for the embassy, and urged that it was best to obey the Lacedaemonians and tear down the walls, . . . and it was voted to accept the peace. After this Lysander sailed into Piraeus, the exiles returned, and the Peloponnesians with great enthusiasm began to tear down the walls to the music of flute-girls, thinking that that day was the beginning of freedom for Greece.

The irony of that last remark is easily recognizable. The long war was over and Athens, the cause of the troubles of Hellas, was at last conquered and her tyranny suppressed; in the exhilaration of the happy moment, however, no one imagined that the very power that was freeing Greece from Athenian domination would accede to the position of ruler herself and that Sparta was not so much delivering Greece from Athens as succeeding her in empire. But this is the wrong ending for a history that was meant to end in 404. It looks forward and not backward. It is not so much the conclusion of an age that started in 431 as an introduction to one that begins in 404. The force of that final remark of sec. 23 is only perceptible when our minds turn ahead to the events that are to take place in the coming decade and the following age. Yet this is the moment to draw the lesson and elucidate the meaning of the war, and not to use the occasion to fashion a transition between that event and those that follow. Xenophon, of course, had an interest in inviting our attention to matters beyond, since his own history continues without interruption directly into the succeeding age. Accordingly, he skillfully constructs an ending that serves his own purposes eminently well but manifests no regard for those of Thucydides.

The same inference is to be drawn from another particular about the way in which Xenophon treats these final events of the war. We have been speaking of the passage in ii. 2. 23 as Xenophon's conclusion. Properly speaking, however, it is Thucydides' conclusion, for Xenophon does not see the war as over until after the fall of Samos (ii. 3. 9), which occurred six months beyond the time set by Thucydides.[114] In the eyes of Xenophon, of course, who intends to carry his narrative on continuously for at least another year beyond the fall of Athens, not to conclude the account of operations before the exact point where they literally terminate is altogether appropriate. To Thucydides, however, who conceived of the war in terms of its internal development and along lines far more comprehensive, to protract the narrative beyond the fall of Athens would have been anticlimactic, and thus he carefully set the limit of his intentions at the last significant event.

Our final point is one we have hesitated to refer to because it has been sufficiently stated elsewhere and also because it is perhaps too obvious to deserve mention at all. To contend that Xenophon conceived his work as the completion of the history of Thucydides is to belittle the judgment of an author who could possibly think that the account we have in the opening section of the *Hellenica* constitutes a history worthy of the great masterpiece of Thucydides; or who could fancy that a lowly and feeble production which at best hardly matches the poorest of his own efforts elsewhere would constitute the

[114] E. Müller, pp. 2, 63.

continuation of the celebrated work of his predecessor merely because this sequel, despite its enormous deficiencies, arranges its exposition in annalistic fashion, or because it avoids μήν , references to sacrifices before battle, words of approximation before numbers, statements in the first person, and other such inconsequential stuff as this. Nor do we evince a high regard for Thucydides when we claim to recognize a duplication of his large ideas, his grand conception, and his power of analysis and expression, in the mean beginnings of the *Hellenica*. If we choose to make such an identification, however, we do so on our own, not Xenophon's, authority and we must absolve from all responsibility the author who nowhere declares, implies, or even suggests, if indeed does not seem to deny at every turn, that there is any connection between his own and the history of Thucydides.

CHAPTER II

XENOPHON AND THE THUCYDIDES PAPERS

When you have assembled all or virtually all the facts, first put them into the form of notes, a mere collection of material without any adornment.
—Lucian (*How To Write History 48*)

One of the oldest solutions which have been proposed to explain the unusual nature of the initial portion of the *Hellenica* is that which holds that Xenophon's account of the end of the Peloponnesian War is based on the notes— ὑπομνήματα[115]—drafted by Thucydides for his own projected history of that period. These notes supposedly came into the possession of Xenophon, who brought them before the eyes of the public, perhaps even along with Thucydides' unpublished history itself. The critical points on which the question turns are: the extent to which Xenophon treated, or "edited," these notes; and the guise under which they were published

---

[115] A term first applied by L. F. Herbst, *Die Schlacht bei den Arginusen* (Hamburg, 1855). See following note.

and the responsibility Xenophon assumed for their "composition." The inherent contradictions of the thesis have occasioned its exponents no little embarrassment as they tend now to the one, now to the other of the alternatives which offer a way out of the difficulties of their position. The theory was apparently originated by Krüger,[116] to whom it was suggested by a passage in Diogenes Laertius (ii. 57) saying that Xenophon came on Thucydides' work and published it instead of concealing it. The new thesis seemed attractive and a number of prominent scholars[117] came to accept it as the solution which best met the difficulties of the problem of Xenophon's sequel. There was, to be sure, a reaction and for a while it seemed to prevail.[118] Of late, however, the theory has enjoyed something of a revival at the hands of such students as Colin,[119] Sordi[120] and Delebecque.[121] Although the issue has been vigorously debated from time to time throughout its history, few new arguments of substance have been urged in support of it since its original treatment by Krüger and Müller. Nor has it ever been successfully refuted.

Most of the effort of those who have impugned the theory has been spent in showing that these opening books of Xenophon's history, for all their peculiarities, cannot be said to be in the form of notes. This objection is sound and it is capable

[116] K. W. Krüger, *Untersuchungen über das Leben des Thukydides* (Berlin, 1832), p. 81; see also K. W. Krüger, "Prüfung der Niebuhrschen Ansicht über Xenophons Hellenika," *Historischphilologische Studien*, I (Berlin, 1836), 245, 263-64. Busolt (III, Part II, 695, n. 1) and Sordi (*Athenaeum*, XXVIII, 45), however, seem to attribute the origin of the hypothesis to Herbst, 23. But Krüger had published his statement of the theory at least as early as the articles stated above, and Herbst, who moreover does not dwell on the point at length, refers us back to Krüger.

[117] Foremost among them were E. Müller; A. Lipsius, *Ueber den einheitlichen Charakter der Hellenika des Xenophon* (Luckau, 1857); W. Meyer; Wilhelm Fricke, *Untersuchungen über die Quellen des Plutarchos im Nikias und Alkibiades* (Leipzig, 1869); and Carolus Henricus Volckmar *De Xenophontis Hellenicis commentatio historico-critica* (Göttingen, 1837).

[118] The chief early opponents of the ὑπομνήματα theory were Nitsche, Grosser, Breitenbach, and Busolt.

[119] Gaston Colin, *Xénophon Historien d'après le livre II des Helléniques* (Paris, 1933), *passim*.

[120] Sordi, *Athenaeum*, XXVIII, 47-52.

[121] Delebecque, pp. 40-74.

of further enforcement; but a more promising approach would be to investigate the extent to which Xenophon treated these notes he presumably inherited from Thucydides. In taking a stand on this question one is in danger of inconsistency, and it is revealing to see how each exponent of the theory handles the problem thereby created.

Krüger's own solution was to put Xenophon through a series of psychological predicaments which exonerated him from the imputation of self-contradictory action. We are told that, having inherited Thucydides' literary remains, Xenophon intended at first only to bring that history down to the end of the war. He then saw, however, that the war, properly considered, ended for Athens only with the settlement made after the expulsion of the Thirty, and he accordingly felt justified in appending to Thucydides not only a history of the end of the war but that of the Thirty as well. Then lest he be accused of claiming credit for the part *(Hellenica* i.-ii. 3. 10) which closes the war, in writing which he had made use of Thucydides' notes, he was compelled to publish the history of the Thirty, which was altogether his own work, as the work of Thucydides also, since he gave both of them to the public at the same time. What then justified Xenophon in joining the remaining five books directly on to these first "Thucydidean" ones with no indication that they were by a different author? By his initial action, Krüger goes on to explain, Xenophon had compromised the situation, over which he was now no longer in control. The mistake committed by the youth left the old man no choice but to join the remainder of our *Hellenica* to the earlier part, whose completion it is. This, however, created still a further dilemma: how was Xenophon to receive credit for the new portion if he joined it directly onto the preceding one? There was no other way out: Xenophon now reversed his initial commitment and put his name to the whole: the close of the war, the Thirty, and all.[122]

The predicament has now been made sufficiently clear. If *Hellenica* i.-ii. 3. 10 is the work of Thucydides, why was it not

---

[122] Krüger, *Historisch-philologische Studien,* I, 263-64.

included in his corpus, particularly if we are to believe that the whole was edited together? And, too, how did Xenophon join his own history to that of Thucydides as though it were Thucydides' own work? Or, if we are to believe that Xenophon published all of our *Hellenica* separately from the work of Thucydides with no suggestion that Thucydides was responsible for Xenophon's own work, how are we to think that Xenophon appropriated bodily the work of another?[123] We are compelled, then, to say that the ὑπομνήματα formed only the basis for Xenophon's account of the end of the war and that his office was not confined merely to putting these notices in order but that he added a substantial amount of his own by

[123] Krüger's reasoning in this matter is decidedly difficult. He has Xenophon publish his own completion of Thucydides—including the history of the Thirty—together with Thucydides' history with no mention of his own name, just as though it belonged to Thucydides: "Ja man möchte annehmen dass er dieselbe ohne seinen Namen als zu der Geschichte dieses Historikers gehörig herauszugeben gesonnen gewesen," which he was justified in doing since he had, after all, written the completion from material Thucydides had gathered, "so dass in gewissem Sinne auch die beiden ersten Bücher der Hellenika Thukydideisch wären." And later on in life he decided to write up the events that had meanwhile occurred, so picking up the thread again, "knüpfte er ohne Weiteres da an wo er aufgehört hatte; und so war es natürlich dass er das ganze Werk *als das seinige* herausgab." (Italics mine.) And we cannot expect Xenophon to have prefixed an introduction to this new edition of all (our) seven books of the *Hellenica,* Krüger states, since the first part had originally appeared separately: ". . . . weil er die beiden ersten Bücher schon früher herausgegeben," p. 264). As to how that would preclude Xenophon's prefixing an introduction, however, I await one's explanation, for nothing appears more natural than for Xenophon to have done so upon the occasion of this new augmented edition, particularly as he is now putting his own name to the piece ("das ganze Werk als das seinige herausgab") instead of, as formerly, "ohne seinen Namen," and thereby taking the credit (blame?) for the first two books. If therefore Xenophon effaced his authorship by "blosses Anknüpfen" of his work onto another, and if he were prohibited on stylistic or aesthetic grounds from inserting an introduction, upon occasion of the second edition, "between," so to speak, Thucydides and the beginning of the *Hellenica,* it is only reasonable to think that the same prohibition would also forbid him from introducing himself at that other point; and that, since he likewise did not introduce himself between the first part and the second part of the *Hellenica,* the ancient public, who were expected to believe that Thucydides wrote *Hellenica* i and ii because it was joined directly onto his Book Eight, would have been also compelled to believe that Thucydides likewise wrote *Hellenica* iii-vii—or else that Xenophon wrote Thucydides' history.

filling in the many lacunae due to the imperfect condition in which Thucydides left his notes. Yet we must remember that the theory was originally resorted to in order to explain how the opening part of the *Hellenica* is so fragmentary and uneven; how it is, in other words, that it appears uncompleted. As soon as we say, however, in arguing for a theory originated to explain that uncompleted condition, that Xenophon undertook the task of completing Thucydides, we become involved in a self-made contradiction. And if we go further and say that Xenophon *did* largely complete Thucydides' history, how can we account for the enormous differences between that work and its "completion" in Books One and Two of the *Hellenica?* For if this early part has been greatly improved since it left the hands of Thucydides, what justification do we have in seeing it as notes, since by the time of its publication it of course would long have emerged from the "note" stage?

We have observed Krüger's treatment of these difficulties and have seen how he ascribed the contradictions to the mutability of Xenophon's conception of his work. He stated that Xenophon would have been faced with the problems of conception and organization at two points: the point at which the history of the war connects with that of the Thirty, and that represented by the division between our Books Two and Three. We shall return to discuss these issues at a later time[124] and for the present will simply state that it is certainly doubtful whether Xenophon would have come to decisions that Krüger says were his and on which Krüger's solution rests. Another way of solving the problem, however, is that represented by the work of E. H. O. Müller, who attempted to satisfy the demands at issue through the original device of assuming both of the two conflicting positions—and he did it in the same book. It is enlightening to follow the equivocal movement of Müller's argument. He begins by taking a firm stand by the side of Krüger in asserting that Xenophon published Thucydides' history as well as the notes Thucydides had made on the rest of the war. These notes Xenophon had

[124] See below, pp. 72-73.

edited by adding some material of his own, to be sure, but only enough to fill the gaps between them. Thus as he merely added to the notes we cannot speak of him as really having completed Thucydides. The effort did not go that far and there is no little justice in the charge that the perfunctory condition of this early part shows his unwillingness to go further in completing Thucydides.[125] In fact Müller sees Xenophon observing an admirable restraint in keeping to the task of merely editing the notes and resisting the temptation to add anything more than enough to put them into connected discourse.[126] Up to this point Müller's position seems to be simple and clear enough. To be sure, we might be somewhat surprised at his allowing that the story of the conspiracy of the cane-bearers on Chios (ii. 1. 2-4) was among the parts that Xenophon inserted himself, and we might well wonder how this comports with Müller's conception of Xenophon only touching up the notes to the point of giving them sequence. Perhaps this was the reason for his prefixing "in general" to the last statement of his position. In any case, as we read further a remarkable transformation takes place as Xenophon now appears to abandon his "commendable restraint" and begins to work up whole speeches and insert them in the text! Thucydides had left summaries of the speeches in indirect discourse; Xenophon, says Müller, turned these into direct dis-

---

[125] E. Müller, p. 4. After giving his assent to the thesis that Xenophon published Thucydides' history, Müller states: "Etenim non video qua alia causa hic induci potuerit ut illam non tam continuaret quam quae in ea deessent expleret. Nec sine justa causa Wyttenbachio ea visa Xenophontei operis indoles, ut scriptorem 'nulla sua praecipue animi sententia et voluptate ductum suscepto Thucydideae historiae continuandae officio defungi voluisse' suspicaretur, etsi hoc tantummodo in priorem Historiae Graecae partem cadit."

[126] Ibid., p. 6 "In universum certe scriptor laudanda modestia exsecutus est editoris officium, contentus plerumque ea quae ex commentariis Thucydideis collegerat in continuae orationis formam redigere." ". . . Xenophontem in scribenda parte priore non indulsisse ingenio suo." Cf. W. Meyer's (p. 21) interpretation of Müller's position: "Prior Hel. pars . . . nihil est nisi ipsi commentarii a Thucydide relicti, quibus singula tantum addidit Xenophon editor, ut Müller vult." Cf. also Breitenbach (I, 28), who interprets Müller's position by saying Xenophon published the notes "ohne selbst etwas Eigenes hinzutun."

course.[127] But to three of them he did more: he elaborated and infused them with his own ideas to a considerable extent. His incentive for taking this liberty was a simple one indeed: he liked their subjects.[128] And our only consolation is that Xenophon left in them a lingering kind of seriousness which you will not find, Müller asserts, in any other speech in the *Hellenica*.[129]

It is at this point that Müller begins arguing openly from his second position. Xenophon, once a mere editor adding just enough to join the notes together and restraining himself with commendable inhibition from meddling, has now in fact become the co-author.[130] This status allowed him to arrogate to himself the liberty of casting out whole all that he found of Thucydides' work that did not please him. This must have been a considerable amount; indeed, there is no question about it: we are in possession of no more than a sort of epitome of all that Thucydides had originally bequeathed to Xenophon![131]

The shifts and turns of Müller's demonstration admirably illustrate the inconsistencies with which the thesis is fraught. It was originated to explain the incomplete and uneven nature of "Xenophon's" history of the war by stating that this "history" is no more, or virtually no more, than Thucydides' own notes. Since to all appearances, however, Xenophon claims it as his own and since it very obviously bears the stamp of Xenophon's handiwork,[132] the exponents of the theory are

[127] E. Müller, p. 7.

[128] *Ibid.* "Tres quae praeterea in parte priore exstant orationes sermone recto compositae, Callicratidae duae et una Euryptolemi, eas Xenophon, quia argumenta ei magis placebant, paulo diligentius elaborasse magisque in suum dicendi genus transformasse videtur."

[129] *Ibid.*

[130] *Ibid.* ". . . non multo minorem ei quam ipsi Thucydidi auctoritatem tribuerim."

[131] *Ibid.*

[132] Cf., for example, the little "Cyropaedian" scene describing the dinner conversation of Cyrus and Lysander in i. 5. 1-7 (it has its counterpart in the informal "garden" conversation between these two in *Oecon.* iv. 20-25); or the address of Callicratidas of i. 6. 8-14, which contains a number of distinctively "Xenophontean" themes that reappear frequently throughout his pages. No better single parallel can be found, however, than *Hell.* v. 1.

compelled to admit that Xenophon went considerably beyond merely editing the notes and took a rather free hand in the composition.[133] At this point, however, we find ourselves no better off than when we began, for we set out wondering why Xenophon left the history in such an insufficient and uneven state, completing certain parts yet allowing others to remain fragmentary and disconnected.[134]

Leaving aside the questions of authorship and of attribution, we have the right to ask whether the condition of this opening part of the *Hellenica* constitutes what would properly be described as notes, although it appears that some have pressed this point too far. One cannot expect loose notes, mere ὑπομνήματα, to exhibit great order or consistency of treatment or indeed even to mention every occurrence that will be described in the finished composition, since the author may not yet have made his note on that matter. Thus the criticism of Underhill[135] on this point is not well taken. Breitenbach[136] makes an argument against the ὑπομνήματα theory by stress-

13-19, an episode which takes place, moreover, under similar conditions: note v. 1. 25. Nor should we fail to recognize there a repetition of i. 1. 27-31, as well, wherein the theme of the leader solicitous of his men recurs. Notice how Xenophon chooses the occasion of replacement of command to give us each of these characterizations.

[133] We should note somewhere along the way that we have not to do here with the notions of those who hold that Xenophon used material left behind by Thucydides but which was incorporated and assimilated into Xenophon's own data in such a way as to be no longer recognizable in the final composition. As the ὑπομνήματα theory is of interest to us only in so far as it attempts to account for the incompleteness, etc., of the first part of the *Hellenica,* it follows that this particular variation of that theory does not concern us. For just as it covers up its traces so thoroughly that we cannot refute it, by the same token it has effaced all evidence in its support. We shall leave it peaceably alone.

[134] It is interesting to read on in Müller who, from this point, after having abandoned his original "ὑπομνήματα" position, begins to argue forthrightly against it: "Nam si horum tam tenue et exile fuisset argumentum quam supplementi Xenophontei, certe ne Thucydidis quidem ars et ingenium suffecissent ut ex illis conficeretur quidquam ceteris libris Thucydidis non prorsus indignum." (Pp. 7-8.)

[135] Marchant and Underhill, p. xxiv.

[136] Breitenbach, I, 28.

ing their greatly uneven character, but since it is ὑπομνήματα
of which he requires consistency his argument loses force. In
any event, his reasoning on this point seems to run as follows:
whatever we may have to say about this early part of the *Hellenica,* about its omissions or about lack of continuity, it has
already been sufficiently established that its most unusual feature is the great unevenness so often referred to. And whereas
it is true that many parts seem fragmentary (in the "note"
stage, that is), a number of them likewise are tolerably complete and cannot be said to be notes, however one cares to
construe that term. The basic story, if so it may be called,
is at least evident throughout, and at times we are treated to a
commodious elaboration.[137]

---

[137] Cf. H. G. Dakyns, *The Works of Xenophon* (London, 1892), II,
xxiv, n. 1. Perhaps we should relegate to a note mention of those who have
given assent to the thesis but have not given an extensive discussion of
their position and have not, therefore, committed themselves on critical
issues. W. Meyer (p. 9) holds that Xenophon used Thucydides' notes, but
he does not go beyond that in establishing the relation between the two
authors. With Volckmar, he thinks that Xenophon endowed this early part
with his own prejudices, distortions, and omissions (pp. 4-7). Josephus
Spiller, *Quaestionum de Xenophontis historia Graeca specimen* (Breslau,
1843), finds Xenophon using Thucydides' notes for the early part of the
Hellenica, but he does not take up the problems consequent to his position
(pp. 5, 38-39). To all appearances he believes Xenophon began without
further ado, for half of his whole treatise (pp. 1-26) is given over to
showing the organic unity between the two works at the juncture. He also
emphasizes (pp. 32-33) Xenophon's conscious attempt to be faithful to
Thucydides' manner in this opening part where he is using his notes. This,
however, apparently did not prevent Xenophon from including the History
of the Thirty, for Spiller includes (pp. 27-34) all of Books One and Two
in this early part which formed a separate piece from the remainder of
the *Hellenica.* Spiller does not attempt to reconcile this inclusion of
material foreign to Thucydides' express intention. There is also the view
of Colin: Xenophon came into possession of Thucydides' works, among
which he found "des notes, plus ou moins complètes, déjà reassemblées
par son prédécesseur," and he undertook to bring the account down to the
point which Thucydides had specified, the capitulation of Athens (p. 105).
As Thucydides left the notes "more or less" complete, we could expect to
be derived from them an account of "more or less" the same fullness and
consistency as Thucydides' other (eight) books. The only explanation
Colin offers for the differences in this regard between Thucydides and
the first part of the *Hellenica* is the prejudice, ineptitude, and dishonesty
of Xenophon, which occasioned numerous omissions and distortions
(passim). But if the condition of the *Hellenica* is due to these causes, why

To summarize the present argument, then: although an author's preliminary notes are seldom at any one time in the same stage of composition or, when considered together, would seldom present a high degree of consistency, nevertheless how likely is it that an author's method would be *so* capricious as to produce the great unevenness in treatment as that represented by the opening part of the *Hellenica,* now in the form of disordered and fragmentary notes, now of relatively consistent narrative? The weakness of this argument lies in its necessary reliance on our subjective appraisal of the habits of men, and some there certainly are who will declare it probable that an author's method of elaborating material for a history would be as irregular as that in question. The argument is valid, on the other hand, if the unlikelihood of the historian's having followed such an irrational method in his work could be more effectively pointed up.

First we must broaden the scope of our consideration so as to include more than the first two books (to ii. 3. 10) of the *Hellenica,* to which our attention has hitherto been confined, for we are in danger of forgetting that the author of these notes is supposedly the same as that of the eight books of history which precede them, and that that history and these notes, therefore, are supposedly part and parcel of the very same composition. Keeping that in mind, let us also recall a few other particulars about these two works. It is a generally accepted fact, for one thing, that the last book of Thucydides' history was never completed.[138] To be sure, relative to other portions of his work the last book might be described as "a mere trunk, still in its first draft,"[139] but compared to almost

call in the ὑπομνήματα theory at all? Why not start out directly with Xenophon, having him use his own data, and dismiss the needless intermediary stage? Or, to put it another way, how is Colin able to divine the existence of original, "more or less" complete Thucydidean material from this paltry, distorted, and abbreviated residue? We might repeat a warning Colin once gave to De Sanctis when he refuted Colin's position on a certain issue: "En pareille matière, il est fort difficile d'arriver à une certitude."

[138] J. B. Bury, *The Ancient Greek Historians* (London, 1909), p. 80, and Busolt, *Griechische Geschichte,* III, II, 642.

[139] Bury, *ibid.*

anything in *Hellenica* i-ii. 3. 10 it is in a state of great perfection. "To pass from Thucydides to the *Hellenica* of
Xenophon is a descent truly mournful,"[140] as any reader of
the two works will affirm. Then let us also remember that
curious tendency we have referred to for the narrative in the
opening part of the *Hellenica* to become more ample as it
departs from its beginning in 411. All these elements taken
together, therefore, would indicate the following process in
Thucydides' composition: having gathered data for the entire
period 421-404, he began to write the history of these years.
In what order he wrote these events and at what point his
writing was interrupted by his death we do not know, but
in the end we are presented with the following aspect. (Our)
Books Five (chaps. 26 to end), Six, and Seven were virtually[141] finished, whereas Book Eight was left still awaiting its
final form; then the "descent truly mournful" nine days a-fall-
ing to the rough places of *Hellenica* i; and from there an
ascent, sluggish and irregular, mounting at its highest to
points unequal to Thucydides in the most unwrought passages of Book Eight. Yet this is of course the contrary of
what we would expect, for as the *Hellenica* departs from its
beginning in 411, it likewise departs from that all but completed portion of the "notes" represented by Book Eight.
Therefore, whether or not it is convenient to account for
the difficulties of Books One and Two of the *Hellenica,* when
those books are considered by themselves, by attributing these
difficulties to some strangely capricious procedure followed
by the author in his composition, it must have been an unusual method of writing indeed that produced the aspect
presented by those books in combination with the others with
which they are said to form a whole.

But there is still one other matter in this connection that

---

[140] Grote, VI, 338, n. 4.

[141] By this I mean to comprehend the difference, which is not greatly in
point here, between the state of perfection of Books Six and Seven, which
were "fully and triumphantly" finished (Bury, p. 80), and that of Book
Five, where "it may also be shown that there was revision to be **done**"
(*ibid.*, p. 85).

deserves our attention. The main stylistic reason why Thucydides' Book Eight is regarded as uncompleted is its lack of speeches,[142] a point on which there was discussion even in antiquity.[143] We conceive, therefore, that before his death Thucydides had brought Book Eight into its present state of completion, having omitted to compose speeches for it, and, although he left the material for the subsequent years of the war (our *Hellenica*, i-ii. 3. 10) mostly in the form of rudimentary notes, some were considerably more developed than others. In fact there is at least one portion that is complete; at any rate, it would be difficult to discover what the author intended to add to the speech of Euryptolemus in i. 7. 16-33, which has every appearance of being finished.[144] So that in addition to our former difficulties we have now to contend with this oration, which stands complete and elaborated in the midst of largely inchoate notes, whereas that other part, all but completed in comparison, of supposedly the same work has not been appointed with speeches. In fine, notes are usually irregular and there are many irregularities in the opening part of Xenophon's history; but the difficulty is that the kind of irregularities which characterize the first two books of the *Hellenica* is not at all the kind which ordinarily characterizes notes.

It remains to give a hearing to others who have shared the views of Krüger in hopes that they can provide the theory with surer support. Volckmar, writing a year after the appearance of Krüger's thesis, also dealt with the topic and like Müller came swiftly to Krüger's support. Along with the completed history Xenophon came into possession of Thucydides' notes for the remainder of the war. These he published as he did the finished history but not before he had expanded them

---

[142] Krüger, *Untersuchungen . . . Thukydides*, p. 74.
[143] The historian Cratippus is supposed to have been following Thucydides' example in this eighth book in not including any speeches in his work. See Dion. Hal. *De Thucydide* 16, 847.
[144] Cf. Breitenbach, I, 28 and Marchant and Underhill, p. xxiv.

and provided them with speeches and adorned them to such an extent that Thucydides' original work was no more than the substratum of the finished whole. But he was faithful to Thucydides in the main points of being accurate, not giving his own opinions, and not dwelling too much on small matters, so that there is a Thucydidean spirit about the whole.[145] This suggests to us the remark of Müller's[146] that Xenophon allowed Thucydides' "gravitas" to shine through the speech of Euryptolemus, even though Xenophon wrote it up himself. In any case, Volckmar does not say how it is that Xenophon, who indulged "proprio Marte" to this great extent, failed to write the events in a consistent fashion and neglected to tell us more about important things, and in a word, to repair all the deficiencies of which we complain so in these parts. He only says that the small things are after the fashion of Thucydides not dwelt on at length, whatever that could possibly mean. Nor was it that Xenophon did not know more and therefore could elaborate the events no further; for we are told that he knew more about the Battle of Cyzicus than he relates to us but that, in good Thucydidean fashion we may suppose, he deliberately omitted large portions and even misinterpreted it in part. In like manner he knowingly passed over the critical mission of Endius,[147] a major episode of the siege of Byzantium, many important events in the life of Alcibiades—all these and many more matters he wilfully and wrongfully withheld.[148] There is, then, no other way of making Volckmar's position consistent than either to say that Xenophon was *not* faithful to Thucydides in accuracy, honesty, and objectivity; or to say that, if he was, the defects in this respect that Volckmar so severely reproves were bequeathed to Xenophon by Thucydides.

Marta Sordi believes that Xenophon left Athens in 401 and did not return until sometime after 369. Thucydides, who had brought his history down to 411, had died in the

---

[145] Volckmar, pp. 12-14.
[146] See above p. 60.
[147] See above, p. 3.
[148] Volckmar, pp. 29-33, with n.

meantime, but his history, she thinks, had not as yet been discovered in the intervening years. When Xenophon returned, however, more than thirty-five years after the end of the war, he discovered the lost history, which he thereupon published together with the notes for the unfinished portion. Pointing to Thucydides' "second introduction" of v· 26. 1, Sordi claims that Thucydides, at the moment he wrote that passage, had already assembled, at least in part, the material on which he was going to base his account for the end of the war. There the historian presents himself as "having written" down to the fall of Athens. Accordingly, Sordi claims that her account of the connection between Xenophon and such notes is not absurd.[149]

Turning to the passage cited by Sordi, let us determine as far as that statement itself goes whether Thucydides is merely indicating his intention of writing the history of the period to 404, which Sordi denies he is doing,[150] or whether the passage by itself constitutes something more than a simple declaration and lends some special support to the ὑπομνήματα theory. Inasmuch as Thucydides, using in his "first" introduction (i. 1) a past tense of the verb, viewed himself stylistically as having already written the account that follows, had he any other choice but to use the same (past) viewpoint in referring to the same circumstance elsewhere? Is it reasonable to believe that Thucydides originally began (i. 1), "Thucydides is writing," and allowed that statement to stand in his MS until he had completed it; whereupon he then could return to the introduction and justly change the tense to, "has written"? By the same token, in the beginning of his book an author could not present himself to the reader in the stylistic present ("I am writing this account in Athens") if he wrote his beginning after he had composed the body of the work. It is wrong to press such stylistic conventions in an attempt to wring significance from them. And what significance has Sordi wrung from the statement in question? She has pressed

[149] Sordi, *Athenaeum*, XXVIII, 47-52.
[150] *Ibid.*, p. 47.

the tense very carefully, but has not seen fit to press the *meaning* of the verb in question. The verb, γράφω, can mean either "to record" or "to compose." Yet it obviously has the latter meaning here since it answers to the statement of i. 1. 1, where the author shows which sense is intended: "composed" (συγγράφω). Perhaps Sordi *is* holding us strictly to the literal meaning, however. In view of the verb (συγγράφω) employed in i. 1, then, we must think that in v. 26 Thucydides began by saying only that he had "recorded" (γράφω) the history in notes, and that he intended to return to this passage after he had completed his history in its final form and change the verb to "I have composed" before giving out the final draft to be published. As this is altogether artificial, we must suppose that Thucydides is here saying that he wrote the history, not just the notes, for the final period of the war, and that on the strength of this passage we have no lost notes for 411-404 to look for, but for Thucydides' lost *history* of that period. As that interpretation is likewise unnatural, we must conclude that insofar as all these matters are concerned the wording of the passage in question proves nothing.

Is there no foundation, then, for the belief that Thucydides was composing his history from notes when he was overtaken by death? Yes, there is, for it is only reasonable to believe that no author could have written a history as fully circumstantial as that of Thucydides without the aid of memoranda, and extensive ones at that. Accordingly, we shall assume that Thucydides had committed to notes data on the final period of the war, and whether he tells us so or not, he was using these records in drafting his history of that period when his work was interrupted by his death. Is it likewise reasonable to assume that Xenophon would have been the first to find, not only these notes, but the history as well, upon returning to Athens (at the earliest) more than thiry-five years after the (earliest) date of the termination of Thucydides' composition? It is not.

Nevertheless let us proceed with Sordi on this questionable hypothesis. Having come upon Thucydides' previously unknown (history and) notes, Xenophon set about completing them. As a long time had elapsed since the events of the end of the war, however, Xenophon could trust neither his own memory nor that of others. In fact Sordi even questions whether Xenophon had participated in many of the events of those years so as to have had any personal memories to draw on at all.[151] Moreover, the narrative of this early part of the *Hellenica* is absolutely devoid "of any personal observation" and is "very far from having the character of personal memories."[152] How, then, was Xenophon able to complete the notes of Thucydides? And do not many particulars appear to be such as are reported by an eyewitness, especially in some of the more elaborated scenes as that of the trial of the generals? No, we are told; there is an "absolute lack . . . of any personal observation." Where, then, was Xenophon able to find the information necessary to complete Thucydides' notes? The Athenian archives; the record office at Athens. This is the only source, according to Sordi, that would have been able to provide Xenophon with precise and reliable information after 369. It was so accurate and detailed, in fact, that all of those minute particulars of the trial that we inquired about would have been recorded: for example, the destitution of the generals, the attitude of the people who were at first convinced by the generals' story, and Theramenes' deception whereby he induced false mourners to appear in the assembly to play on the sympathy of the crowd.[153]

We shall leave it to those to do so who care to believe that the Athenian public records were so descriptive as to be able to yield information of this sort;[154] we must not, how-

---

[151] *Ibid.*, pp. 41, 45.

[152] *Ibid.*, p. 42.

[153] *Ibid.*, p. 43.

[154] The examples given above were cited by Sordi. It is interesting to see what other minutiae the Athenians were accustomed to record in these surprising public documents: that the generals were not granted the hearing prescribed by law (sec. 5): the government's own action described as illegal in the government's records!; that the false mourners hired by Theramenes were pretending to be relatives of the deceased (secs. 8-9); that the Council's "probouleuma" had been extracted by bribery (sec. 9); that the crowd clamored that "it was monstrous if the people were to be pre-

ever, lose sight of our main problem: the question of the unusual character of the early part of the *Hellenica* and the ὑπομνήματα theory as its solution. Sordi admits that this part suffers from strange faults: more or less serious gaps, the "inequality" of the treatment, the chronological irregularities, etc., but all this can be very easily explained, she goes on to say, by the fact that Thucydides' notes were only notes, and in an embryonic state at that. So as Breitenbach objects (and Sordi acknowledges the objection) that even notes could be expected to present more regularity than we meet with here, Sordi replies that these were especially undeveloped notes: still in an "embryonic" stage.[155] Yet we have seen that the only logical interpretation of Sordi's insistence on the expression, "has written," of v. 26. 1 is that, although there remained the final task of actually joining them all together in a continuous account, Thucydides' data had been so far assembled and his notes were in such a state of completion that he could virtually say that he had already written his history of the end of the war; and that in Books Five to Eight we have a specimen of the history which could be written from these notes. At this point we can only repeat the observation of the "ὑπομνήματ-ist" E. Müller[156] who so eloquently protested that not even the art and genius of a Thucydides would suffice to turn the mean and sorry (he almost said "embryonic") stuff of *Hellenica* i.-ii. into an account at all worthy of the great history. But there is a still more perplexing difficulty that must be reconciled with Sordi's thesis. If, as Sordi believes, the "more or less serious gaps," the chronological confusions, and "the very inequality of the account, which Breitenbach has rightly pointed up," the disturbing irregularities, in a word, of our *Hellenica* i.-ii. 3. 10

vented from doing whatever they wished" (sec. 12); that the "mob" broke out again with shouts of approval (sec. 13); or that the Prytanes acted as they did because they were "stricken with fear" (sec. 15). Frankly, if I found such subjective statements in a presumably dispassionate public document, I should reject it as completely untrustworthy evidence for a historical account; Sordi *(ibid.,* p. 45) finds it "precise and reliable."

[155] Sordi, *Athenaeum*, XXVIII, 48.

[156] See above, p. 61, n. 134.

are due to the rudimentary condition of the notes that Thucydides left behind for his history of the end of the war, what are we to say about Xenophon's part in the composition, since he is said to have written using Thucydides' notes merely as the "basis"[157] for his account? They served as the "fundamental nucleus,"[158] which Xenophon "elaborated"[159] and "completed"[160] before publishing. With that clearly in mind, then, it is now time for us to turn back to the matter of Xenophon and those replete documents of the Athenian record office, and ask: if there is at least some truth in Müller's celebrated animadversion based on the *present* condition of these notes, what must they have appeared like originally before the work of Xenophon, who had these uncommonly detailed records to draw on for his elaboration, expansion, and completion? If the striking "inequality" is so greatly in evidence now, after all of Xenophon's laborious research and arduous concentration of data[161] from these minute accounts, what must have been the condition of the notes—the notes, indeed, that Thucydides was using to write his history—when they first came into Xenophon's hands? Or, if we are to suppose that they were substantially detailed, what did Xenophon do with these notes? Why did he not pass them on to us? Are we to suppose that the trial of the generals, the one episode that Sordi discusses, was a somehow exceptional incident, even though she says it is only an example, and was therefore reported with unusual fullness? Was not the Battle of Cyzicus an exceptional battle? Or was the fruitless diplomatic journey of i. 3. 13ff., which never even reached its destination, more exceptionally important than the Battle of Cyzicus or the Battle of Notium, the confused accounts of which are each accorded less attention by one third than that given over to the embassy? Perhaps our problem, then, is neither one of Thucydides' defective notes

[157] *Ibid.*, p. 45.
[158] *Ibid.*, p. 48.
[159] *Ibid.*, p. 45.
[160] *Ibid.*, p. 52.
[161] *Ibid.*, p. 41.

nor of Xenophon's incompetent editing, but of the *Ungleichmässigkeit* of the Athenian record office.

Sordi makes still another argument in attempting to show
that the early part of the *Hellenica* was written from notes
prepared by Thucydides. She finds an accuracy in names and
figures in this portion that occurs with less frequency in the
remainder.[162] It will be more convenient to deal with this
question later;[163] for the present, however, we shall merely
note that such a tendency could just as well be explained using
Sordi's thesis[164] that Xenophon is consciously attempting to
imitate Thucydides' manner in this opening part of the
Hellenica. In addition, as Sordi conceives of Xenophon having written this part from data recorded in archives where
precise designations would be given, there is sufficient reason
for accounting for such a characteristic without reference to
any notes of Thucydides'.[165]

There is a final point of Sordi's thesis which will bear
discussion here. No one has failed to notice that the account
of the period of the Thirty, in ii. 3. 10-4. 43, is much more
expansive and generous of particulars than that of the end of
the war. Suddenly military operations become clear and are
described with an abundance of detail that enables us to make
a plausible reconstruction of the activities. The terse notices
that previously served to describe major engagements have

---

[162] *Ibid.*, pp. 42, 49.

[163] See below, pp. 80-81.

[164] See below, p. 146.

[165] It is curious to note how Sordi, *Athenaeum,* XXVIII, 42, where she
is trying to make a case for her thesis that for the early part of the
Hellenica Xenophon drew on archives and not personal memory, cites
certain characteristic particulars therein to support her argument. On p. 49,
however, where she is attempting to establish that Xenophon must have
used Thucydides' notes for this part and could not have come by the
information himself, which must have been gathered by the same historian
who was so accurate in Book Eight, she cites these very same particulars!
They are: officers' names are given; the number of days involved in or
having elapsed between certain events; the precise time of day at which
events occur. So I can only repeat that if Xenophon could have derived
this documentation from the archives, what use do Thucydides and his
ὑπομνήματα serve? Why was the theory invented if we can explain our
problems sufficiently without it?

now given way to an interest in the development that is commensurate with the importance of the encounter. The fact that one-half as much space is devoted to the events of this one year as is given to the previous six together is alone instructive in this regard. The great inequalities are gone. There are omissions, but they are rational ones deliberately left to avoid matters that, however important in themselves, are foreign to the story, which is clear throughout. An interesting confirmation of this change in spirit will be established by consulting the lists of problems and irregularities that students of these first two books have compiled. Despite the fact that about one-half as much attention is given by Xenophon to the year of the Thirty as to the previous six together, fully two-thirds of these difficulties occur in the earlier account. Moreover, the difficulties that we encounter in the later account are usually minor; those in the previous part great. Sordi[166] declares that there is no unnecessary description in the first two books to ii. 3. 9. Indeed there is not; in fact, there is often a deplorable want of *necessary* description as well. There are, however, no superfluous details in the history of the Thirty;[167] and yet practically all the essential ones are included also. In view of all this we are surprised to find that Sordi believes that Xenophon wrote both of these accounts at the same time[168] and in doing so drew exclusively upon a single, identical source: those curious archives of the Athenian record office.[169] And as this narrative of the Thirty is of a fullness that approaches that of Thucydides, it is strange to find that, as soon as Xenophon no longer has Thucydides' notes to draw on, his account becomes ample, coherent, and detailed. In addition, Sordi[170]

[166] *Ibid.*, pp. 11-12, 42.

[167] *Ibid.*

[168] *Ibid.*, pp. 49-50: The continuity between these two accounts, in fact, is so strong that Sordi cites it as evidence that they were written at the same time, Xenophon never stopping between the war and the Thirty but writing continuously from i. 1 through to the end of ii.

[169] *Ibid.*, pp. 42, 45.

[170] *Ibid.*, pp. 50-51.

discountenances the thesis of Colin[171] that Thucydides died as early as 399 and points to passages that she believes indicate a later date. But even if Thucydides died as late as 399, would not one, nevertheless, justly wonder whether the combination of six years (411-404) of Thucydides' own labors during the war (v. 26), five years, at the least, in the archives after the war, and let us say three to five years of Xenophon's further "intensive" and "laborious" lucubrations among the same documents after 369 would have sufficed to produce an account a little more endurable than that which by Sordi's own admission still even now suffers from more or less serious gaps, confusions, and inequalities? In fine, the ὑπομνήματα theory, whose only *raison d'etre* is to explain the irregularities of the opening part of the *Hellenica,* has at Sordi's hands not only not helped to solve those difficulties but rather intensified them by affording many reasons why they should not exist.

Perhaps it was the problems consequent to Sordi's thesis, whereby Xenophon in 369 is the first to discover Thucydides' history, that encouraged Delebecque to adopt the extreme alternative position and carry it through to its logical conclusions in hopes of making out a plausible case for the failing ὑπομνήματα. Abandoning Sordi's separation of the work of the two authors, Delebecque posits a close relation between them; a remarkably close relation, in fact. Xenophon and Thucydides, he says, were actually the co-authors, if not of the finished portion of Thucydides' history proper,[172] at least of the concluding portion, which we have come to know as Books One and Two of "Xenophon's" *Hellenica.* Here the two "historians," if so they may be called, were engaged in a conspiracy of distorting history in order to vindicate Xenophon's reputation from the aspersions that accrued to him from his complicity in the deeds of the Thirty Tyrants. Xeno-

[171] Colin, p. 102.
[172] Delebecque, pp. 53, 74; it is only because we are unable to determine exactly whether Thucydides died in 403 or 402 that we cannot tell how long Xenophon worked alone in his revision of "Thucydides'" history before he was compelled to publish it in 402.

phon's method was subtle; he did not from the start of the narrative assume complete control, but only gradually, as he departed from the opening in 411 and from the distinctively Thucydidean portion of the account.[173] We detect his influence increasing as that of Thucydides wanes: the account becomes less exact;[174] Xenophon becomes careless and often does not trouble to consult records or to confirm his information.[175] He does not work out problems of chronology nor give much attention to establishing the temporal relations between events.[176] But these matters are trifling. Thucydides had chosen Xenophon as his collaborator because, in addition to being a Socratic, he was young and of the strongly philo-Laconian, aristocratic party, as was Thucydides himself.[177] After the war Thucydides had returned from exile[178] a sick old man,[179] whereas Xenophon was still able to serve his party by entering the service of the Thirty Tyrants as a knight.[180] But the course of events suddenly changed as Thrasybulus and the democrats descended on Phyle and on the Piraeus; then finally Pausanias and the end of the aristocratic regime. This was in 403. There was for Xenophon no denying that he had served the Tyrants. There was an amnesty, to be sure, and the democrats were supposed to forget the past; but it was not altogether effective and hatred did exist.[181] Xenophon was at this time working with Thucydides,[182] who died before the work was finished, leaving the task of finishing it to Xenophon.[183] Moreover, that Thucydides had committed to Xenophon, his trusted intellectual heir, the task of completing the work was a widely known fact.[184] Sometime

---

[173] *Ibid.*, pp. 43, 48.
[174] *Ibid.*, pp. 43-44.
[175] *Ibid.*, p. 44.
[176] *Ibid.*, pp. 41-42.
[177] *Ibid.*, p. 53.
[178] *Ibid.*, p. 61.
[179] *Ibid.*, p. 52.
[180] *Ibid.*, p. 61.
[181] *Ibid.*, p. 64.
[182] *Ibid.*, pp., 52-53.
[183] *Ibid.*, p. 53.
[184] *Ibid.*, pp. 53, 74.

between the return of the democrats and the death of Thucydides, Xenophon must have conceived the plan of using
the history as a unique means of at once redeeming his position in the eyes of the party in power without betraying his
true principles and proving false to his secret ideals.[185] His
method was one of coloring, suppressing, and distorting history in such a way as to show off events and characters in a
light favorable to democracy, in doing which he hoped to
gain the sympathy of those in power, who knew he was the
author.[186] It is in the history of the Thirty, of course, as being
the most politically sensitive period, that Xenophon's distorting tendency is most in evidence; but as we are concerned
here only with Xenophon's use of Thucydides' notes, we will
limit our consideration to the period that ended with the war.
Even in this part Xenophon was already executing his mean
purposes, being careful to exonerate Thrasybulus, for
example, in the eyes of the people from the deception he
practiced on them during the trial of the generals in 406,
although he was fully as responsible as Theramenes.[187]

We shall attempt no refutation of this thesis at present;[188]
our task is simply to indicate its implications for the
ὑπομνήματα theory. Our question is whether Thucydides
authorized Xenophon to make this use of his notes. Delebecque does not answer directly. He points to those examples of
Xenophon's political distortions in the first book of the *Hellenica*. Then,[189] in discounting the usual assumption that Xenophon did not begin writing his part (i.e., *Hellenica i.-ii.* 3. 10)
of the history until after the death of Thucydides, he posits
the contrary, saying that Thucydides could easily have lived

---

[185] *Ibid.*, pp. 69, 73.
[186] *Ibid.*, p. 74.
[187] *Ibid.*, pp. 71-73.
[188] That is, the thesis that Xenophon wrote the biased account that
Delebecque says he did. We are here only interested in its relation to the
ὑπομνήματα theory. Moreover, other relationships between Xenophon and
Thucydides predicated by Delebecque (as Xenophon's imitating Thucydides'
style in this early part of the *Hellenica*) can be explained as well by the
thesis that Xenophon was merely completing Thucydides without any
reference to Thucydides' notes.
[189] Delebecque, pp. 52-53.

until 402 or at latest 401 and that the date of the composition of the first two books (402) does not pre-suppose the death of Thucydides.[190] Although when the occasion to do so arrives Delebecque hesitates to state his mind on the matter outright, nevertheless the combination of these several statements of his seems to indicate that such is his position.[191] In any case, there seems to be nothing in his thesis that stands in the way of the possibility that Xenophon "had the assent of his predecessor" in giving the history "an increasingly personal slant."[192]

But there is yet another consequence that those who accept Delebecque's hypothesis must be willing to assume. If Delebecque has Xenophon shamelessly[193] contrive a "historical"

---

[190] *Ibid.*

[191] Compare also this statement (Delebecque, p. 64): Just as certain parts of the work of Thucydides make sense when one imagines them to have been written shortly after the defeat of Athens, likewise it is just at that same time that these two books have their fullest meaning; and "il faut s'y reporter par la pensée pour saisir les sentiments de l'auteur et l'objet de son ouvrage." The "pensée, sentiments et l'objet" he defines as Xenophon's use of history as a personal apology for his complicity in the deeds of the Thirty Tyrants. When this fact is understood, we are told, certain distortions, omissions, and pretenses that Delebecque finds can be explained (pp. 64-73).

[192] *Ibid.*, p. 74.

[193] I stand by this description. Delebecque says (p. 73), "On se gardera de jeter la pierre à ce témoin un peu tendancieux plus qu'historien impartial," owing to the political situation at the time he wrote. Allow me, then, to be the first to cast a stone. It is one thing for a historian who finds himself constrained to write—and Thucydides' work had to be completed—to sacrifice a bit of objectivity to spare himself from ruin; it is quite another for one to seize upon a period and to become its historian solely to ingratiate himself with the leaders of the day. Delebecque (p. 64), noting that however much the combination of Xenophon's ideas with those of Thucydides in the part up to ii. 3. 9 makes it difficult there to tell which "pensée" is distinctively that of Xenophon, nevertheless observes that "il est évident que sa pensée sera plus apparente dans la partie qui lui appartient en propre puisque c'est là que, dépassant les intentions de son prédécessor, il veut en venir." Then he asks ironically whether, "était-il obligé par des raisons d'art ou de science à coiffer une histoire, limitée par Thucydide et entrant dans le passé, du récit dangereux d'une guerre civile toute fraîche? A l'historien désintéressé se substitue un citoyen d'Athènes qui veut exprimer sa pensée." And again (p. 73): "Après avoir atteint l'object de celui-ci et achevé le récit d'une guerre de vingt-sept ans, il saisit l'occasion d'aller au delà, ... Sous couleur d'achever

account to serve a personal and ulterior purpose and, moreover, publish that account in the name and under the signature
(if not with the approval) of Thucydides, there is nothing to
prevent our thinking that Xenophon did not perpetrate the
same fraud in the distinctively Thucydidean portion of their
cooperative project of the history of the Peloponnesian War.
Noting that Thucydides may well have been dead when Xenophon published the entire ensemble in 402, Delebecque wonders whether Xenophon did not intend to complete Book
Eight and bring it and the remainder into a concinnity of
views as well as of style before he was prematurely constrained to publish.[194] It appears, therefore, that if Xenophon
acted according to Delebecque's thesis and if there were anything in Book Eight that Xenophon felt embarrassed his prejudicial exposition in the *Hellenica,* he would not have
scrupled in the least to alter it to suit his purpose; so that the
latter portions of Thucydides have probably suffered the
corruption of Xenophon's distortions. Nor can we even call
attention to the fact that Book Eight is still incomplete, as
evidence against this possibility, for Delebecque has already[194a] suggested that Xenophon was capable of just such
a device—disingenuous imperfection—for disavowing a connection.

It is not our intention here to attempt a refutation of Delebecque's thesis, as a more useful purpose is served in simply
drawing from it all its implicit effects, that one may be sensible
of the consequences for which one must be responsible in
adopting such a position. We have seen what an impostor

Thucydide, et d'ailleurs sans trahir sa pensée politique, il écrit, en 402,
sachant qu'il sera lu par les démocrates revenus en 403 au pouvoir. Il ...
dissimule l'apologie derriere l'éloge et le blâme." So, in fine, Delebecque
asks us to forgive Xenophon for distorting history in an account Xenophon
wrote for the very purpose of distorting history. And who was this tender
stripling, anyway (born, says Delebecque alone, as late as 426: p. 24),
who was so distinguished and important among those of Athens in 403
as to need special exculpation in the eyes of Thrasybulus? There is nothing
in Delebecque's conception of Xenophon's conduct in this matter that is
not highly reproachable.

[194] *Ibid.,* p. 74; cf. also p. 53.
[194a] *Ibid.,* p. 56.

the theory makes of Xenophon, if not of Thucydides his accomplice, who, moreover, must have been as egregious a misjudger of men as was Socrates, for Delebecque describes Xenophon as a "profound" disciple of both.[195]

There are other features of Delebecque's version of the ὑπομνήματα theory that invite challenge, but which need not occupy us long. For example, he appeals to Diogenes Laertius in support of the remarkable thesis that Thucydides designated Xenophon as his intellectual heir,[196] whereas in rejecting Diogenes' far more probable testimony about the date of Xenophon's birth he calls attention to that authority's uncritical attitude.[197] Or again, pointing to the "has written" of v. 26. 1, he takes Thucydides to imply thereby that he had already essentially composed the history down to 404.[198] Finally, by comparing Xenophon's treatment of certain persons and places in *Hellenica* i. and ii. with his treatment of them in *Hellenica* iii. and iv. and in the *Anabasis,* Delebecque professes he can tell us whether Xenophon had known those places or persons before writing the former account.[199] But what of the Thucydidean factor? Thucydides had already dealt with many of these persons (Hermocrates, Clearchus, Tissaphernes, etc.) and his narrative shows an acquaintance with many of these places (Thracian Chersonese, the Hellespont, Byzantium, etc.). If, therefore, Thucydides had treated these figures in the history and given a certain interpretation to their personalities, was Xenophon, who was continuing that work, at liberty to impose some different construction on their character?[200] Moreover, if Thucydides' notes for the first part

---

[195] *Ibid.,* pp. 27, 52-53, 80, n. 22.

[196] *Ibid.,* p. 53. Also see below, pp. 84ff. Diogenes was more skeptical about this than is Delebecque.

[197] *Ibid.,* p. 23.

[198] *Ibid.,* p. 52.

[199] *Ibid.,* pp. 29-39.

[200] Is not this precisely what Delebecque is saying himself on p. 46? He finds that Xenophon treats Hermocrates with favor and remarks that in this we can think that if Xenophon "écrit suivant une ligne thucydidienne c'est qu'il suit des notes rédigées par Thucydide, dont on connaît l'intérêt et peut-être l'admiration pour le personnage d'Hermocrate." Here he gives five references to Thucydides.

of the *Hellenica* were as "extensive"[201] as Delebecque sup-
poses them to be, would they not have contained interpretive
material that Xenophon was obligated to respect? A negative
answer unsettles all the more our belief in the ὑπομνήματα
theory. Delebecque has told us that Thucydides had already
himself written the essential narrative of the war before
Xenophon came to the work,[202] and that Xenophon definitely
added only four events: the Battle of the Arginusae and the
trial that followed, the return of Alcibiades, and the siege of
Athens. These scenes are so circumstantially described that
it appears that in narrating them Xenophon was drawing on
his own memory and that, accordingly, he had witnessed them
himself.[203] The others, then, are the result of Thucydides' research alone, since they are not really so detailed and, besides,
they use specific figures and exact numerical documentation,
which Xenophon in his less rigorous manner was unaccus-
tomed to give attention to and to seek out.[204] But what of
some of these latter episodes that employ vague, uncertain
"Xenophontean," shall we say, and not "Thucydidean" documentation? He can explain them all away. One occurs just at
the very beginning of the *Hellenica* in i. 1. 1. Here we are
told that, although it was, to be sure, Thucydides who had
gathered the information and although he recorded it accurately, Xenophon must have used it in a negligent fashion—
hence its present condition.[205] Or again, when in i. 5. 11-15
our information is indefinite in a passage that should not belong to Xenophon, we learn that the deficiency must be owing
to a gap in Thucydides' notes.[206] And if we should ask why
Xenophon, who took so much interest in these passages he
was writing from his own experiences, did not trouble to do
the little research necessary to furnish the account with specific
numbers, Delebecque would presumably remind us of his
other contention that Xenophon had no relish for laborious

---

[201] Delebecque, p. 52.
[202] *Ibid.*
[203] *Ibid.*, pp. 46-48.
[204] *Ibid.*, pp. 44, 46, 48.
[205] *Ibid.*, p. 46.
[206] *Ibid.*, pp. 44, 47.

research;[207] and so on. If we accept all these reservations, then, one for each possible objection, he professes he can show a tendency for Xenophon to become progressively more inexact and indefinite about numbers and quantities the further he departs from the distinctively Thucydidean portion (i.e., after 411). He gives a catalogue[208] of the episodes in which the principle is supposed to be demonstrated, but anyone caring to consult this list will find that it is not so. For the Battle of the Arginusae, occurring near the end of the first book and, moreover, one of the few descriptions which Xenophon supposedly wrote from his own memory, the precision, according to the catalogue, is "very great"; in the next episodes in which there is a question of numbers we find the precision "perceptibly declining"—before it begins to rise until it is "middling" and finally ending "right exact." Or again, the Thucydidean Battle of Notium, in i. 5, suffers an "éclipse de précision"; that of the Xenophontean Battle of the Arginusae, which follows it (i. 6), enjoys an exactness "très grande." There is, then, no meaningful correlation between the relative location of the episodes in *Hellenica* i.-ii. 3. 10 and the precision of the quantities found in those accounts. The detailed, Xenophontean accounts are supported by precise figures; *a fortiori,* the briefer accounts as well could have been written by the same author. There is in Delebecque, then, no evidence for the ὑπομνήματα theory.[209]

---

[207] *Ibid.,* pp. 44, 48.

[208] *Ibid.,* p. 44.

[209] Here we must pause to bid adieu to the guide who has so patiently seen us through the perplexities of the last few pages, the gifted French historical novelist, Delebecque. And yet, with whatever admiring spirit we may credit his romantic endeavor, in the end his work must be taken as again marking the necessity of erecting hypotheses on reality. The wispy, diaphanous clumps of gossamer of which Delebecque's reveries are necessarily woven, the delicate little puffs of wonder that stand him as fact offer such unsure support for the momentous conclusions they are made to carry that it is all too often obvious that his theories are without any foundation whatsoever. Passing over lesser matters, our interest naturally centers on what is the crux of Delebecque's hypothesis, whether Thucydides was responsible for Xenophon's distinctive management of the history to serve a selfish end. The hypothesis demands that he was, but it is too monstrous

An argument that is persistently made in favor of the ὑπομνήματα theory is that based on an inscription placed at the beginning of the *Hellenica* in certain manuscripts, describing what follows as Ξενοφῶντος Θουκυδίδου παραλειπόμενα to state outright. Delebecque begins his discussion of this point by imagining that Thucydides became old and sick, so he engaged Xenophon, who was also aristocratic and philo-Laconian, to work with him on the great history. Delebecque discounts the usual view (which is "arbitrary") that Thucydides died before Xenophon became concerned in the labor, and substitutes the "natural" explanation that he did not. The two met often over the work, Delebecque goes on to say, and collaborated on the unfinished portion. Thucydides schooled Xenophon sufficiently until finally the student had "very forcibly seized the profound meaning" of the history, and then distinguished him at last as the executor of his intellectual heritage by committing the great labor to him entirely (pp. 52-53). Thucydides left him extensive notes for the remaining portion, and these Xenophon supplemented and completed, in doing which he, the trusted intellectual heir of Thucydides, converted the history to his own personal use. Did not Thucydides, therefore, condone his doing so? Delebecque several times approaches the point of finally telling us, but we never get it out of him. But why not? There is as much evidence for settling this issue as there was for deciding all those that led up to it. And what was the nature of that evidence? In that page (53) and one-half (52) cited above in the attempt to extract Delebecque's position, one has to puzzle over statements introduced with the following reservations: "It invites us to suppose"; a certain solution "is perfectly compatible" with a certain proposal; or "In such a case we would. . . ." We encounter questions: "But is it not natural to suppose . . .?" "Would it be surprising if . . .?" "How would they have been able . . .?" "Si" is used six times, "possible" thrice, "semble" twice, "naturel" thrice, "peut-être" four times, and "pouvoir" five times—all in a page and a half. What is one to do, for example, with a sentence such as: Ces conclusions, *possibles* sans être sûres, sont *peut-être* confirmées par le fait que ... ["fact:" at last!] l'influence *semble* [foof! our Nereid vanishes and we are left holding only her kerchief] ..."? Or there on p. 74 and the matter mentioned above of the extent to which Xenophon foisted off his own personal apology in Thucydides' name: "Lead us to believe"; "the enlightened public, at least"; "the apology is only conceivable if . . ."; "one would not see . . . unless"; "and if it is indeed Xenophon who published Thucydides' work, signed by Thucydides, one could fancy that . . . either . . . or . . ."; "if there was collaboration, it would not have . . ."; "Did Xenophon intend . . .? We shall never know. If Thucydides was, . . Xenophon would not have had . . . ." At this point on p. 74 a note is indicated, to which we eagerly turn and receive the documentation which resolves our confusion at last: "It would be important to know under whose signature this first part of the *Hellenica* was published; that of Xenophon? Or of Thucydides? And at what date was the beginning of the *Hellenica* attached on to it? It is not certain whether the problem is capable of a solution." Thus enlightened we return to the text: "It is therefore possible, in fine, if it is necessary to express one's opinion [well, we λληνικῆς ἱστορίας. [210] The word, παραλειπόμενα, could mean either, "that which was ommitted" or "left out," or, "that which vas left behind." In the former case the meaning would be nnocent enough and would simply refer to the fact that Xenophon wrote up the *period* that Thucydides omitted. If he latter sense is meant, however, the passage could be taken, s some prefer, to support the theory that in the early part Xenophon was using *material* that Thucydides had "left be-ind" upon his death. It is even maintained that the designa-ion goes back to the very moment of publication, there being o way otherwise to account for the origin of the tradition.[211] f this were true, however, we would be obliged to believe all uch stories; [212] nevertheless, it is quite possible that the tradi-ion, if not original, is very old.[213] A clue to which meaning he term, παραλειπόμενα, has in this connection, however, is iven us in a passage found in Dionysius of Halicarnassus' *De Thucydide* 16 (847), where that critic says that Cratippus lourished at the same time as Thucydides, καὶ τὰ παραλειφθέντα ὑπ' αὐτοῦ συναγαγὼν γέγραφεν. [214]

[on't want to work a hardship exactly] on a very delicate point, but in eing very careful not to say anything for certain, that Xenophon did not nly write, in 402, the first two books of the *Hellenica,* but that he also ublished as one ensemble, that same year, the eight books of Thucydides nd the two books of his own *Hellenica,* all probably [i.e., possibly robably] in the name of Thucydides." What does the man believe? erhaps some of those "if's" are meant as "since's," and some of the is it not's?" mean "is," but which ones? One hesitates to say in any one ase, "Delebecque believes," in fear lest he reply, "I said, 'If!'" And yet n defending himself on some point he always has the liberty of quoting ne of these elusive intimations as though it were a statement. And when he inally dares state his position definitely on a matter, as one would expect e commits the same fault in reverse, being overly positive on dangerously enuous issues. On the same p. 74 he refers to the notions that Xenophon inished Thucydides' history and published it, as "data": "données non outeuses"!

[210] Colin, p. 7. See Marchant and Underhill, p. xiii, for a description f the MSS and their titles.

[211] Delebecque, p. 74.

[212] I suppose the story recorded by Marcellinus (*Vita Thuc.* 43) that hucydides' daughter (save the mark!) wrote Book Eight likewise goes ack to the moment of publication, therefore.

[213] Marchant and Underhill, p. xiii.

[214] It is interesting to find that the author of the anonymous *Vita Thuc.* 5) uses an equally ambiguous word to describe those affairs after 411

Finally, what are we to say about our statement in Diogene: Laertius,[215] the one that has been taken as the foundation of sc many extravagant conclusions? It is the usual practice of stu dents of these problems to pass it over with a smile and pro ceed to important matters, if they mention it at all.[216] Perhap they are right in doing so; even Diogenes himself, who ca: seriously record as genuine certain chatty letters purportin: to be the Correspondence of the Seven Wise Men, here ap

which Thucydides κατέλιπε to others to write; namely, he says, Xenopho and Theopompus. Without the latter name appended to that of Xenophon': this passage could also have become grounds for controversy much th same as that of the MSS' titles. There is also a statement in Dionysiu Letter to Pompey (778) in which "the Hellenica" is distinguished fro that which κατέλιπεν ἀτελῆ Θουκυδίδης. But in another place (De vet script. censura, 427) he explains his meaning by saying that one way i which Philistus imitated Thucydides was τὸ τὴν ὑπόθεσιν ἀτελῆ καταλιπεῖ In fact, Dionysius several times admonishes Thucydides for not fulfillin his promise to narrate the full twenty-seven years of the war, and Thucydides had at least left a rough sketch of the period he omitted, would have gone a long way toward redeeming his promise and absolvir him from the charge of neglecting his obligations; and the absence of an indication that Dionysius knew of any such outline is especially strikin in places where he would certainly have mentioned one if it existe (Pompey 771; De Thuc. 837, 847, 867). Still, the evidence of the obscu notice of Diogenes would be preferred, by those who uphold the ὑπομνήματ theory, to negative testimony extending over the length of two protracte disquisitions, ones written by an authority who was closer to Thucydid by some two hundred years, at that. Moreover, not only does Dionysi not mention any παραλειπόμενα but no other author uses such a ter either, even though there are many references to the Hellenica in ancie literature (see L. Dindorf, JCP IV [1832] 254-56). Finally, the Gree title of the two books of Chronicles in the Old Testament is the Para pomena. Besides covering the period (from Adam to ca. 973 B. C.) omitte from the beginning of the books of Kings, and relating a number events passed over in the narrative of the latter, they carry on the histo of the Jewish nation for about twenty-five years after the end of the boo of Kings (from 561 to 538: Pfeiffer, Intro. to Old Test., pp. 374, 382) the time of Cyrus the Great. The books of Chronicles were the Para' pomena and any later employment of this title could not have failed recall that original use and be reminiscent of it; and its original use clear shows that the sense intended is the continuation of something, and not t literary remains of someone.

[215] ii. 57: λέγεται δ'ὅτι καὶ τὰ Θουκυδίδου βιβλία λανθάνοντα ὑφελέσθ δυνάμενος αὐτὸς εἰς δόξαν ἤγαγεν.

[216] Ludwig's comment (JCP, XCV, 152) is typical: "We are to relega this statement to the realm of the fabulous."

parently demurs: he passes on the information to us with, "it is said." Even aside from the uncommon character of the notice, Diogenes may have been uncertain about the very meaning of the words themselves, nor has anyone else since been quite sure, either.[217] But construing them in whatever sense one likes, we are left with an assertion that we have seen to be quite unacceptable. And yet, if such a statement is completely unfounded, one may ask, to what does it owe its origin? How do such baseless stories begin?

There is a distinct tendency in ancient tradition that seeks to organize phenomena of similar character by establishing relationships between them and contriving identities to link them together. The Battle of Salamis, for instance, has served as the focus for the attachment of many such correspondences. The Battle of Himera, in which the barbarian was mightily repelled from the shores of western Greece, was said to have been fought on the same day as its equivalent in the east.[218] Aegospotami was thought to answer to Salamis in its effect for Athens: as Salamis enabled the Athenians to erect their walls, Aegospotami compelled them to dismantle them. Accordingly,

---

[217] The διβλία are always taken as referring to Thucydides i-viii, but why could they not designate what came to be called the παραλειπόμενα? If modern scholars have misunderstood the relation of Xenophon and Thucydides to Hellenica i and ii, why could not the same mistaken thoughts, about Thucydides writing Hellenica i-ii, have also occurred to some ancient writer, who then went on to embellish his notion with the pretty fiction reported by Diogenes? And can not most of the difficulties (δυνάμενος ὑφελέσθαι, αὐτός) of this obscure sentence of Diogenes, be cleared up considerably by understanding them in this light? I. e., instead of taking the δυνάμενος in a concessive sense, let it and the λανθάνοντα have here a causal force, thus: "Since the work (i. e., the παραλειπόμενα of 411-04) of Thucydides had not yet been discovered, Xenophon (finding it) was therefore able to appropriate it stealthily and publish it in his own name (αὐτός)." Moreover, the unusual condition of Thucydides' final book and the inexplicable termination of the history occasioned several attempts to account for these peculiarities by attributing the last book to various authors other than Thucydides, and Xenophon was among them (Marcellinus Vita 43). So if some of the ancients could have believed that Xenophon wrote Book Eight, why could not some also have thought that Thucydides wrote Hellenica i and ii?

[218] Herodotus vii. 166.

Lysander was later reported to have commenced the dismantlement of the Long Walls on the very anniversary of the day on which the Battle of Salamis had been fought seventy-six years before.[219] Of the three great tragedians, Aeschylus was later said to have fought in the battle,[220] Sophocles led the chorus around the trophy on Salamis,[221] while Euripides, in order to maintain the fanciful association, was born on Salamis on the very day of the victory.[222] It is the same propensity, then, that is at work in so arranging the lives of Herodotus and Thucydides as to enable the younger to have been present at Herodotus' recitations at Olympia.[223] And even in our own day in fact, we can see the workings of the very same tendency. From antiquity we have inherited the substance for a similar story, and it had only to await the imagination of a Volckmar to receive its determinate transformation. As Euripides,[224] so too Thucydides was said to have been killed in the wild, barbaric north.[225] Plutarch[226] gives the location more exactly: Hyle Scapte. Now as Herodotus[227] says that this village was on Darius' route, and as Xenophon[228] adds that Agesilaus' army, which Xenophon himself accompanied, took that same course, all the rudiments are at last at hand for a marvelous synthesis: Thucydides was murdered

[219] Plutarch *Lysander* 15.

[220] Pausanias i. 14. 5.

[221] Athenaeus i. 20^f.

[222] Philochorus *Vita Euripidis* 1.

[223] The urge was ever at work and the common trade and distinction of these two celebrated figures provided too inviting an opportunity to be forgone; so that eventually a connection was inevitable. The substance had been supplied by Lucian (*Herodotus or Aëtion* 1), who recorded that Herodotus used to give readings from his history at Panhellenic festivals to the gathered spectators; and of course who would most appropriately be among them but little Thucydides? Souidas (s.v. Θουκυδίδης) duly pictures him there, accordingly, holding his father, Olorus', hand and weeping tenderly at the moving recitation! Subsequent writers were agreeable to the story, of course, and it was repeated consistently thereafter.

[224] Diodorus xiii, 103. 5.

[225] Marcellinus *Vita Thuc.* 32-33.

[226] *Cimon* 4.

[227] vi. 46. 3.

[228] *Ages.* 2. 1.

by Agesilaus and Xenophon recovered the ὑπομνήματα![229]

Such charming fables, in fine, whether ancient or modern, are to be seen simply as manifestations of the ubiquitous tendency to gather notable events and persons about some common association and to press the conformity to the point of striking coincidence. In the case of the three tragedians we see the process complete; in that of the three historians[230] we find it incipient and undeveloped but moving, nevertheless, toward its inevitable consummation. Just as Herodotus and Thucydides came in time to be connected, so too Thucydides and Xenophon are in the process of being furnished with a similar unity in the form of the βιβλία λανθάνοντα of the ancients and the ὑπομνήματα of the moderns. Naturally such tendencies are properly the province of folklore and are only of incidental interest to the student of history; when such legends are looked upon seriously, however, they impede progress toward solution of our difficulties. Its sole justification being to explain the unusual character of the *Hellenica,* the ὑπομνήματα succeeds only in confounding the problem roundly by distributing the trouble it is supposed to remove. With Xenophon alone we have our difficulties enough; adding the element of Thucydides compounds them beyond all hope of solution. The theory, like its very title, is simply modern invention of no authority in antiquity and with no justification internally, as it was devised to satisfy a need that never existed.

[229] Volckmar, p. 12. After ventilating his remarkable thesis Volckmar pretends to be repelled by the horror of this enormity and hastens to add in all humility that it is incumbent on him to support his charge, as it would not be at all proper without the weightiest reasons to lay such a crime at the feet of the Lacedaemonians. Here are his reasons: Thucydides had been an Athenian general in the war; Xenophon passes over Agesilaus' progress into Greece with silence, although, as Xenophon himself said, it took a month. But Thucydides associated with the Peloponnesians for the greater part of twenty years *during* the war (v. 26), so that we have little reason to think that the Lacedaemonians would be so vindictive toward him after the war, and nine years after at that. The case of Alcibiades, besides, is enough to tell us that exiled Athenian commanders were not unwelcome among the Peloponnesians (or am I taking all this too seriously?).

[230] By Lucian's time they had become a triad. See *Quomodo historia sit conscribenda 2-10.*

CHAPTER III

SOURCES AND COMPOSITION

> One problem a historian is faced with is to decide what to
> include in his account and what to omit from it.
> —Dionysius of Hal. *(To Pompey* 771)

A number of circumstances of Xenophon's life have combined to form the basis of some interesting problems. It is
generally agreed that he spent the days of his early youth in
Athens during the closing years of the Peloponnesian War,
perhaps even engaging in some of the operations of that conflict. The next period in his life opened with his departure for
Asia to accompany the expedition of Cyrus on a venture that
was finally to return him to Greek Asia in charge of the
Cyrean troops. There he committed his army to Thibron when
that commander had been dispatched from Lacedaemon to
organize a campaign against the satraps on behalf of the
Greek coastal cities. Had Xenophon yet been banished from
Athens? Was he still able to return to his native city at this
time, as some would have him do? This possibility offers the
opportunity of assigning to this period Xenophon's acquaintance with Thucydides' history, and Xenophon's own completion thereof in the first two books of the *Hellenica*. In any
event, we find him (again?) in Asia at the side of Agesilaus,
who succeeded to the command in that region. It was at this
period that the conflict known as the Corinthian War broke
out, compelling Agesilaus and Xenophon with him to return
to Greece. If Xenophon had not been exiled before this time,
the fact that he was in the company, if not in some position
of command, of the forces of a state hostile to his own would
certainly then have brought down the penalty upon him. How
long he remained in the company of Agesilaus we do not
know, nor do we know where his residence was between the
opening phase of the Corinthian War and the time that he

was settled at Scillus in Triphylia by his Lacedaemonian hosts. Here he remained for some years at least, but he may have been constrained to forsake his pleasant retreat when Triphylia fell away from Spartan control in 371. There is a tradition that he thereupon took up his residence in Corinth, near to his native city, and this invites speculation about whether he ever returned to Athens, at least for visits, if his exile had been revoked.[231]

The interesting problems referred to above, however, are not those which grow out of the occurrences of Xenophon's life, but come about rather when these particulars are combined with those of his literary activity. Even more than in the case of Thucydides before him, Xenophon's historical writings are about movements and events in which the author took part, so that many opportunities are afforded us for interpreting these writings in the light of the circumstances of the historian's life. Perhaps the most important single event in this regard is the moment at which Xenophon committed the Cyrean troops to Thibron, for, as this event is mentioned in both the *Anabasis* and the *Hellenica,* it is the point at which the two works meet. Xenophon could well have been present at almost every scene described in the *Anabasis;* thereafter he was probably a witness to at least some of the events he relates, but to how many of them? Are the pages of Books Three and Four of the *Hellenica* as autobiographical as those of the *Anabasis?* If so, were these two histories intended to form a continuous, identical work? Do these two books of the *Hellenica,* moreover, form a section to themselves separate from the following books? Were the parts of the *Hellenica* written all at one time, therefore, or was each one written separately? All these questions touch on issues that are at the heart of the problem usually referred to as the composition of the *Hellenica.*

The indications we have for attempting to establish the date or dates of composition may be said to be either direct

[231] See Roquette, pp. 15-30, for a discussion of the problems relevant to the periods of Xenophon's life.

or indirect. Of the former variety are the specific allusions to historical events, contemporary literary works of others, and matters discussed in other writings of Xenophon himself. Foremost among the indications of this sort, of course, are the very historical events themselves, which constitute a *terminus a quo* for the section in which they are described. Of a more indirect nature are considerations of the author's conception of his history, general reflections of movements or ideals current during the age, and changes in the author's reaction to subjects that he dealt with more than once and at supposedly different times during his life. In the following discussion many of these indications will be examined to see whether we do indeed possess any strong evidence for determining the process whereby Xenophon came to write and assemble the last five books of the *Hellenica* and whether there are sure signs for dating any stages in the composition.

One is naturally led to a study of sources. If the origin of a writer's information can be determined, it can be correlated with what may be known of his life and used as an indication of the time and place of writing. Perhaps we can learn something, too, of the version, or side, of the story that the author is reporting to us and from whose viewpoint he is relating his account. This consideration is of particular significance in the case of Xenophon because of his prolonged association with Peloponnesians and his residence in their territory. As these circumstances afforded him access to knowledge about the activities of the Peloponnesians, to what extent did they also prevent him from learning about events taking place elsewhere? Here it becomes clear that such a problem is bound up with that of the date of composition of the history, since Xenophon's changes of residence as well as the alterations in the political situation would have affected the availability of information from the various quarters of Greece.

The most exhaustive study of the sources for the last three books of the *Hellenica* was made by Albert Banderet.[232]

---

[232] Albert Banderet, *Untersuchungen zu Xenophons Hellenika* (Basel, 1919).

His method of inquiry was one of drawing conclusions about the provenience of the historian's information by examining the reported facts themselves and on the basis of their content making inferences about their source.[233] As an illustration of this procedure we might select his exegesis of *Hellenica* v. 1. 21ff., which relates certain activities in the Saronic Gulf during the Corinthian War. As the vessels of Teleutias left the Piraeus after a daring raid, part of them went directly to Aegina with the captured merchant ships, whereas the others sailed down the coast of Sunium capturing still others, and since we are not told the number of ships that were conveyed to Aegina but are informed of the number of triremes which escorted them thither, Banderet infers that Xenophon's informant must have been with the contingent that sailed toward Sunium. For the operations on Aegina itself, where the Athenian Chabrias executed a successful ambush, the witness is likewise on the Peloponnesian side. He knows the number of ships that Chabrias brought to Athens before departing for Aegina, but he does not know the size of the armament Chabrias conducted from Athens to Aegina. This tells us that Chabrias must have originally departed from some port in the Peloponnesus, such as Corinth, where Xenophon could have learned the number of ships with which Chabrias arrived in Athens. The Aeginetan and Spartan losses are given separately, moreover, indicating that the informant for the battle on Aegina was on the Peloponnesian side.[234] This example adequately illustrates Banderet's procedure; he continues in this fashion, examining the particulars of each episode with a view to determining whether they indicate a Peloponnesian or Athenian source. "The narrative betrays the Spartans as its source";[235] "it is easy to suppose that one of the φυγάδες was the informant"; "the chief source derives from Sparta, from the Spartan army, from the company of Agesilaus, from

---

[233] ". . . ich Abschnitt für Abschnitt der Prüfung unterwarf und die Frage nach den Quellen und der Entstehung mir vorlegte" (*ibid.*, p. 8).

[234] *Ibid.*, pp. 10-11.

[235] *Ibid.*, p. 18.

his staff"[236] are statements typical of the conclusions that his method yields.

In the course of his examination Banderet discovers a kind of principle according to which Xenophon supposedly organized his account. He gives us his statement of this principle in connection with his discussion of Xenophon's failure to mention the Second Athenian Confederacy. He believes that Xenophon narrated history only in terms of significant events and that an account of such an event would have been considered meaningful only if it contained enough particulars to constitute a fully-rounded and internally consistent episode. Because the foundation of the Confederacy in 378/77 was concurrent with the outbreak of hostilities between Athens and the Peloponnesus and because this state of affairs interrupted communications between the two regions, Xenophon, an exile from Athens, was at that time prevented from acquiring a significant amount of information about the origin and nature of the new league. Since he therefore did not have enough facts to compose an account which would convey the essential understanding of the affair, his method dictated that he say nothing about it at all. In fact, although he could allude to the existence of the Confederacy indirectly,[237] he could not mention it outright.[238]

Finally, Banderet comes to the following conclusion about the nature of the *Hellenica*.

What is the result of these investigations? . . . There is hardly one section that is like another; they are each one begotten of the times and reflect in many ways the point of view of the person who served as Xenophon's source of information. . . . We gain no deep insight into Xenophon's conception of his work as a historian.[239]

We have considered Banderet's inquiry first, not because he was the first to attempt an analysis of the *Hellenica*, but rather because his work best represents the analytic position. If his work is sound we are not to think of the *Hellenica* as

---

[236] *Ibid.*, p. 19.
[237] On p. 43 Banderet notes seven such allusions.
[238] *Ibid.*, pp. 43-44.
[239] *Ibid.*, p. 8.

having any real unity or organization.[240] But are his findings
valid? We must first consider his method. At the basis of
Banderet's examination of the *Hellenica* lie two assumptions
which he everywhere makes without explicitly stating so. They
are conditions which are in fact inherent in the analytic approach, which confines its attention to the particulars of the
account in their immediate setting and forms conclusions only
on the basis of considerations arising directly out of them.
These assumptions are: that Xenophon reports to us all he
learns, and that he reports to us only what he learns of an
event at the time of its occurrence. Let us examine Banderet's
first detailed critique, that of *Hellenica* v. 1. 21-24, with a
view to determining the validity of a method based on these
assumptions. We recall that, since Xenophon's informant, according to Banderet, does not report the number of ships captured in the Piraeus, he must be aboard one of the ships that
continued to Sunium and not in one of the "three or four"
escorting triremes. For if he had been aboard one of these
latter vessels he would have known the number of captured
merchantmen; and had Xenophon learned that number, he
would have reported it to us. But may we not ask why Xenophon did not also inform us of the number of vessels captured by the party the informant was in that sailed down the
coast? For he definitely says that this contingent too captured
merchantmen, "some of them full of grain, others of merchan-
dise." Yet no number is given here either. We cannot assume,
therefore, that the historian has recorded every particular of
which he was informed. Moreover, after the exciting raid had
been so successfully executed and when all elements had returned to Aegina (sec. 24), can we not imagine that the full
number of vessels that were captured would have been calculated? Indeed, one could suppose that it was ascertained
with great interest and repeated as often as the tale of this
surprising adventure was rehearsed. No such number, how-

---

[240] Here we should exclude from consideration the position of those who
believe the main portion, if not all, of the *Hellenica* was left unfinished,
since we cannot tell whether the author intended to give it a unified exposition.

ever, is anywhere found in Xenophon's account. Strangely, it is only those numbers that are inconsequential to the narrative of an exciting exploit that are given.[241] Xenophon makes an approximation of a distance (sec. 21) and of the number of escorting triremes (sec. 23). But the grand total number of ships captured and the amount of the booty—these, the important and impressive figures, we are not told; the historian refers to these quantities only in the vaguest terms.

At this point, however, one might object that, although we may not have the right to assume with Banderet that Xenophon has reported all he was able to learn, we can rightly expect that every *important* fact be reported; and seeing that the total number of ships captured is wanting from the account, we may therefore conclude that Xenophon never received a report of this figure. Yet, however compelling this possibility might appear and however useful such a principle would be in historical criticism generally, it too must be rejected. For would not just such a particular as the full number of the ships that were seized be the very one most subject to corruption owing to the tendency for those who relate stirring adventures to lend interest to their stories through exaggeration?[242] There is good likelihood, then, that Xenophon did receive exact reports of these matters but, as they were conflicting and suspicious, he chose not to repeat them. Attempts to infer the point of view or presence of the historian's source according to Banderet's method are therefore fallacious, since

[241] Although the smallness of the number (12) of Teleutias' triremes would, to be sure, have enhanced the danger for the participants in the raid (cf. v. 1. 19-20) and thus would have been liable to diminution by a raconteur, it was known to Xenophon from other connections (cf. v. 1. 5-6).

[242] At least Thucydides thought so (v. 68. 2): "As for setting down a definite figure, either for the several contingents on either side, or for the grand totals—that is more than I could have done, with accuracy. There was no getting at the strength of the Lacedaemonians, thanks to the secrecy of their administration; as for the figures for the others again, there was no trusting them, because men are so prone to exaggeration touching their own numbers" (Woodhouse). For another such important total reported to Thucydides which he refuses to record for the same reason, see iii. 113. 6.

we cannot even assume that Xenophon reports to us all of the important information that he received.

The same may be said of Banderet's study[243] of the ambush of the Peloponnesians by Chabrias (v. 1. 10-13), wherein the attempt is made to establish that Xenophon had access to information from the Athenian side. There are no few objections that might be made to Banderet's analysis of this episode, but it will be sufficient to draw attention to one particular that admirably demonstrates the contradictions this method leads to when it is conscientiously followed. As Xenophon does not inform us whence Chabrias came (sec. 10) before stopping at Athens, we know that the informant was not on the Athenian side. And the fact that the composition of the armament that Chabrias brought with him to Athens was known to Xenophon indicates that the voyage must have originated somewhere in the Peloponnesus, "probably from Corinth."

The other of the two assumptions on which the analytic type of criticism employed by Banderet is founded is that the account of events in the *Hellenica* represents the extent of the author's information about those events at the time of their occurrence. Banderet has explained Xenophon's failure to record the foundation of the Second Athenian Confederacy, for example, on the ground that Xenophon could not learn enough about that movement to write a full episode about its creation and its operation. First of all, however, it would hardly seem true that an author of the type that Banderet conceives Xenophon to be, would be so methodical as to refrain from relating a matter unless he had enough particulars to describe it as a well-rounded episode. In any case, it would be impossible to bring even the most well-known omissions in the *Hellenica* under Banderet's explanation. Let us look at his treatment of three representative incidents. In referring to Xenophon's supposed lack of knowledge of the Athenian Confederacy, Banderet discusses Xenophon's situation "in the winter of 378/77,"[244] when the Confederacy was organized.

---

[243] P. 11 and n. 6.
[244] *Ibid.*, p. 44.

In the case of the foundation of Megalopolis, which Xenophon "does not mention in definite terms," Banderet's argument is introduced with: "At the time when these events took place, Xenophon. . . ."[245] And, finally, concerning the fact that there is no record of the foundation of Messene in the *Hellenica,* Banderet notes that "by that time he [Xenophon] had already taken up his residence in Corinth. . . ."[246] The critical element in each case, then, seems to be the historian's whereabouts and consequently his access to the facts at the moment each event occurred. But why could not Xenophon have obtained information about these undertakings, ones of such magnitude and of such importance to his account, at some later date? Besides, in each of these three cases Banderet grants that Xenophon later acquired information about the events of which he had imperfect knowledge at the time of their occurrence.[247] There is therefore no reason to believe that there is in the *Hellenica* any relation between the inclusion or omission of the report of an event and the author's knowledge of that event at the exact moment of its occurrence.

Moreover, we are under no obligation to concede that any supposed organization of his history in terms of episodes would mean that, if Xenophon had but limited knowledge of the Athenian Confederacy at the time of its foundation or even at any later date, this would have been an impediment to his making mention of as much as he in fact knew.[248] Actually,

[245] *Ibid.,* p. 70, n. 46.

[246] *Ibid.,* p. 81

[247] See especially p. 70: Xenophon was in Corinth when Megalopolis was founded and "von einem Namen Μεγάλη πόλις hörte man damals noch nichts." When the Megalopolitans later join Epaminondas, Xenophon names them "ohne eine Erklärung beifügen zu müssen oder an einer früheren Stelle ein erklärendes Wort einzuscheiben." Why? He would of course have been obligated to do so. It is curious, too, that Xenophon's being in Corinth during the foundation of Messene was no reason for him not to have heard of that event (p. 81), whereas the fact that he was in Corinth when Megalopolis was founded is given as a reason why he did not know of it and "nichts anderes berichten konnte, als er es tut" (p. 70, n. 46).

[248] An interesting confirmation is found on pp. 39-40, where Banderet admits that Xenophon discussed the Battle of Naxos without really knowing too much about it; in fact he does not even know where it happened

a number of passages offer themselves as appropriate locations for such a notice, although there is none more fitting than the raid of Sphodrias in v. 4, which was, in fact, the very occasion for organizing the Confederacy.[249] So that if we were to find in v. 4. 34, "Therefore the Athenians furnished the Piraeus with gates, set about building ships, organized an alliance of maritime states, and gave aid to the Boeotians with all zeal," it would appear as natural a sentence as Xenophon ever wrote.

Nevertheless, for those to whom Banderet's procedure is acceptable, promising results await. Concerning the account of the siege of Phlius (v. 2. 3), we learn that Xenophon's source "is informed about everything exactly; he relates in detail the covert allusions in the calculated answers of his general to the increasingly apprehensive Phliasians; he had intelligence of a strong dissension in the Spartan camp, and how Agesilaus reluctantly becomes commander; he participates in the first negotiations for surrender; he knows of Agesilaus' resentment bred of checked ambition, the secret threads of which, . . ."[250] and so on. All of which enables Banderet to affirm that the character of Xenophon's account is simply a reflection of his sources.[251] Little room is left for Xenophon's own predilections, or style, or judgment, or interests; or discretion in selecting information, or liberty to omit it. How unlikely it is, therefore, that Xenophon, who is merely the representative of his informants, could have a fundamental

(we know it was Naxos from Diodorus xv. 34), nor of the siege whereby Chabrias induced Pollis to fight, nor the losses, nor Chabrias' action so reminiscent of an incident in which Xenophon once took the greatest interest—retrieving those on the wrecks—nor even the significance of the success for the Athenian Confederacy (see p. 43). Ignorance on none of these points, however, prevented Xenophon from telling what little he did know of the battle.

[249] Beloch, III, Part II, 147-150; Grote, VIII, 96-97; and J. B. Bury, A History of Greece (3d ed. rev. by R. Meiggs; London, 1956), pp. 563-64. Banderet, p. 43, mentions this incident as the first reference in Xenophon to "diesen neuen Aufschwung athenischer Seemacht."

[250] Banderet, pp. 19-20.

[251] Ibid., p. 8.

purpose in writing, or that the *Hellenica* could have a grand organization and unity.[252]

If Banderet's work is to be taken as representative of this method, then, we must conclude that the attempt to determine from the *Hellenica* alone, as it were, the sources of Xenophon's information and his use of it has been unsuccessful. We need not despair of a solution to these problems, however, for there exist other approaches, which offer, besides, more encouraging prospects of results. These attempt to arrive at solutions using the *Hellenica* in connection with other writings, whether those of Xenophon himself or of contemporary authors. The possibilities of this method have been pointed out by Rapaport,[253] whose conclusions were obtained by a comparison of some passages of the *Hellenica*, other works of Xenophon, and works of contemporary authors as well. He first of all noted that we have what appears to be a distinct contradiction between two different passages in Xenophon. The first is found in *Hellenica* i. 7 in the story of the trial of the generals after the Battle of the Arginusae. Here we are expressly told that only eight generals were tried (secs. 1, 34), and Socrates appears to be one of the ordinary Prytanes (sec. 15). Turning to the *Memorabilia*,[254] however, we find that the

---

[252] Banderet fancies that he can tell more about the personality of Xenophon's witness (he seems to know there was only one) to the Battle of Leuctra than, one might suppose, he knows about Xenophon himself: (p. 59) "Hier spricht wieder ein Augenzeuge, ein Teilnehmer am Heereszug; er spricht zu jemand, der die Ereignisse im grossen und ganzen schon kannte, im Plauderton, zu einem Freund, dem gegenüber er sich gehen lässt, bei dem er Verständnis zu finden glaubt und geneigtes Gehör, wenn er auf der einen Seite kleinliche Kritik übt an dem spartanischen Feldherrn und sich die Niederlage klar machen will, ohne von der Stichhaltigkeit seiner Gründe überzeugt zu sein." If the nature of the *Hellenica* can be resolved into the character of its sources to the extent to which such statements as this imply, then we might raise the question whether we can rightly speak of Xenophon as the "author" of the *Hellenica*, seeing that his office was merely to transcribe deputations of witnesses and report them to us verbatim without exercising any judgment or giving any arrangement of his own. As we speak of a "Homeric" question perhaps we may speak of a "Xenophontean" one.

[253] Arthurus Rapaport, "Xenophontea," *Eos*, XXVII (1924), 19-22.

[254] i. 1. 18, iv. 4. 2.

number of generals tried on that occasion is reported as nine, and Socrates, moreover, now appears as *epistates*. In an attempt to resolve this puzzling conflict, Rapaport calls on two other authorities for the period in question, Aristotle and Plato. The latter makes an incidental allusion to the affair in the *Apology* (32ᵇ), where his topic is the activities of Socrates. There, however, the number of generals is given as ten, and Socrates is described as one of the Prytanes. Aristotle[255] confirms Plato's version of ten generals but adds another particular that tends to increase the difficulties, for he speaks of there being some generals condemned who did not participate in the battle. Whose account, then, is correct, and what are we to make of the two conflicting statements of Xenophon? Are there any conclusions we can draw about Xenophon's method and sources from these differing versions of the same event?

Rapaport ambitiously sets about the task, uniting all the various elements to produce some impressive results. To begin with, he infers that, since the *Hellenica* contains a fuller documentation and shows a greater familiarity with the incident in question, it must have been written after the corresponding passages in the *Memorabilia*.[256] At the outset, however, an objection is raised by MacLaren.[257] He rather conceives that Xenophon wrote the passage in the *Memorabilia,* which MacLaren admits to be inexact, long after the trial, and, having forgotten the particulars thereof, turned to his own account of the episode in the *Hellenica,* written much earlier, to recapitulate the proceedings. But his forgetfulness must have been no match for his carelessness, since MacLaren goes on to say that he misread even his own words and concluded that there had been nine generals on trial, not eight. This seems most unlikely. Xenophon may well have been present at the trial, to begin with, and it is difficult to believe that he could ever have forgotten such a prominent aspect of the affair, particularly as he had once written an elaborate account of all

---

[255] Ἀθ. Πολ. 34. 1.

[256] Rapaport, *Eos*, XXVII, 20-21.

[257] *AJP*, LV, 256-60.

the transactions. And in spite of all of that to have the author misunderstand his own account is too much.[258] Moreover, MacLaren will have still another difficulty to reckon with, for Rapaport notices that, whereas there is nothing said of Socrates' special position of *epistates* in the *Hellenica,* he is so distinguished in both passages in the *Memorabilia.* In addition, Rapaport thinks it is probable that the *epistates* had the power to prevent a proposal from being put to a vote, and how could the generals have finally been condemned, he therefore asks, if Socrates, the *epistates,* had not agreed? The version of the *Hellenica,* where Socrates is not designated as *epistates,* represents, then, a later clarification of his role. This time, however, MacLaren is better prepared. Pointing out first that Rapaport relies on no real evidence for his assumption about the powers of the *epistates,*[259] MacLaren goes on to show that

---

[258] MacLaren's reconstruction of Xenophon's erroneous calculation, however, is perhaps acceptable—if only we attribute it to someone other than Xenophon. Reading no more than the first sentence of i. 7, one could get the impression that there were only nine generals concerned, naively subtracting one (Conon) from ten. But if he reads the *second* sentence, he is immediately undeceived, for here it is specified (six plus two), replete with names and all. "Had he read a little farther . . ." (Yes, *one* sentence); yet "he carelessly neglected to do so." Hardly Xenophon, then. Besides, the fact that Xenophon, unlike Plato and Aristotle, was solicitous about specifying the exact number and felt it necessary to consult an authoritative account, argues a careful regard for the truth that is belied by inattentiveness so great as his not troubling to read two consecutive sentences in the record after having taken the trouble of seeking it out. MacLaren also suggests, though not too seriously, a scribal error "arising from the similarity in sound between 'eta' and 'theta'." But this always seems to be an unfair way out of a controversy; as would be, too, arguing that the words ("nine generals") are an intrusion of a marginal comment into the text. So, until more convincing reasons are advanced to explain the contradiction, Rapaport and Sordi, who agrees with him (*Athenaeum,* XXVIII, 44), must have their way. We need not, however, grant to the latter her point that the *Memorabilia* represents Xenophon's personal recollections (rather than results of investigation) because of the general way in which the story is there told (*ibid.*). It is not there in point, of course, to give a fully detailed account of the trial (as in the *Hellenica),* when one is interested only in Socrates' behavior. These are, after all, simply memoirs of Socrates, not a history of Greece.

[259] Actually, Rapaport does refer (*Eos,* XXVII, 20) to a statement in Aristotle's 'Αθ. Πολ. 4. 1, which is supposed to throw light on the matter, although the words he quotes are not found at that place in my

the fact that Socrates is not designated as *epistates* in the *Hellenica* does not constitute an objection to his argument, for he cites Thucydides vi. 14, where the *epistates* is addressed merely as Prytanis. And at this point we may also mention the view of Delebecque, who finds Xenophon's according Socrates the distinction of *epistates* to be evidence of a later conception that Xenophon formed of his great teacher after Socrates had impressed his significance upon his pupils by his sacrificial death.[260] However that may be, we should also observe that the powers of the *epistates* would have been known to Xenophon from his general acquaintance with such things as an Athenian citizen as well as from the many times he personally attended meetings of the Assembly, and his supposed ignorance of these matters is an issue much broader than his memory of this one trial, to which, however, discussion of the problem is usually confined. And how likely is it, too, that Xenophon would have forgotten significant particulars about the role of his own master?

We have more to hear about Xenophon at this early period, however. Writing the episodes in the *Memorabilia*, Rapaport continues, Xenophon found it necessary to specify the number of generals convicted at the trial. Although he did not know this number himself, he had heard various reports about it, and among these was the version (ten) of Plato. And although he did not think it was accurate, it was nevertheless partly under the influence of this account that Xenophon chose to record the report of nine generals (rather than that of a lesser number, let us say). Yet if that is so, how did Aristotle come to accept the account of ten generals that Xenophon rejected? This version Aristotle simply took over from Plato: "who could possibly deny" that he did so, in fact, seeing that Plato

(Oxford) edition. Nor can I quite discover how his conclusion follows from the sense of the passage he quotes; in fact he seems not altogether certain himself. MacLaren ignores the point completely, and I think rightly so.

[260] Delebecque, pp. 36-37. Cf. Hatzfeld, *Xenophon: Helléniques,* I, 62, n. 2, who also finds Xenophon adorning the story later by giving Socrates the higher honor in the *Memorabilia.*

is "a most reliable authority"? This interpretation also explains another erroneous statement of Aristotle's, that even those generals who took no part in the battle were convicted, for it shows that Aristotle felt it necessary to alter the rest of the story to conform to the report of ten generals convicted, rather than relinquish that datum. But in the meantime he had learned from still another (erroneous) source that there had been eight generals present at the battle. It was necessary, therefore, to reconcile this report somehow with Plato's statement that ten generals were convicted, and this he did by saying (wrongly) that some generals who were not present at the battle were also condemned. This was presumably much the same calculation, therefore, that led to Xenophon's account in the *Memorabilia*.

But we have not yet pursued our inquiry far enough, Rapaport encourages us, for it is soon to bring us to a truly rewarding conclusion. Accepting the opinion of those who assign the *Memorabilia* to a date shortly after the Battle of Leuctra, Rapaport believes that it was not until much later that Xenophon began investigating records in preparation for his account in the *Hellenica*. It was only now that he discovered the true facts about the trial, which he has recorded for us in detail in his definitive version. It now became apparent to Xenophon that Plato had been wrong about the number of ten condemned, and it was this version that had given rise in turn to Xenophon's inaccurate report of nine.[261] This figure, accordingly, he now changed to eight. And, finally, discovering that, although Plato had been wrong about the generals, he had nevertheless been right in not saying that Socrates was the *epistates,* Xenophon changed his original account and identified Socrates simply as one of the Prytanes.[262] Now all

---

[261] Rapaport, *Eos,* XXVII, 21. The only documentation he produces for this confident assertion is a statement of Wilamowitz' saying that it is not so.

[262] *Ibid.,* pp. 20-21. As the relationships of the elements of Rapaport's system are complicated, I have sought to render the scheme more comprehensible by graphic representation. The traditions are indicated by

this at last brings Rapaport triumphantly to his conclusion, and it is one that puts him right on the side of Wilamowitz and Eduard Schwartz, the most learned men of the age:[263] if parts of the *Memorabilia* were written after 365, the *Hellenica* was composed even later.[264]

Rapaport's deductions need not detain us long. He is of course wrong in thinking that Plato's account had any influence on Xenophon's, which opposes that of Plato in every respect. Conflicting versions contradict, not confirm, one another.[265] And why would Aristotle not have known of the

triangles, whereas circles enclose deductions made by the writers as reconciliations of conflicting reports.

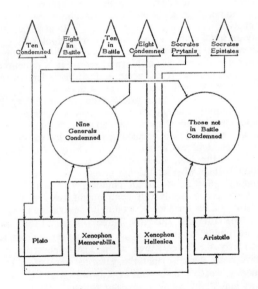

[263] "Cum doctissimis aetatis nostrae viris." *Ibid.*, p. 21.
[264] *Ibid.*, p. 22.

[265] The following is offered in an attempt to save Plato's version of ten generals. First, we must remember that Plato is here writing about Socrates not about the generals or about their trial. Could there not have been a popular notion abroad that there had been ten generals involved in the affair? Indeed, we have evidence that there was such a current impression

more authoritative account of the *Hellenica?* Certainly the
Constitution of Athens was written after the *Hellenica,* with
which it betrays a familiarity on several points.[266] Moreover,
Aristotle's account is even more erroneous than Rapaport
notes, for whereas Xenophon (i. 7. 32) has Euryptolemus
say that there was only one general who was rescued from
the sea, Aristotle speaks of several (34. 1). Clearly then,
Rapaport's arguments, to say nothing of their following a
dubious logic, are deficient besides, since they have not taken
into consideration all of the facts and the possibilities con-

from the very fact that two of our authorities so have it. Allowing that
possibility, then, what would Plato, if not Socrates himself, have probably
said in referring to the incident when his sole purpose was to recall the
occasion to the mind of his audience? Pedantry and scholarly relevance are,
after all, somewhat out of place when one's life is at issue. As a parallel
(and to compare small things with great) we may think of the propriety of
the pronounciation and spelling of certain words that exist in two forms.
When we make use of them in an informal setting it is sometimes advisable
to choose the more popular if less accurate form in order not to call undue
attention to the word and detract from the, albeit informal, thought.
(Cf. perhaps "It is I" and "It's me.") However that may be, there is
still another possibility that ought to be given a hearing. Our texts of
ancient authors do not use a special designation for proper nouns, as we
(in English, at any rate) are accustomed to do by capitalizing the first
letters. For example, whereas we so treat "the Thirty," "the Five Thousand,"
"the Demos" and the like, these are not specially distinguished in the
texts. My point is this: whether the ten generals were not really conceived
of as a standing group of a certain number? If the Eleven at any one
time was not composed of its full complement (owing, for example, to
the death of one of its members), would it, nevertheless, not still be referred to as the Eleven? Did the Three Thousand become the Two
Thousand Ninety-nine when Critias struck Theramenes' name from the
roll, or the Thirty the Twenty-nine when Theramenes died? Likewise it
may well have been the case that the generals were often thought of as
the Ten Generals, whether their number was always at full strength or not.
Thus Socrates and Plato could have been following usage in referring to
the collective action of the Board of Ten Generals, quite regardless of
how many were in office at the time of the battle, or how many participated
in it, or how many were condemned because of it, since *collectively* all
these things applied.

    [266] So conclude Kurt von Fritz and Ernst Kapp, *Aristotle's Constitution
of Athens and Related Texts* (New York, 1950), pp. 182-83. Of 36. 1 and
most of 2, for example, they state, "This passage seems to be taken over
almost literally from Xenophon."

sequent to them. We must look elsewhere, therefore, if we are to arrive at acceptable results from the method of comparing the *Hellenica* with other writings.[267]

Perhaps the approach that seeks to analyze the *Hellenica* by using the works of other authors is too pretentious. Our knowledge of the dates of publication of ancient works, of the practice of issuing several editions, and of the relations that

[267] Actually there are some attractive possibilities for establishing relations with the *Hellenica* in the writings of Isocrates. There is an interesting similarity of wording, for example, in the ἀντιρρόπως ῥώμ ἐπικυδέστεροι of Hell. v. 1. 36 and the ἐπικυδέστερα and ῥώμης of *Panegyricus* 139, but no one has been able to arrive at any useful conclusions about it. The most determined effort was made by Gustav Friedrich, "Zum Panegyrikos des Isocrates," *JCP*, CXLVII (1893), 1ff. Friedrich begins with section 126 of that oration, which is often taken as one of the indications that confirm the usual date, 380, for the work. He first (pp. 6-7) moves the date of the oration back to 385 and solves the resultant difficulty of section 126 (actually he includes the entire passage secs. 122-32) by saying it was inserted in the second edition. The way is now open for him to argue his thesis, that the second part of the *Hellenica* was published in 384 (p. 17), since he can show that Isocrates did not know the *Hellenica* when he published the *Panegyricus* in 385. He first tries to show that Isocrates did not know the *Anabasis* when he wrote the *Panegyricus* and decides (p. 8) that since Isocrates did not then know the *Anabasis* he did not know the *Hellenica*, without, however, establishing the relative order of the *Anabasis* and the *Hellenica*. To this he adds a few comparisons of indefinite value before concluding (p. 9) that Xenophon must have known the *Panegyricus* in writing Hell. v. 1. 36, since Isocrates did not know the *Anabasis* in 385. Now the fact that Isocrates does not follow the *Anabasis* does not mean he did not know it, any more than Aristotle's not following the *Hellenica* means that he was ignorant of that source. Actually, however Isocrates could just as well have been recalling the passage in Xenophon as the contrary: to say nothing of the possibility that both of them could have been under the common influence of a third author, which would throw off all calculations completely. Finally, I would discuss the work of Piero Treves, "Per la cronologia di Senofonte," *Mélanges Desrousseaux* (Paris, 1937), pp. 470-72, except that I do not understand his reasoning; namely, (1) whether he believes that Erianthus did in fact make the demand (to destroy Athens) at the congress of the allies in 405, or not; (2) was the demand in fact disavowed by the ambassador at Athens in 395, or not? or is it only that Xenophon *says* it was disavowed? (3) what is the point

existed between contemporary writers is drastically limited, and we cannot expect plausible results from methods that rely too strongly on these uncertain particulars. A safer, if more modest, procedure would be to consider only works within the corpus of the same author, whose identity provides the unifying element that renders comparison more valid. We have already considered the *Memorabilia* in this connection, and we shall have occasion in time to speak of the *Anabasis*.[268] But it is the *Agesilaus* that offers by far the most attractive possibilities, owing to the striking similarity that work bears to a great section of the *Hellenica*. A number of attempts have been made to pursue the significance of this resemblance, although few observations of any importance have been made since the elaborate studies of Rosenstiel,[269] Seyffert,[270] and Opitz.[271] If, to the extent to which they are parallel, the two writings were an exact transcription of one another, our problem would be of a measurably different and less perplexing nature. The disparities that occur are often slight, yet they are sufficiently distinct to show that they were intended and did not arise through carelessness or oversight. In the opinion of those who have given close attention to the matter, in fact, most of these variations are stylistic and correspond simply to the difference in the nature of each work: the *Hellenica* is written in the plainer manner of a history, whereas the en-

---

in his saying that the party of Ismenias was not philo-Athenian? (4) what leads Treves to think that Isocrates got the "phrase" from Xenophon and not the reverse? in fact, what is his evidence for any connection between the two at all? (5) how is Xenophon supposed to be giving us to believe that the Athenians in 395 knew the exact wording of the Theban proposal of 405? (6) and finally, if Xenophon knew this "phrase of Erianthus," why does he not reproduce it? for there is no similarity in the wording of *Plataeicus* 14. 13 and *Hell*. ii. 2. 19.

[268] See below, pp. 154ff.

[269] Friedrich Rosenstiel, *De Xenophontis Historiae Graecae parte bis edita* (Jena, 1882).

[270] Walter Seyffert, *De Xenophontis Agesilao quaestiones* (Göttingen, 1909).

[271] Alfonsus Opitz, "Quaestiones Xenophonteae: de Hellenicorum atque Agesilai necessitudine," *Breslauer Philologische Abhandlungen* (hereafter cited as *BPA*), XLVI (1913), 1-88.

comium prefers a more ornate style of expression. But there is one type of divergence about which opinion is somewhat divided. Passages in the two works will often correspond to one another with virtual similarity except for a certain apparently meaningless and unnecessary substitution of a single word in the one work for its synonym in the other. These pairs of variant synonyms are (ἐφ) ἕπεσθαι *(Ages.)* for (ἐπ) ἀκολουθεῖν *(Hell.);*[272] περί *(Ages.)* for ἀμφί *(Hell.);* [273] and μείων *(Ages.)* for ἐλάττων *(Hell.)*.[274] Moreover, the synonym in each set that is preferred by either work in the parallel passages is also the word that that respective work prefers elsewhere.[275] Rosenstiel noted that in the *Hellenica* the words in each set which are used more often than their synonyms are those which are more characteristic of Attic prose usage of the fourth century and that their synonyms are the forms oftener or exclusively employed in older Attic (ἕπεσθαι) or in dialects other than Attic (ἀμφί, μείων). Xenophon's greatest literary activity, Rosenstiel said, was during the years 401-371, a time when his contact would have been exclusively with non-Attic speaking Greeks, and since *Hellenica* ii. 3. 11-v. 1. 36 was also written and published during that time, it would have been written in the same style as that of the rest of his works. Removing to Corinth sometime after 371, however, Xenophon resumed intercourse with his native city,

[272] As, for example, *Ages.* 1. 32: cf. *Hell.* iii. 4. 24; 2. 2: cf. iv. 3. 3; 2. 3: cf. iv. 3. 5.

[273] E.g., 2. 3: cf. iv. 3. 4; 2. 4: cf. iv. 3. 8; 2. 11: cf. iv. 3. 17.

[274] 1. 13: cf. iii. 4. 11. There are no other parallel passages that contain either of these two words.

[275] Using the statistics of Seyffert (pp. 7-8) we find that neither ἀκολουθεῖν nor any compound thereof is found in the *Agesilaus,* whereas ἕπεσθαι and its compounds are found four times (cf. also 2. 12). περί (local? See Rosenstiel, p. 17) is there (2. 2) found once, however; ἀμφί (Rosenstiel, *ibid.)* occurs four times (cf. also 2. 13). Ἐλάττων is found once (2. 7), whereas μείων is found six times (cf. also 1. 1, 2. 1, 7, 24 [cf. *Hell.* vi. 4. 15]; 6. 3). In the *Hellenica* ἀκολουθεῖν and its compounds occur forty-seven times, ἕπεσθαι and its compounds twelve times; περί sixty-nine times ἀμφί five times (ii. 3. 46, v. 3. 6, 13, v. 4. 7, 29); and ἐλάττων thirty-four times, μείων twice (i. 5. 4 and vii. 4. 2).

which by now had probably recalled him from exile, and renewed acquaintance with his own dialect. When he finally undertook to complete the *Hellenica,* in addition to writing the events that had occurred since the first publication, he revised the earlier part as well. This revised and expanded version, then, Xenophon at that time published, and this is the edition, in fact, that has come down to us. Sometime after his death, however, an anonymous rhetor wrote the *Agesilaus,* basing considerable portions of Chapters One and Two of that work on the old, first edition of the *Hellenica,* which is no longer extant. And thus it is that the *Agesilaus,* though having been modelled on the *Hellenica,* nevertheless shows a preference for words Xenophon characteristically used in works written before our *Hellenica.*[276]

What are we to make of these variations? Should we with Opitz and Seyffert recognize in the differences between the two works no great significance as to the stages of the writing of the *Hellenica,* or are we to believe with Rosenstiel, Friedrich, and De Sanctis that the variations in the choice of synonyms provide a definite indication of the period at which that work was composed? A starting point for consideration is provided by the work of Rosenstiel, one of whose conclusions was that the *Agesilaus* was not written by Xenophon.[277] Friedrich, while accepting much of Rosenstiel's reasoning about the relation between the two works, objected to a solution that deprived Xenophon of the authorship of either, and he set about making a case for Rosenstiel's approach by which both works could nevertheless be attributed to Xenophon. Pointing to *Agesilaus* 1. 6, where Agesilaus, who must have been approaching forty years of age at that time, is spoken of as " νέος," Rosenstiel thought that Xenophon, who had known the King intimately, would not have made such an error, and he took the passage as evidence that the *Agesilaus* had been written by another hand. Friedrich, however, notes that the same word is used in similar circumstances in Aris-

[276] Rosenstiel, pp. 26-33.
[277] *Ibid.,* pp. 52-53.

totle's *Constitution of Athens*,[278] and since νέος has a somewhat different meaning from merely "young," he thinks it
could properly have been used of Agesilaus when he came to
the throne. Accordingly, Friedrich believes that Xenophon
first wrote *Hellenica* ii. 3. 11-v. 1. 36 but that he did not, as
Rosenstiel had thought, publish it immediately. Xenophon's
hesitation in giving this part to the world was due to the fact
that it was written in a somewhat venturous style which dif-
fered considerably from the usual Attic prose style of his
day. This was Xenophon's first publication, Friedrich believes,
and since he would have been apprehensive about appearing
to depart too severely from the ordinary Attic usage,[279] he
reviewed the work on second thought and substituted the
regular Attic forms for the dialectal and obsolescent ones that
he had used in the original copy. The original draft Xenophon
put by and made no use of it until he was writing the
Agesilaus, and, having by that time overcome his initial dif-
fidence, he confidently indulged in the unorthodox vocabulary
that he had withdrawn from the published *Hellenica*.[280]

A possible objection that they must counter who follow a
reasoning similar to Friedrich's arises from the question of
priority: why could it not be that the *Hellenica* was written
after the *Agesilaus* and thus naturally use a "later" vocabulary? Friedrich answers by pointing to a number of parallel
passages in the two works in which the version of the *Hellenica* appears to him to be clearer and therefore corrected.
He first of all cites *Hellenica* iv. 3. 8, and iv. 3. 7, which according to him represent an improvement in sense over the
corresponding passages (2. 4 and 2. 3) in the *Agesilaus*. One
way in which this is so is illustrated by the fact that in the

---

[278] Gustav Friedrich, "Zu Xenophons Hellenika und Agesilaos," *JCP*,
CLIII (1896), 297, n. 9. Cf. 'Αθ. Πολ. 26 and 27.

[279] At this point Friedrich (*JCP*, CLIII, 298, n. 11) remarks that the
appellation, "the Attic Bee," by which Xenophon came to be known, must
have been given him at a much later date. But does "Attic" in this connection refer to the dialect or the locality? I wonder if this epithet is not
equivalent to "the Stagirite" or "the Mantuan"; or rather, perhaps, to the
"Wasp of Twickenham"?

[280] Friedrich, *JCP*, CLIII, 298.

first of these two parallel versions the verbose expression, "they were captured alive," of the *Agesilaus* was shortened to "they were captured" in the *Hellenica*. Friedrich finds another indication for the priority of the *Agesilaus* in a tendency illustrated by the changes in wording of the last two parallel passages cited where "trying to turn around" of the *Agesilaus* became "trying to do this" in the *Hellenica*. Here, then, a more concrete expression has given way to an abstract one in accordance with the natural development of an author's style and thought.[281] Finally, in the difference between the fullness of some of the parallel passages, Friedrich detects the usual tendency for an author to shorten and abridge his manuscript before publishing it. We learn more about the Battle of Coronea, for example, in the *Agesilaus* (2. 13ff.) than in the *Hellenica* (iv. 3. 20ff.). This practice, Friedrich explains, is a common one and we can quite naturally suppose that Xenophon followed it too. But what of the final part of the *Hellenica,* which was written after the *Agesilaus?* In this case it was Xenophon's feeling for consistency that required that the remaining portion should observe the same stylistic form as that of the earlier part, and thus this section shows a much closer affinity with the earlier part than with the *Agesilaus.*[282]

One might receive the impression from statements of Friedrich's that, with respect to the choice of words which we have noted, there is a great difference in the style of the two works in question, and that, whereas the later vocabulary is exclusively preferred in the *Agesilaus,* the standard Attic forms alone occur in the *Hellenica*. If this were true it would give point forcibly to the argument that it was more than considerations of genre that so carefully determined that a special vocabulary was to be exclusively employed or strictly avoided. A perfect regularity, however, does not exist. In the *Agesilaus* the form, ἐλάττων, is found once (2. 7), and περί occurs also at least once (2.2), perhaps twice (1. 33). But it is not so much the occurrence of these words in the *Agesilaus* on which

---

[281] Friedrich, *ibid.* Cf. also *Hell.* iii. 4. 16 with *Ages.* 1. 25; Hell. iv. 3. 6 with *Ages.* 2. 3; and particularly *Hell.* i. 5. 1 with *Ages.* 2. 18.
[282] Friedrich, *JCP,* CLIII, 299.

Friedrich builds his argument as upon their absence from the *Hellenica*, since the cause of all the changes is said to be Xenophon's reluctance to employ a novel and non-Attic prose style in his first publication. It must be noted, however, that Xenophon does make use of these supposedly non-Attic elements openly and freely in the *Hellenica*: μείων is not unknown, ἀμφί is found five times, and there are at least twelve occurrences of ἕπεσθαι.[283] At most, then, we have to do with an inclination to prefer certain words to their synonyms, and there does not exist any systematic avoidance of words of either group. Our problem, accordingly, is decidedly a more moderate one than we might have been led to suspect, and one that presents no difficulties that could not be satisfactorily explained by any number of more natural solutions than the involved plan proposed by Friedrich. Moreover, Xenophon's standard in his choice of words in the *Hellenica* was supposedly that of "the other Attic writers,"[284] but is this really true? Friedrich notes that the three non-Attic synonyms do not occur in Isocrates,[285] and it is of course true, as is usually stated, that the style of the Orators represents the most conservative Attic. But is the *Hellenica* oratory? And is not Thucydides an Attic author? Turning to Thucydides, then, for a more appropriate comparison with the *Hellenica*, we find in this matter of the synonyms that, "with the exception of ἕπεσθαι,"[286] Thucydides' style is about the same as that of Xenophon's in the *Hellenica*.[287]

It is, as Seyffert remarks,[288] no coincidence, then, that the agreement in these matters between these two histories is as strong as we find it to be. More than any other work of

[283] Seyffert, pp. 7-8.

[284] Friedrich, *JCP*, CLIII, 298.

[285] *Ibid.*, p. 297.

[286] Even here, however, we note the similarity: ἕπεσθαι is found twelve times in the *Hellenica* and fifteen times in Thucydides (Seyffert, pp. 7-9).

[287] *Ibid.*, p. 9.

[288] *Ibid.*

Xenophon's "this sadder and more sober production"[289] would by its nature prefer the plainer and less venturous form of expression that tends to impart an aura of reserve and impersonality to an account the effectiveness of which depends highly on an appearance of objectivity.

Friedrich also notes a deliberate avoidance in the *Hellenica* of a poetic manner and a tendency to prefer the more Attic and thus more prosaic turns of expression.[290] A thorough study of the styles employed in the *Hellenica* and in the *Agesilaus* was made by Opitz, and the results of his study are convincing and instructive. It would not be fitting to review his entire book here, but a few examples will suffice to illustrate his findings. For want of a better method of selection, in fact, we might examine the very passages Friedrich offers himself in support of his hypothesis. He points to the expression, ζῶντες ἡλίσκοντο, in *Agesilaus* 2. 4, and he takes the omission of ζῶντες in the corresponding passage (iv. 3. 8) in the *Hellenica* to represent the removal of an illogicality in a later, corrected version. Now when Friedrich says that in the later publication, the *Agesilaus,* Xenophon made use of a vocabulary that he had avoided in the earlier *Hellenica,* we might allow that such a procedure occurred. But who would also be willing to believe that the author who in a previous edition had eliminated a certain word as an illogical pleonasm, would in a later edition deliberately reinsert that identical blunder? Accordingly, we must think either that the *Hellenica* was written before the final draft of the *Agesilaus,* or that the presence of ζῶντες in *Agesilaus* 2.4 does not constitute a careless mistake. But of course if it is not such an error, Friedrich's reasoning must likewise collapse, since it is based on the assumption that the reading of the *Hellenica* was a

---

[289] Dakyns. II, xxxiii. Actually, what other historical works are there to mention? Even the *Anabasis,* particularly in its latter half, is much more of a "Prunkschrift" than a history of the order of the *Hellenica.*

[290] "In den Hell. ist also immer der ionische bzw. poetische Ausdruck vermieden, und das sind demnach auch alles Änderungen im Sinne des Atticismus und der Stilgesetze der attischen Prosa." Friedrich, *JCP,* CLIII, 298.

correction of the version which was later adopted for the *Agesilaus*. But to return to Opitz and enlightenment about *Agesilaus* 2. 4 and ζῶντες: actually, there are two "corrections" of the supposedly later work made in the former one, and not one correction only. Whereas the *Agesilaus* reads, ὥσθ' οἱ making an elision of ὥστε, in the *Hellenica* this unnecessary omission is avoided, just as the "unnecessary" ζῶντες is there likewise dropped. Now we are ready to ask what the real meaning of the variations between the *Hellenica* and the *Agesilaus* is and according to what principle the changes were made. When we put our two passages together for comparison, the difference between the pedestrian style of the history and the ornate elaboration of the eulogy becomes at once surprisingly clear:[291]

Hellenica iv. 3. 8

ὥσ-τε οἱ μὲν ἀπ-έ-   θνῃ-σκον αὐτῶν;
οἱ δὲ καὶ ἠ- λί-σκον-το.

Agesilaus 2. 4

ὥσθ'οἱ μὲν ἀπ- έ-   θνῃ-σκον αὐ- τῶν,
οἱ δὲ καὶ ζῶν-τες ἠ- λί- σκον-το.

Perhaps no clearer case than this neatly contrived isocolon could be made for thinking that the differences between the two works are not such as to require our plotting intricate schedules of draftings and publications, but answer easily and naturally to the difference in genre. But to make that perfectly clear in the present example, we might look with Opitz at *Memorabilia* iii. 12. 2—written, according to Friedrich, after our passage in the *Hellenica*—to see whether Xenophon conceived the omission of ζῶντες as a correction. There we find: πολλοὶ δὲ δι' αὐτὸ τοῦτο ζῶντές τε ἁλίσκονται.[292]

---

[291] Opitz, *BPA*, XLVI, 51.

[292] It is interesting to note the difference in approach represented by Opitz's and Friedrich's views about the difference in the wording of the other "discrepancy" cited by Friedrich: *Ages.* 2. 3 and *Hell.* iv. 3. 7. Friedrich saw the conversion of "turn around" (*Ages.*) to "to do this"

It is by the same difference between the character of the *Hellenica* and the *Agesilaus* that any affinity in one or the other for concrete or abstract expression would be accounted for. Euphuistic panegyrics would affect the abstract, whereas histories, being plain and literal, would seek out the concrete, however much the development of an author's thought and style "ought"[293] to show the opposite tendency. Friedrich's argument, that we are permitted to infer that the version in which "we learn more about the Battle of Coronea than in the *Hellenica*" is the earlier one since it is a "frequent occurrence" for a writer to abridge as he goes along, is likewise inadmissible. And again we must repeat how strange it is that Xenophon should have found errors in the original manuscript, which he corrected for the *Hellenica,* irregularities, which he eliminated, and verbiage, which he removed— only to adopt, without change, the uncorrected, irregular, and verbose manuscript for a later publication! And yet Friedrich's reason for thinking that the first part of the *Hellenica* (i-ii. 3. 10) was never published by the author is that Xenophon would have first corrected it and would never have given it to the public in its imperfect condition.[294]

By what criteria, moreover, Friedrich has determined that the second part of the *Hellenica* was Xenophon's first work,

(Hell.) as an attempt to avoid repetition and thus an improvement. Opitz, *BPA,* XLVI, 51, is not offended by the harmless repetition but notes rather the disturbing clumsiness of: seeing the enemy upon them (1) some fled, (2) others turned around, and (3) others trying to turn around were captured; (4) Pol. and others, however, turned around. It was an awkward attempt at anaphora; in writing the *Agesilaus* Xenophon noticed the blunder and cleared it up by simply eliminating the offending second clause.

[293] The concrete "pflegt der frühere zu sein" (Friedrich, *JCP,* CLIII, 298). It almost goes without saying that I cannot accept Friedrich's argument that these alterations represent changes from the concrete to the abstract. Opitz can of course account for them on stylistic grounds, such as *(BPA,* XLVI, 71) analyzing *Ages.* 2. 18 as a long studied period and thus an expansion of *Hell.* iv. 5. 1. Besides, there must be many parallel passages that would show just the opposite tendency as well, if one cared to look for them. A hurried survey of one page toward the end of *Ages.* (1. 27-32) discloses four: 1. 27, πολεμικά: *Hell.* iii. 4. 18, τὰ πολεμικά; 1. 28, μηδέν iii. 4. 19, οὐδέν; 1. 30, κατά: iii. 4. 22, εἰς; 1. 32, ἐπί: iii. 4. 24, εἰς.

[294] Friedrich, *JCP,* CLIII, 295.

he has kept successfully hidden from us. He would argue from his own view, that the case is proven by the deliberate avoidance of Ionic words, but we could not grant an assumption that is used to prove itself. He notes that the first part is very different on stylistic grounds from the other two;[295] yet according to all comparative stylistic studies the second part of the *Hellenica* comes toward the end, not the beginning, of Xenophon's literary career.[296] All of Friedrich's arguments, then, must be regarded as ill-taken and unacceptable.

But the position of those who argue for the priority of the *Agesilaus* cannot be dismissed without our giving a hearing to the arguments of De Sanctis,[297] who generally looks with favor on Rosenstiel's conclusions but who like Friedrich is somewhat distressed at a solution which requires that someone other than Xenophon wrote the *Agesilaus*. De Sanctis wisely notes that it is not easy to determine the nature of the relation between the two works, despite the fact that a close relation exists. Our quest for solutions, then, will not be easy and it must make use of all possible approaches. Accordingly, De Sanctis subjects the parallel passages in the two writings to a thorough collation in an attempt to determine the influence of one on the drafting of the other. First he compares *Agesilaus* 1. 28 with *Hellenica* iii. 4. 20. In the latter passage Agesilaus gives an order to the Spartan commanders that seems to apply rather to the soldiers, whereas in the *Agesilaus,* where there is no mention of the commanders, the order is rightly directed to the soldiers themselves. Thus, De Sanctis concludes, the *Agesilaus* at this point represents the original version and in copying the *Hellenica* from it Xenophon confused the grammatical reference by inserting the notice about the commanders. But since the intrusion did not greatly disturb the

---

[295] *Ibid.,* p. 299.

[296] Dittenberger, *Hermes,* XVI; Roquette; Stahl, *PA,* XVI, 35-36.

[297] Gaetano De Sanctis, "La genesi delle Elleniche di Senofonte," *Annali della R. Scuola Normale Superiore di Pisa, Storia e Filosofia,* Serie II, Vol. I (1932).

sense, the error thus introduced was not noticed and therefore no change was made in the wording to correct it.[298]

Hellenica iii. 4. 15 and *Agesilaus* 1. 23-24 also narrate the same episode between them. De Sanctis finds the reference in the *Agesilaus* to "skulking warfare" to be somewhat inappropriate, seeing that the encounter of the two armies, though related in *Hellenica* iii. 4. 13-14, is here omitted. Yet the measures Agesilaus took to provide against fighting a "skulking warfare" were occasioned by that unsuccessful skirmish with Pharnabazus. In this case, therefore, it would seem that the *Hellenica* was serving as an exemplar for the *Agesilaus,* in the composition of which an allusion was made unclear by an inadroit omission of its antecedent.[299] The account of *Agesilaus* 1. 23-24 is also unclear. We learn that the King proclaimed that any individual in the cities who would supply a horse and rider would be freed from his obligation to serve in the cavalry. Agesilaus then declared that certain cities must provide a cavalry contingent, and we therefore become confused about the relation of the first order to the second. Looking to the *Hellenica* we find the difficulty resolved simply by the omission of the second order. It would appear, then, that the sense has been disturbed this time by the addition of the second proclamation to an account originally written with no expectation of the later insertion.[300]

There are indications of a different type that also prove useful to De Sanctis in determining the relative order of composition of the two similar writings. In *Agesilaus* 1. 6-7 the causes of the King's expedition to Asia are mentioned, yet significant elements of the story, which are related in the *Hellenica,* are passed over without notice. Nothing is said, for example, of the part played by Lysander in initiating the enterprise. In addition, one gains the impression from the *Agesilaus* that the expedition was a measure of defense, sent out to forestall the Persian preparations, whereas in the *Hel-*

---

[298] De Sanctis, *ibid.,* p. 16, is apparently following Seyffert (pp. 6-7) at this point.

[299] Cf. Seyffert, p. 4.

[300] De Sanctis, *Annali di Pisa,* II, 1, 20.

lenica (iii. 4. 1) less is said that would support such an interpretation of Spartan motives. Although he admits that the more circumstantial account is not necessarily the original one, De Sanctis cannot resist the impression that the *Agesilaus* here represents an abridgement made for the purpose of converting the longer narrative into a biography of the hero.[301] And he believes that this conclusion is strengthened upon our examining the two treatments of the truce concluded by Agesilaus and Tissaphernes. In the encomium (1. 10-11) the tendency to set off the deeds of Agesilaus favorably is again in evidence, for there Tissaphernes promises πράττειν εἰρήνην and to effect a settlement, whereas in the corresponding version (iii. 4. 5-6) his promise is only to ἔχειν εἰρήνην and to *try* to bring about a settlement. Thus as these conditions go unfulfilled, in his biography the King appears morally in a better light when he renews hostilities. Even in the *Hellenica* justice is not done to Tissaphernes, to be sure, but not so strong a case is presented for his antagonist. The problem is therefore whether a more prejudicial account would be substituted for a less prejudicial one or the contrary, and De Sanctis argues that we might more reasonably expect that a strongly biased version would succeed one less so, for if the replacement were made in the opposite direction it would hardly have stopped short of correcting the distortion completely.

Finally, De Sanctis turns to the critical passage found in *Agesilaus* 2. 7-8, in which Xenophon interrupts the narrative of the manoeuvres prior to the Battle of Coronea to interpret the actions and intentions of Agesilaus at this juncture. Up to this point the narrative in the two works is approximately the same; the interpretive passage, however, is not found in the *Hellenica*. In the wording of the statement in the *Agesilaus* that resumes the narrative after the inserted passage, there is also a slight departure from the equivalent statement in the *Hellenica* (iv. 3. 16). There Xenophon declares that he will also describe the battle and how it proved to be like no other of his time. The wording in the *Agesilaus* is virtually

the same except for the substitution of "for" for "how," giving,
". . . narrate the battle, for it proved. . . ." At first glance it
might appear that there is no significance to the change in the
wording, but when we look more closely at the succession of
the clauses in the *Hellenica* we discover that our statement
is the answering clause to the one that preceded: "This
then (μέν) was the force on both sides, and I will also
(δέ) narrate the battle. . . ." Turning to the *Agesilaus*, we
find that Xenophon there also details the forces on both sides
but that the enumeration is separated from the statement introducing the battle by the long interpretive insertion. Thus
the balance of the thoughts is broken; the statement introducing the battle comes in more suddenly, and the abruptness is
softened by justifying, so to speak, its existence with the ex-
planatory "for." It appears from this comparison, therefore,
that the text of the *Hellenica* at this point precedes that of
the *Agesilaus*, for which it served as a guide.[302]

Having finished his critique based on the arrangement of
thought in the two works, De Sanctis takes up the "verbal"
argument of Rosenstiel and others. Noting that the *Hellenica*
prefers the forms that were characteristically used in the
closing years of the Fourth Century whereas the more conservative synonyms predominate in the *Agesilaus*, he takes
this as an indication that the latter work was the first composed. On the other hand, he finds the diction and style of the
Agesilaus more perfected and artful, betraying the later, more
elaborated version.[303]

De Sanctis therefore wonders what solution can be found
to explain how the *Agesilaus* in most respects seems to have
been written after the *Hellenica* whereas there are other indications that it was the first of the two works to have been
composed. In most of the parallel passages where a difference
between the two accounts produces a confusion of sense in
one of them, it is the version of the *Hellenica* that appears to
be earlier. Yet there are times when the account of the *Hel-*

<hr />

[302] *Ibid.*, pp. 20-21.
[303] *Ibid.*, pp. 22-23. Cf. Seyffert's identical conclusion, pp. 11-12.

lenica is unclear because of an addition of matter not found in the *Agesilaus*. An example of the latter, we may recall, is the announcement in *Hellenica* iii. 4. 20, where Agesilaus' proclamation meant for the soldiers is actually made to the newly-arrived Spartan commanders, owing to the insertion of the section describing their advent. Finally, according to its style the *Agesilaus* is shown to be later whereas in its preference for the older synonyms it precedes the *Hellenica*. De Sanctis, like Friedrich before him, must reject the solution of Rosenstiel, for he thinks it inadmissible that the realistic scene depicting the Battle of Coronea could have been written by one who had not been present at the fray, but he is not averse to a solution that predicates a single manuscript as the source of both works. In fact De Sanctis believes that such was indeed the case: the text from which the *Agesilaus* was written was the same one which later, after reworking and extension, was to appear as the *Hellenica*. This subsequent elaboration, however, was not systematic nor thorough; it was casual and the changes thereby wrought were made according to no conscious tendency. Therefore we should not expect, says De Sanctis, that all the synonyms should have been changed to their later equivalents.[304]

Thus we have before us the latest and most refined statement of what may be referred to as the "matrix" theory of the composition of the *Hellenica* and the *Agesilaus,* whereby an archetype containing the basic substance of the common account suffered a succession of parturitions under conditions that produced now one version, now another. When we ask which work was copied from the other, then, the hypothesis replies that both were delivered instead from a common source, which served as the basis of both accounts. Such is the ideal statement, though each exponent conceives the process differently.

---

[304] De Sanctis, *Annali di Pisa*, II, I, 23-25. This last objection would be more valid against Friedrich, who attributed the tendency to avoid the conservative vocabulary in the *Hellenica* to a conscious effort on the part of the author.

We have seen that De Sanctis argues that there are both indications of the priority of the *Agesilaus* as well as evidence that it was written after the *Hellenica*. In support of the former contention he cites two proofs: one was the "synonym" argument; the other was the awkward wording of Hellenica iii. 4. 20, which describes the arrival of the new Spartan commanders upon the completion of the first year of Agesilaus' expedition. The insertion of this notice was what supposedly disturbed the reference, so that Agesilaus is wrongly made to command the generals, not the soldiers, to prepare mind and body for the coming campaign. MacLaren,[305] however, disagrees with this interpretation, for it appears to him that the message was rightly intended for the generals. They had "just come from the peace and quiet of Sparta," he reminds us, and it therefore would have been fitting for them to be ordered to engage in physical exercise. Moreover, MacLaren points out, Agesilaus does not actually bid the generals to ready themselves for the fighting, but according to Xenophon's account the King announces to them that a campaign is imminent by way of suggesting that it would be well to fit themselves for it. But of course it makes no difference whether the order specified the preparation or was intended only to suggest it to the generals, so long as we admit that it would be incongruous to expect that preparation of them. And even if it had been appropriate to make such a demand of the generals, it still remains that, according to the wording in the *Hellenica,* the order was not addressed as it is in the *Agesilaus* to the party to whom above all it was appropriate, namely the soldiers. MacLaren replies to this that the generals would have told the soldiers also, and he cites *Anabasis* vii. 1. 13-14, besides, to show that officers in Greek armies could not keep secrets and that the soldiers could overhear what was being said "in council."[306] The meeting in the *Anabasis,* however,

---

[305] *AJP,* LV, 255-56.

[306] He makes a general observation from this single incident: "We may reasonably doubt, after reading *Anab.* vii. 1. 13-14, whether a group of officers could prevent the soldiers from learning about matters discussed in council" (*Ibid.*). What this indicates, of course, is merely that it sometimes happens that secrets are not kept; but this is of no value to us in our present case.

was a much more general assembly than that of the *Hellenica,* since all the captains were present as well; in the *Hellenica* Agesilaus addresses the thirty generals. His address to them, moreover, is here introduced by προεῖπεν, "proclaimed," whereas a command or announcement to a small group of officers is introduced with εἶπεν, προεῖπεν throughout these sections being reserved for public proclamations.[307] In addition, Agesilaus' ostensible purpose in informing the generals of the imminent campaign was that they should put their bodies and minds into condition for fighting. His real purpose, however, was to mislead Tissaphernes as to the object of the march, and Xenophon does not even bother to inform the reader that word of the campaign had reached Tissaphernes' ears but assumes that the reader has already received the impression that the order, given in the *Hellenica* only to the generals and not to the soldiers, became publicly known.[308] And we have no right, therefore, to deprive De Sanctis of his point by declaring with MacLaren that "we may be sure that Agesilaus took good care that Tissaphernes heard of this intended march toward Sardis,"[309] when De Sanctis' point turns, not on what Xenophon means to say, but what in consequence of a careless slip he in fact does say.

Is it true, then, that Xenophon made a mistake at this point in copying the *Hellenica* from the *Agesilaus?* Probably not. We may allow the possibility that, in writing in the *Hellenica* that Agesilaus announced "to them," Xenophon was under the influence of the equivalent passage in the *Agesilaus* and that mentally "the soldiers" was present to him; but it is difficult to explain the omission of "this also," which is found in the *Agesilaus,* and which refers to the proclamation to the soldiers. That is to say, just as Xenophon changed "to the generals" to read "to them," in referring to the generals, he likewise omitted the "this also," which would be appropriate

[307] Cf. iii. 1. 28, 2. 16; and iii. 4. 3, 11 (twice), 15, 19. 20, 21.

[308] In other cases of this same ruse Xenophon specifically points out the deliberate measures that were taken to assure that the enemy would be apprised of the ostensible objective: *Hell.* v. 4. 48; iii. 4. 11, 12 (note "soldiers"); *Ages.* 1. 14-16, 28.

[309] *AJP,* LV, 256.

only in an announcement to the soldiers, to whom Agesilaus has previously been making announcements. It therefore seems that when Xenophon wrote the *Hellenica* passage, he was aware that he was having Agesilaus address no longer the troops but another group to whom he had made no previous announcements. Of course Xenophon is still guilty of the oversight whereby a public announcement is made only to the generals—here we must be careful to distinguish—but it is doubtful whether the error was committed under the influence of the wording of the *Agesilaus*.

How, then could such an error have come about? Through any number of ways no doubt, but Seyffert[310] has noted a similar *constructio ratione* in a passage that is common to both the *Hellenica* (iii. 4. 19) and the *Agesilaus* (1. 28), where a proclamation intended for the army is actually made to the heralds, rather than given to them to be announced to the soldiers.[311] There is little need, therefore, to presuppose the existence of the *Agesilaus* in order to account for the vagaries of thought and wording of the *Hellenica* at this point.

---

[310] Pp. 6-7.

[311] I hope that I am right in attributing this observation to Seyffert, although I am not certain about his reasoning on pp. 6 and 7. Referring to the statement, "He also made this announcement to the soldiers," in *Ages.* 1. 28, he says: "Exspectamus etiam antea dictum esse ' προεῖπε τοῖς στρατιώταις' [rather than 'προεῖπε τοῖς κήρυξι'], tum optime annectebantur 'προεῖπε δὲ καὶ τοῦτο τοῖς στρατιώταις'." Does this not suggest that by saying, "also this," Xenophon implies that the next previous announcement was addressed to the soldiers? The only possible objection that occurs to me here is that this announcement to the heralds was indeed intended for them alone and was not to be relayed to the army. Could it not be that the heralds were themselves the ones who conducted the auctions of slaves? But still, the καὶ τοῦτο is out of place, taking the "heralds" announcement as one will. For if the previous command was meant for the heralds alone, the next previous proclamation to the soldiers goes all the way back to sec. 21, too far back to expect our retention. But if the heralds are supposed to have proclaimed the message to the soldiers, then we have an instance of synesis that would justify the existence of another one no more violent; namely, the public proclamation made to the generals. That said, I might also record the fact that, if I have interpreted Seyffert aright on this point, with which I am in agreement, I cannot, however,

It remains, then, to consider whether according to a comparison of the style of each work it can be maintained that the *Agesilaus* preceded the *Hellenica*. Many studies have been made of the evolution that Xenophon's style underwent both within single works as well as from work to work. In the former connection we shall in time have occasion[312] to examine De Sanctis' refutation of the findings that appear to contradict his position; for the moment, however, we shall be concerned with the light that has been shed on the problem of the relative order in which Xenophon's writings were composed. The criterion usually adopted as the basis for determining the growth of Xenophon's style is his use of particles, which in the most elaborate studies[313] includes no less than forty-eight variations and combinations of eleven separate particles. In their employment, it seems, Xenophon evinces a steady progression so that, whereas in his earlier works he is sparing of their use,[314] by the time of his latest writings they appear in ample frequency on his pages. The conclusions based on these observations are given additional support from the fact that this tendency apparent in Xenophon's writings is consistent, at least in some respects, [315] with a general tend-

approve of the remainder of his arguments in these same pages, where he is too anxious to refute the notion that the *Agesilaus* preceded the *Hellenica*. As he is led to argue that the version of the *Agesilaus* is wrong because of the influence of the pre-existent *Hellenica,* he states that Agesilaus "militibus ipsis consilium suum exponit, quod parum accurate dictum est." But of course it is accurate and we need not go to such lengths to prove our case. It is enough that both versions seem to have their difficulties to obviate our trying to explain those of each by the influence of the other. And if that obliges me to account for the slip in the *Hellenica* through the influence of the internal wording, I should think that Xenophon was under the impression of the previous word, "soldiers": ". . . στρατιώτας, καὶ προεῖπεν αὐτοῖς . . . ."

[312] See below, pp. 137-38; 165ff.

[313] Best represented by the work of Roquette. For a succinct conspectus of all findings see his charts.

[314] The *Cynegetics* and the first part of the Hellenica are cases in point; see Roquette, *ibid.*

[315] Notably as applies to the particle μήν, alone and in combination. See Dittenberger, *Hermes,* XVI, 321-45, and R. Müller. In the works mentioned above as being early, this particle is not found even once.

ency shared by other writers of the age. And according to these studies[316] the *Agesilaus* was written not before but considerably after the middle section of the *Hellenica*, contrary to the conclusion of the "synonym" argument. Thus two statistical methods are in contradiction; which one is correct?

Between the two it is not difficult to decide. The indications of an author's stylistic development that recommend themselves to us most strongly are those that are more sensitive to unconscious dispositions and to tendencies which operate unawares on the writer's habits; and certainly the manner in which an author unobtrusively studs his page with particles,

---

[316] One would have to consult the elaborate tables of the statisticians for a full exposition, but a rough digest will do for present purposes. The *Agesilaus* is just over one-fourth the length of the second part of the *Hellenica*, which is the part it was largely modelled on. This part of the *Hellenica* (including oratory) shows 686 occurrences of the 48 particles and variants studied, whereas if it were merely written as late as the *Agesilaus* we would expect it to have 950 (3.9 times the 244 of the *Agesilaus*) of them, to say nothing of its being written later than that work (cf. Roquette, p. 39). Mήν, perhaps the most significant of all, occurs 27 times in this part of the *Hellenica*, 57 times in the *Agesilaus*. I of course do not believe that these mechanical calculations are at all decisive in studying the development of an author's style, but they can be effectively cited *quid pro quo* against one who himself cited statistics and who could moreover say of them, "Tale statistica è assolutamente probante" (De Sanctis, *Annali di Pisa*, II, I, 23). But to show the extent to which naughty caprice reigns in these matters, I cite an instructive little story recorded by H. W. Fowler, *A Dictionary of Modern English Usage* (Oxford, 1957), p. 713. Someone describing Lord Morley's preparation for a new edition of his works states: "He was determined to make it a carefully revised edition, and made one or two attempts at revising it himself. . . . He then asked me whether I would care to help him, and explained what my part of the work would be. It sounded rather dull, for he was particularly keen on having the word 'which,' wherever there was the possibility, exchanged for 'that.' . . . He was always ready and very willing to go with me . . . through a book page by page, 'which' hunting." Now the rule that "that" should only be used to introduce restrictive relative clauses and that "which" is to be reserved for unrestrictive ones is something we might expect of the older, more conservative writer, whereas to ignore the distinction would be the later tendency, whether in general or within the development of a single writer's style. So what must the poor Rosenstielian do a millenium hence when confronted with this change of wording in the two editions? His grammar (the *Agesilaus*) in hand, he will cleverly assign the second edition, with its purist, "older" vocabulary, to an earlier stage and have the actual first one written last.

which serve to fill out and enforce the meaning rather than to convey the content of it directly, would be a more reliable guide than his preference for now one verb and now its synonym, a verb, moreover, as important and indispensable as "follow." At any rate, the combined evidence of eleven particles and their forty-eight variants is entitled to at least equal authority with three synonyms, the most important of which is a prominent verb.[317]

All our discussion up to this point, however, has been concerned with the temporal relation between the synonyms; that is to say, that a correlation exists between the vogue of each word and the passage of time whereby the one word is associated with older usage and its synonym eventually supplants it. De Sanctis, following Gautier, Seyffert, and Rosenstiel, rightly calls attention to this temporal relation, and he relegates the drafting of the *Agesilaus* to a time prior to that of the *Hellenica,* seeing how the *Agesilaus* uses certain earlier words and eschews their later equivalents. But the reader will be surprised to know that, for all the attention given to this one distinction, there is a difference between the synonyms that is far more significant than their temporal relation. It is that the synonyms in the *Agesilaus* are more poetic, and their equivalents of the *Hellenica* are the ones more common in Attic prose.[318] Now exposing to view this important fact brings

---

[317] This point is pursued further below, pp. 137-38; 165ff.

[318] Cf. Rosenstiel, p. 26: "Praepositiones ἀμφ' et περί non tam significatione quam dialecto et sermonis genere, quibus usurpari, differunt. Illa enim in dialecto Ionica et in poetico sermone locum habet et a dialecto Attica fere aliena est, haec contra omnibus et dialectis et scriptoribus communis." Seyffert, p. 3: "Pro Attica enim voce 'ἐλάττων' in Agesilao non Attice 'μείων' insertum est." And, speaking of the substitution of ἕπεσθαι for ἀκολουθεῖν, on p. 7 he says, "Ergo etiam hic videmus Xenophontem certa quadam ratione commotum in *Hellenicis* formis Atticis usum esse, in Agesilao non Atticis." Rosenstiel, p. 26, is more inclined ("licet enim suspicare") to make the difference between ἕπεσθαι and ἀκολουθεῖν correspond only to a change in vogue in the course of time; but he notes that ἀκολουθεῖν does not appear in the tragedians Sophocles and Euripides when their prose contemporary Thucydides is using the two with perfect indifference. Opitz (*BPA*, XLVI, 1-88) points out still other reasons why the *Agesilaus* synonyms are more appropriate in the embellished elocution of that work. Ἕπεσθαι is more versatile since it is deponent, whereas

our whole problem at last into proper adjustment. The *Agesilaus* is an encomium. Its wording is in part based on that of the *Hellenica,* in the adaptation of which, however, there is hardly a sentence that was not altered to attain some rhetorical effect. There is great artistry in the construction of periods,[319] an evident consciousness of hiatus,[320] an elegant alteration of tense;[321] figures are abundant, [322] the clausulae are consciously rhythmic,[323] and there are numerous substitutions of poetic words for their prosaic equivalents.[324] What is more, there are whole sections added as embellishments of episodes related in the *Hellenica.*[325] All this indicates, then, that the

ἀκολουθεῖν is active, he says (p. 33), and illustrates this principle by citing the second clause of *Ages.* 2. 2 (cf. *Hell.* iv 3. 3), where we find almost (nine) all of the main words ending in -οι, including the last two, whose agreement was achieved by changing the αὐτόν of the *Hellenica* to αὐτοί and converting ἀκολ. to ἐφεπόμενος. He gives other instances showing how the deponent -ομενος is more adaptable than the active. Then, on p. 49 he observes: "Vidimus, ne extrema vocalis praepositionis cum primavocali vocis insequentis concurreret, vocalem praepositionis in Agesilao, ubicumque fieri potuit, elisam esse. Ita explicatur, quod Xenophon, qui in Agesilao maxime in praepositionibus adhibendis ad hiatum vitandum animum intendit, ubicumque in Hellenicis praepositionem περί invenit concurrentem cum voce, cuius prima littera vocalis erat, eam praepositionem uno loco, quem modo tractavimus, excepto *(Hell.* IV 3, 4: *Ages.* II 2) commutavit in ἀμφί, quia huius praepositionis littera finalis elidi poterat, non poterat praepositionis περι." Friedrich *(JCP,* CLIII, 298) sums it up: "In dem Hell. ist also immer der ionische bzw. poetische Ausdruck vermieden."

[319] Cf. Opitz, *BPA,* XLVI, 7, 21, 67; Seyffert, pp. 13, 21, 39.

[320] Opitz, *BPA,* XLVI, 11ff.

[321] Opitz, *ibid.,* p. 14, notes nine places in the *Agesilaus* where a verb in the imperfect in the *Hellenica* was brought over for stylistic purposes as aorist in the *Agesilaus* (cf. Seyffert, p. 3).

[322] As homoioteleuton (Opitz, *BPA,* XLVI, 5, 21ff.), alliteration (pp. 9, 16), antithesis (pp. 7, 15), chiasmus (pp. 17, 47), isocolon (pp. 30, 51), etc.

[323] Opitz, *ibid.,* pp. 20, 61ff.

[324] As μαστεύω *(Ages.* 1. 24) for ζητεύω *(Hell.* iii. 4. 15); σέβω (1. 27) for σέβομαι (iii. 4. 18); πίων (1. 28) for μαλακός (iii. 4. 19); ἐξαμείβω (2. 2) for διαλάττω (iv. 3. 3); ναός (2. 13) for νεώς (iv. 3. 20); κτῆνος (2. 18) for βόσκημα (iv. 5. 1). See the respective places in Opitz for the poetic associations for each word.

[325] The best example of this is at once the best single passage to which one could go to understand the nature of the *Agesliaus.* It is 2. 14, a passage that "plena est verborum elegantissimorum . . . plenaque verborum poeticorum praecipue ex Homero et tragicis sumptorum" (Opitz, *BPA,*

changes made in converting portions of the prosaic *Hellenica* to the *Agesilaus* were made for the purpose of adapting them to the rhetorical setting of a eulogy. With that established, we are now ready to be told of another change made in bringing over passages from the *Hellenica* to the *Agesilaus;* that, of course, of our now famous three sets of synonyms. If mention is made only of their temporal[326] implications, we must contrive elaborate schemes to explain how works which were written later than others were actually written before them. The other, but somewhat unimaginative solution is simply to suppose that the synonyms of the *Agesilaus* were chosen because they were more poetic.

In order to consider the final problem before us we shall be obliged to make certain assumptions. We must admit that the circumstance that all other indications show the *Agesilaus* to have been written later than the *Hellenica* does not establish that it probably was, in view of the fact that the three synonyms, if more poetic than their earlier equivalents, are also those used by older writers (yet what poetic words are not also older ones?); then we must admit that the conclusions of those who have examined Xenophon's use of the forty-eight particles are invalid and, by virtue of their opposition to the "synonym" statistics, cannot be taken as establishing that the *Hellenica* was written before the *Agesilaus;* and we

XLVI, 66). After giving these words and their parallels from Hesiod, Aeschylus, etc., Opitz (p. 67) then analyzes the passage rhetorically as an elaborate period of nine parts.

[326] I do not at all mean to imply that there is no temporal significance to Xenophon's preference of one set of these synonyms to the other; the other, more reliable statistical studies indicate that Xenophon's style, like that of pratically all other writers, shows a development with the years, and I see no reason to deny that these synonyms could have escaped the effect of the same tendency. But if the later ones were at all prosaic (and the poetic vocabularies in languages are drawn from the older words, not the modern ones), and if the earlier ones had poetic connotations (and they had strong ones, too), this stylistic consideration in the composition of a work like the *Agesilaus* would unquestionably prevail, while the mere temporal implication would lose significance altogether.

must also be willing to still the promptings of a kind of senti-
mental monition, if so it may be called, that somehow bids
us for seemingly simple problems to resist the constraint of
involved solutions that require an inverted and unnatural
construction of things. Making these allowances, then, we
recall that De Sanctis has Xenophon compose the archetype
for the second part of the *Hellenica* and the *Agesilaus* sometime prior to 380.[327] From this archetype Xenophon first produced the *Agesilaus* by leaving out parts that did not accord
with the nature of an encomium and by adding flattering little
scenes and stylistic embellishments suitable to such a piece.
And there was the further consideration that the style in which
the archetype was originally written and in which the *Agesilaus,* which was taken from it during an early stage, was written was the style Xenophon employed during the early period
of his literary career. As an indication thereof we have the
synonyms: those which Xenophon employed in his earlier
writings[328] and those which are found in the *Agesilaus,*

---

[327] *Annali di Pisa,* II I, 24, 29. He has the second part end with v. 1. 36;
but, since he accepts the findings of Opitz, according to which the *Agesilaus*
uses the *Hellenica* up to at least v. 4. 49 (and not merely to v. 1. 36, as
Rosenstiel had claimed), De Sanctis believes that the third part was at
least in its first draft when the encomium was written upon the death
of Agesilaus.

[328] A remark could well be made at this point to prevent the reader from
concluding that De Sanctis' statements regarding the relative time of the
composition of the *Hellenica* among the works of Xenophon represent the
most well-established views. De Sanctis *(Annali di Pisa,* II, I, 23) compares
the *Hellenica,* with regard to the employment of the synonyms, only to the
Anabasis and the *Cyropaedia,* two works which he classifies as undoubtedly
belonging to Xenophon's early period. Many there are, however (e.g.)
Dakyns, I, 1vii, 1xx), who would put the final part of the *Hellenica* in the
same period as that of the *Cyropaedia,* while according to the particle
studies (see Roquette, pp. 30ff.) the second and third parts of the *Hellenica,*
the *Cyropaedia,* and the *Anabasis* as well are among Xenophon's latest
productions. So, *quot homines tot sententiae.* But even if the *Anabasis* and
the *Cyropaedia* were among Xenophon's early works, comparisons of them
or of any others of Xenophon's works with the *Hellenica* would not
necessarily establish anything about the chronological development of
Xenophon's style as exemplified by his preference for certain of the
synonyms, if the following significant, even alarming, observation of
Seyffert's is true. That student of the problem finds that the incidence of
the synonyms in the *Hellenica* differs, not only from that in the *Anabasis*

whereas those that correspond to a later time are the ones usually preferred in the *Hellenica,* which was drawn from the archetype after the *Agesilaus.* What had the archetype undergone, then, in the meantime? Xenophon had kept it by him, returning to it from time to time, completing it, retouching it, adjusting his account of events as he received additional information, and generally revising the whole in anticipation of an eventual publication. And it was in the course of all this reworking that the earlier words, like ἕπεσθαι and ἀμφί, were largely replaced by their synonyms, either those which over a century or so had been coming into vogue generally or those which had encroached peculiarly upon Xenophon's own style. The *Hellenica,* parts two and three, was consequently given its final shape at a time when Xenophon's preference lay heavily in favor of the newer forms. There is no reason to believe that this gradual replacement of the older words was done deliberately or that the reworking to which the text was subjected was consistent throughout, and therefore, De Sanctis goes on to say, we have no right to demand with Opitz that all of the earlier synonyms should have been substituted with their later equivalents.[329]

The last two books of the *Hellenica* constitute the final stage of its composition and represent the full maturity of Xenophon's style.[330] The *Agesilaus,* De Sanctis says, shows the stage of development, so far as the preference for our synonyms goes, which our author's style had attained when that work was composed, whereas the *Hellenica,* Books Three to Five, which represents the extent of the archetype at the time the *Agesilaus* was written, is intermediate, originally

or the *Cyropaedia,* but from that "in reliquis fere omnibus scriptis" of Xenophon (p. 9). It is clear, therefore, that, whatever may have determined the choice of the particular synonyms used in the *Hellenica,* their occurrence there is in no way connected with the relative time when the *Hellenica* was composed.

[329] *Annali di Pisa,* II, I, 22-25. The latter statement seems to imply that, if the retouching had been everywhere thorough, all the synonyms would have been replaced, and that Xenophon's final style was the complete reverse of that represented by the *Agesilaus,* where virtually none of the later equivalents occurs.

[330] De Sanctis, *ibid.,* p. 23.

composed in one style but partly re-written in another.[331] Consequently, the change in style between the *Agesilaus* and the last two books of the *Hellenica* represents the development of Xenophon's style during the years that separated their composition. It must have been a considerable change. In the *Agesilaus* Xenophon made no use whatsoever of ἀκολουθεῖν whereas in this last period he uses it exclusively—twenty-nine times—and employed the ἕπεσθαι of the *Agesilaus* not even once.[332] The change indicated by these statistics— and "such statistics are absolutely decisive"—then, is considerable indeed and represents an appreciable development in the author's style. De Sanctis, in fact, thinks that it indicates a transition all the way from Xenophon's "earliest writing" to his "latest productions."[333]

But over what period of time did this great revision of Xenophon's style take place? The latest event mentioned in the *Hellenica* (vi. 4. 37) occurred in 358; accordingly, the composition would have continued until that date, but no later than 355.[334] And the *Agesilaus?* It of course would not have been written until after the death of its subject, although there is no telling how long after. The death of Agesilaus, at any rate, took place in the year 360.[335] Now if the last two books of the *Hellenica* were written no later, though probably earlier, than 355, and if the *Agesilaus* was written no earlier, though possibly later, than 360, the interval of time that separated their composition was at most five years, though probably less; in fact, it could even have taken place in the very same year. Be that as it may, there is in this matter of dates a major problem awaiting our consideration; for even the extreme possible limit of five years between the composition of the *Agesilaus* and that of the last part of the *Hellenica* is far too short an interval to allow for the thorough trans-

[331] De Sanctis, *ibid.*, pp. 23-25.

[332] De Sanctis, *ibid.*, p. 23; Seyffert, p. 7. The same is true for the other synonyms: *ibid.* p. 8.

[333] *Annali di Pisa*, II, I, 23.

[334] The date of the death of Tisiphonus of Pherae, who was still living when Xenophon wrote iv. 4. 37. Cf. De Sanctis, *ibid.*, II, I, 27.

[335] Beloch, III, II, 125.

formation in Xenophon's style proposed by De Sanctis' theory, which recognized only the temporal correspondence of the synonyms. Nor is that all: at what period do these (at most) five years fall in Xenophon's life? At the very end. This is no callow novice now turning his hand to his first literary essay; these few years do not come during the writer's formative days, when his style is not confirmed and he is still taking the measure of his abilities. Rather, they occur late in his settled maturity, when as an old man he is at the end of his literary career and at the close of his life. And this would be clearly impossible.

There is, therefore, no more support for the hypothesis that the *Hellenica* was written after the *Agesilaus* than there is need for it. The reason that Xenophon preferred the older synonyms for the encomium is only that they were more poetic.

CHAPTER IV

THE DOCUMENTARY HYPOTHESIS

> No sensible author would begin a history of Greece and, after getting a certain way along in it, would convert it into the biography of a king.   —Polybius (viii. 11)

The unity of the last five books of the *Hellenica* is not great. The events narrated in this part are, to be sure, related to one another and are appropriate for inclusion in a general history, and in that respect their account cannot be said to lack basic organization. It is only when we examine the work carefully and seek to determine the precise relation between the episodes that we have difficulty understanding the historian's plan. Although the same want of proportion that characterizes the narrative of the early books is in some measure evident in these later five as well, it is not precisely that same "quantitative" inequality that here disturbs us. In the first part of the *Hellenica* important events are too often accorded so little attention that not even their main features are delineated. In the later parts with their more expansive narrative, almost all events of great importance that are included in the account are adequately expounded, although it also not infrequently happens that insignificant ones are dwelt on at too great length. But the unevenness that characterizes the last five books lies rather in the difference in manner in which the author treats the scenes he describes and in the mood he imparts to them as he manages them now in one style and now in another. This variation in treatment has given the last five books a curious episodic nature which has long held the attention of scholars causing them to wonder whether it can somehow afford us any indication of the author's purpose in writing, of the influences and impressions under which he wrote, and of the order in which he wrote, rewrote, and assembled the various parts of his history.

The most thorough analysis of the composition of the *Hellenica* ever made is that represented by the views of De Sanctis in combination with those of Sordi,[336] who, accepting many of the former's arguments, proceeded to elaborate them and add a considerable number of her own. We have seen[337] how De Sanctis argues that the middle section of the *Hellenica* (iii-v 1:36) was written considerably earlier than the last two books. In support of this belief he cited the replacement of the synonyms by their later equivalents and he compared the wording of the parallel passages, *Agesilaus* 1-2 and *Hellenica* iii-iv. To these proofs, based on the comparison of the *Hellenica* with the *Agesilaus,* De Sanctis also adds some internal evidence derived from the *Hellenica* alone. He calls on the witness of practically all the critics, who are united in distinguishing the last five books into two parts written at different times. We really do not even need the testimony of the experts to discern a difference, however, for it is in fact quite apparent, De Sanctis points out, in view of the profound difference in style, in freshness, and in manner of composition that one encounters upon leaving Books Three and Four and passing to the cold, fragmentary, and negligent account in the last two books.[338]

[336] *Athenaeum*, XXVIII, 3-53; *ibid.*, XXIX, 273-348.
[337] See above, p. 121.
[338] De Sanctis, *Annali di Pisa*, II, I, 26.

This is a general indication; but there is also another of a more specific character. We have referred to it before; it is found in iv. 3. 16, where the author comments on the Battle of Coronea. Here Xenophon refers to that conflict as being "like no other of our time." Although the encounter at Coronea was an impressive struggle and may have had no rival in any battle easily within memory in 394, such a statement would be difficult to justify after the momentous clash at Leuctra and altogether untrue after Mantinea in 362. The presence of this statement in our text together with the other arguments noted, then, leaves hardly a doubt at all, according to De Sanctis, that one part of the *Hellenica* was written shortly after the Peace of Antalcidas (386), when Xenophon was still in the vigor of his days and in possession of that same freshness of spirit we find in the *Anabasis* and in the *Cyropaedia;* and that the other part was written much later, approximately a quarter of a century, when Xenophon, a tired old man, was saddened by the termination of his leisure at Scillus and disappointed by the frustration of his political ideals upon the fall of Spartan hegemony.[339]

At this point De Sanctis takes note of an objection made by Hatzfeld,[340] who called attention to an inscription[341] recording a dedication by the Spartan king Pausanias to his deceased son, Agesipolis. In v. 3. 19 we learn that the death of Agesipolis took place in 381, and in iii. 5. 25 we are told of the death of Pausanias himself in Tegea. This indicates, according to Hatzfeld, that the composition of the events leading up to the Peace of Antalcidas, recorded in v. 1. 36, did not take place immediately after the termination of the period which ended with that event in 386. Those who make a division at that point, however, lay great emphasis on the conclusive nature of the Peace. They think that in that year and shortly thereafter the impression must have prevailed that the events of the preceding years had at last reached their consummation,

[339] *Ibid.,* pp. 20-21, 27.
[340] J. Hatzfeld, "Notes sur la composition des Helléniques," *Revue de Philologie,* IV (1930), 120, 125-26.
[341] *Fouilles de Delphes,* III, 1, 509.

and Xenophon would therefore have concluded his narrative at that point. Against this Hatzfeld notes that the inscription referred to above shows that the composition of the part of the *Hellenica* in which the death of Pausanias is recorded could not have occurred earlier than 381, and however decisive the results of the Peace may have appeared until that year, they would not have appeared so afterward, when it would have been all too obvious that the convention of 386 was no more than a momentary pause in a steady march of events that had started long before and was not to reach its climax until 362.

To answer this objection, De Sanctis[342] calls on his theory that Xenophon, having written the events down to 386, did not publish his draft immediately nor continue the narrative down to 362 until much later.[343] He quite agrees with Hatzfeld that the notice of Pausanias' death given in iii. 5. 25 indicates a date after 381 for the composition of that notice, but we need only suppose that Xenophon, in one of his later perusals of the manuscript, had noticed the omission of a reference to Pausanias' death, which had occurred in the meantime, and that he simply inserted mention of that event in the pre-existing account. Reading the notice about Pausanias' exile and his death in Tegea in iii. 5. 25, we receive the impression that no great length of time separated the two events, since the one is recorded immediately and summarily after the other. By showing that Pausanias did not die shortly after being banished, Hatzfeld confirms the contention that the notice in question was awkwardly inserted at a later time, since no effort was made to fit it carefully into its new context.

Since Hatzfeld has failed to carry his point in opposition, De Sanctis persists in thinking that we are to distinguish a definite break in composition at v. 1. 36. So if the middle section of the *Hellenica* can be ended at that point, De Sanctis goes on to ask where we are to locate its beginning. Does this "middle" (if so it be) section include everything from i. 1 to

---

[342] *Annali di Pisa*, II, I, 27-28.
[343] De Sanctis believes that sec. iii-v. 1. 36 was written about 384-380. *Ibid.*, p. 29.

v. 1. 36, or are we to distinguish one or more parts, or phases of composition, within this section? There are two places that offer themselves as likely points at which to make a division. We may either let the final phase of the Peloponnesian War (i. 1-ii. 3. 10) constitute a section to itself and reserve the history of the Thirty for the beginning of the next part; or we may put those two episodes together as the first stage of the composition and have the next section, starting with Book Three and describing the Spartan expedition to Asia, begin the part that ends with the Peace of Antalcidas. De Sanctis favors the latter alternative and he sets out to reckon with the objections that have been made to this arrangement. The major impediment before him is of course the firm conviction of many scholars that, along with the break in the thought that occurs at or about ii. 3. 10 with the end of the Peloponnesian War, there occurs also at that point a definite change in the style. To deal with this problem De Sanctis turns to a statement of Hatzfeld's,[344] who is interpreting the stylistic studies of those such as Dittenberger who have made an investigation of Xenophon's use of certain verbs, particles, and the like,[345] and whose work is usually taken as indicating a division at ii. 3. 10. De Sanctis first calls attention to Hatzfeld's discussion of the conjunctions and adverbs, which show only insignificant changes in rate of occurrence after ii. 3. 10. And, although the statistics for the other category of particles, syntax, and style, indicate that in the later books Xenophon feebly approaches the manner of writing he employed up to ii. 3. 10, we nevertheless note only a gradual transition after that point in both categories. De Sanctis, therefore, does not find this conclusion very indicative of a change in style after the narrative of the war.[346] The stylistic tables compiled by Roquette, which also show a change in style after ii. 3. 10, likewise are of doubtful significance, De Sanctis further observes, especially when we consider the fact that in the history of the Peloponnesian War Xenophon was not very much

---

[344] Hatzfeld, *Revue de Philologie* (hereafter cited as *R de P*), IV 220-21.
[345] See above, pp. 125-27.
[346] De Sanctis, *Annali di Pisa*, II, I, 29-30.

interested in what he was describing, so that a change in style with the end of the narrative would be understandable. The whole nature of the first part, besides, with its dry, fragmentary narrative helps to explain any difference in style observable between it and what follows, without our having to suppose any great interval of time in the composition. And this conviction grows even stronger when we recall that for the history of the war Xenophon made use of the annalistic arrangement, which suppressed his spirit.[347]

Even if there were any convincing conclusions to be drawn from the witness of these statistics on Xenophon's use of particles, abverbs, and prepositions, however, De Sanctis thinks that there is another consideration that renders those findings invalid. This is the "synonym" argument, which, as we have seen,[348] De Sanctis believes is proof that the draft for the middle part of the *Hellenica* was not published immediately upon being written, but that Xenophon kept it by for many years, adding to it and re-working it. It is this retouching, then, that has confused the statistics and made Books Three and Four appear to represent the second stage of Xenophon's style in the composition of the *Hellenica*. The condition of any part of our text of the *Hellenica,* therefore, reflects the author's style, not at the time of the original composition, but only at the time of the final revision. Nor have we any other means of determining in what parts the author's hand fell more heavily than in others as he repeatedly reviewed his original draft than by supposing that he must have returned more often to the episodes in which he took a special interest. And why, De Sanctis asks, could this not have been the case with Books Three and Four? We must therefore reject the particle statistics, according to De Sanctis, for determining the relative order in which the parts of the *Hellenica* were composed.[349]

There is one conclusion indicated by the statistics, however,

[347] *Ibid.*, p. 30, n. "La minore frequenza di certe particelle nei primi libri si spiega anche in parte dal carattere cronachistico, frammentario e asciutto di questa parte; . . . l'animo del narratore, non più vincolato al procedere cronachistico e più interessato a ciò che narra è diverso."

[348] See above, pp. 109, 121.

[349] *Annali di Pisa*, II, I, 30-31.

that De Sanctis believes can be accepted as reliable. As Hatz-feld rightly points out, there is an affinity between the style of the final two books of the *Hellenica* and that of the first two.[350] There are independent reasons for thinking that the first two books were written after those that immediately follow, and this statistical indication serves to confirm the impression that the order of the books does not represent the order of their composition. In order to pursue this topic De Sanctis must first establish where Part One ends. Having rejected considerations based on style, De Sanctis examines the problem from the standpoint of content. Are we to look for a termination at ii. 3. 10 with the end of the war or should we include the history of the Thirty (to ii. 4. 43, the end of the book) as well? De Sanctis chooses the latter alternative. It is evident, he maintains, that the settlement of factional disorders forms a satisfying conclusion for a history of internal conflict, which Xenophon brings to a close on a lofty note of conciliation. Moreover, the poor chronological connection[351] between the end of Book Two and the narrative of the Asian expedition shows that the two parts were not written at one time, but separately, and that their inaccurate juncture was made artificially at a later date. Nor is Xenophon content to end his account of the Thirty merely by recording the peaceful termination of strife, but he gives special point to the prevailing toleration and magnanimity of those times by noting that the conciliatory spirit of the *demos* continued in effect down to the very moment at which he wrote. At the very outset of the narrative that follows, however, De Sanctis detects a feeling toward the *demos* that is completely different from that which could have inspired the compliment paid to it at the end of Book Two. In a vein of animosity Xenophon records that, in response to a Spartan request for a troop of cavalry for the Asian expedition, the Athenians gladly sent three hundred knights who had taken service under the Thirty, and that they thought that it would be no loss to the *demos* if those troops should go off and perish in some foreign land.

[350] *Ibid.*
[351] See Schambach, p. 20.

The complete reversal of the author's sentiment that this passage indicates can only be explained by supposing that the spirit of resentment came first and the friendly one came later. Accordingly, De Sanctis sees no possible alternative to his thesis that the first two books were written after, not before, the two that follow.[352]

If the "middle" part of the *Hellenica* was actually the first one written, then, De Sanctis has some interesting things to tell us about the circumstances of its composition. The story that begins with Book Three is that of the expedition to Asia of 399 to 394, and it is during this period that the Cyrean soldiers, having returned from the Black Sea and Thrace, took service under the Lacedaemonian commander, Thibron (iii. 1. 6). The two expeditions, the Cyrean and the Lacedaemonian, are at this point connected, and Xenophon was a participant in both. It appears to De Sanctis, therefore, that Xenophon would not have concluded his memoirs with the end of the Cyrean adventure but would have continued to record his experiences after taking service under the Lacedaemonian commanders. Later, in Scillus after 386, upon becoming acquainted with the history of Thucydides, Xenophon decided to continue the unfinished work of that historian and to connect it with his own memoirs of later times by means of a history of the intervening years. His own memoirs of the years 399 to 386, where he is no longer the leading figure, were suitable for incorporation into a general history, since interest centers on others and on events of a more general and less personal character. It was the nature of the circumstances themselves, therefore, that imposed the character of a general history on what had begun as personal memoirs, and even the author himself did not perceive the transformation. Having detached this section of his memoirs from the rest, Xenophon joined them to the history of Thucydides by means of the first two books of our *Hellenica*.[353]

This is essentially the manner in which De Sanctis conceives how Xenophon came to produce his history. Sordi accepts

[352] *Annali di Pisa,* II, I, 25-26.
[353] *Ibid.,* pp. 31-33.

many of De Sanctis' conclusions, although taking exception to some, and she goes on to elaborate the thesis considerably. Her first task is to establish that the style of Books Three and Four differs markedly from that of the rest of the *Hellenica*. She calls attention to the greater use of dialogue, which distinguishes these books from the others. She then refers to the "almost complete lack" of direct discourse in iii and iv, a mode of expression she thinks Xenophon purposely avoided in writing informal memoirs, because of the sobriety and great elevation of tone that is associated with direct quotations. Yet direct speeches do occur in this part: iii. 5. 8-15 and iv. 2. 11-13; but these need not be seen as exceptions nor be taken as evidence that Xenophon was using his memoirs for these two books, since these speeches are found in the midst of scenes that Xenophon did not witness. After iv. 8. 1 the style of narrative changes: the purely descriptive element prominent in the preceding chapters is gone; dialogue disappears; and there is an abundance of direct discourse. Whenever Xenophon makes a subjective appraisal or passes judgment in iii-iv. 8. 1, he is careful to give his opinions indirectly and impersonally, while in the other parts of the *Hellenica* he presents his thoughts directly in the first person. Moreover, although "methodological" statements, wherein the author remarks on his procedure, sometimes occur in the *Hellenica*, none is found in this section. Finally, she notes that, whereas in other parts of the *Hellenica* certain statements are found in which the author distinguishes between that which is of importance to the narrative and that which is not, no such statement exists in iii-iv 8. 1, although there are several occasions for making one.[354]

The *Agesilaus* makes an interesting comparison in these respects with the part of the *Hellenica* that corresponds to it. In the former work we find a number of subjective remarks made by the author in the first person that are lacking in equivalent passages in the *Hellenica*. There is also the curious circumstance that practically every dialogue related in the

[354] Sordi, *Athenaeum*, XXVIII, 12-23.

Hellenica disappears entirely from the corresponding scene in the *Agesilaus* or is at most reported in indirect discourse. The *Agesilaus,* which was written later than the middle section of the *Hellenica,* bears a closer relation to the other parts of the *Hellenica,* therefore, than to the memoirs of the third and fourth books.[355]

All this signifies, Sordi concludes, that the middle section of the *Hellenica* constitutes the nucleus of the whole work. This part to a great extent was written from Xenophon's personal memoirs, which were expanded with accounts of contemporary events in Spartan history, such as the Conspiracy of Cinadon (iii. 3) and the Battle of Corinth (iv. 4). With De Sanctis, she views this section as an extension of the story of the *Anabasis,* written together with the account of that episode and not originally intended as a general history. These books have a distinct nature all their own, and there is likewise a "profound continuity of style," as well as of general tone, and of method, common alone to the other parts of the *Hellenica.*[356]

In one respect, however, Sordi takes issue with the conclusions of De Sanctis, and it is an issue of major importance. The latter thinks that Xenophon converted his memoirs into a general history in a rather informal or even unconscious and imperceptible manner as he was gradually induced by the nature of the account itself or by sugestions that occurred to him as he was completing the history of Thucydides: by a gradual process, in a word. Sordi on the other hand believes that Xenophon from the outset had planned a grand history, unified in conception and coherent in its design. The *Hellenica* was in fact written as the formal completion and continuation of the history of Thucydides. When in executing his plan Xenophon arrived at the events of the early fourth century, he had at hand the account of his own experiences and observations, which he had written some time before as the continuation of the story of the *Anabasis* and which he had never published. These unused memoirs were hereupon incorporated

[355] *Ibid.,* pp. 22-23.
[356] *Ibid.,* pp. 23-25.

into the history, to which they were now adapted by the insertion of accounts of events which had occurred in mainland Greece contemporary with those of the memoirs.[357]

One problem remains, for according to her thesis it is incumbent on Sordi to show that certain sections of the memoirs that differ from others in style and tone are indeed later insertions and are not simply distinguished by the fact that Xenophon was not a witness to the events related in them. Is there evidence that the sections which would not have formed parts of the original memoirs were introduced into an account written previously? Sordi is confident that traces of such an adaptation can be detected. She points to the passages, iii. 5. 3-25 (from the mission of Timocrates through the Theban-Athenian alliance to the Battle of Haliartus, 395) and iv. 2. 9-23 (from the council at Corinth to the Battle of the Nemea, 394). When we examine iv. 2. 1, to begin with, the point in the narrative where Agesilaus' operations in Asia are about to resume, we find a remarkable statement: "When the Lacedaemonians had learned for certain both that the money had come into Greece and that the greatest states had formed an alliance for war against them, they reasoned that their state was endangered and that it was necessary to conduct a campaign." The reference of course is to the coalition of Corinth, the expedition of Pausanias and Lysander, and the Battle of Haliartus: yet these events Xenophon had just narrated in full! Therefore, Sordi contends, as there is no need for such a repetition of events but lately given in detail, such an unnecessary summary is certainly in indication that the fuller exposition did not exist in the original account. The inappropriate recapitulation represents what was the only reference in the original version to the events in Greece contemporary with those that Xenophon was witnessing at the side of Agesilaus in Asia. We note as well that this section, with its direct discourse, its rapidly moving account, and its clarity and precision, differ in spirit noticeably from the narrative of affairs in Asia.[358]

[357] *Ibid.*, pp. 24-25, 52-53.
[358] *Ibid.*, pp. 25-27.

There is also another consideration that Sordi introduces at this point: the earlier sections were written when the author was "profoundly philo-Laconian," whereas the later additions reveal "the reverse of the coin" in this regard. As in the *Anabasis,* the numerous references here to the Spartan ascendancy[359] show the author's disposition toward Sparta at the time he wrote the memoirs. The speech of the Theban ambassador (iii. 5. 8-15), however, interprets that Spartan hegemony in its true light: "twofold subjection: the tyranny both of governors and of decarchies" (iii. 5. 13). Hence this speech must have been written much later, after Xenophon had undergone an abrupt awakening to reality and had dismissed his fanciful illusion of Sparta as the disinterested benefactress of Greece.[360]

So much, then, for the first passage. Turning now to iv. 3. 1, Sordi believes she has detected yet another unnecessary summary, this time of the Battle of the Nemea, related in full in iv. 2. 13-23. It is detailed; it is related in indirect discourse; it suffices as a compendium such as would be appropriate in an account to which the battle were only incidental.[361]

Finally, it is possible that the section iii. 2. 21-31 is a later insertion into Xenophon's original memoirs. The later reworking in this instance, however, seems to have eliminated the epitome of the original draft, if indeed this episode was mentioned at all in that earlier account. Still, there is the fact that it is introduced by phrases that isolate it from its context.[362]

We have already noted that Sordi calls on the findings of De Sanctis to confirm her thesis of a considerable lapse of time between the composition of the memoirs in iii and iv and of the additions thereto of a more general nature. She follows him in believing, for example, that Xenophon's appraisal of the Battle of Coronea (iv. 3. 16) must have been written

[359] *Hell.,* iii. 1. 3, 5, 20, 4. 5.
[360] Sordi, *Athenaeum,* XXVIII, 28-29.
[361] *Ibid.,* p. 30.
[362] *Ibid.,* pp. 30-31.

before the Battle of Leuctra.[363] She accepts De Sanctis' reasoning based on confusions in wording that were resolved in the *Agesilaus;* she uses the "synonym" argument and she cites the change in the author's disposition toward the popular party at Athens to which De Sanctis had called attention.[364] The same political feelings, moreover, that motivate Xenophon in the first part are evident as well in the last three books.[365] To these arguments she adds the difference in Xenophon's manner of exposition in the middle part, wherein he departs from the annalistic method observed in the first two and last three books.[366] These other books must therefore have been written at one time and at a different time from the middle part, when Xenophon was inclined to follow the concurrent system of narration. She notes also that, because of the care with which the adaptation was carried out in these later chapters, it is difficult to determine the point in the *Hellenica* at which the memoirs are no longer used. We can still perceive the earlier account up through iv. 7; yet perhaps the acquittal of Sphodrias in v. 4. 25-33 formed a part of Xenophon's memoirs, too. Sordi also proposes that the original draft, the memoirs, would have still been in the condition of a sketch rather than a finished account at the time of its incorporation into the *Hellenica.* Finally, she cites the example of Xenophon's using with slight modification parts of the *Hellenica* for his biography of Agesilaus: this illustrates that author's habit of introducing into a later work material that was originally written as part of an earlier one.[367]

There remains for Sordi the problem of the other books of the *Hellenica;* she must now examine these to see whether they offer any difficulties for her analysis of their composition. There is of course the formidable opposition of the statistical studies, which both set off i-ii. 3. 9 distinctly from the remaining books and show a convincing continuity existing between

[363] *Ibid.,* p. 33.
[364] *Ibid.,* pp. 32-34.
[365] *Ibid.,* p. 52.
[366] See above, pp. 30ff.
[367] Sordi, *Athenaeum,* XXVIII, 31-36.

those remaining ones as well. Although believing that some exception can be taken to the arguments based on these studies, Sordi admits that they contain some points to which her thesis is not equal. Some of those stylistic phenomena (like γέ, δή and ὥστε), rather than making a sudden appearance at the begining of the second part, show a gradual increase in frequency as we pass from the first two into the subsequent books, and Sordi accordingly believes that their incidence is a natural one and need not be explained by assuming a great lapse of time between the composition of the early part and the rest. In addition, she calls on the revisions proposed by De Sanctis to nullify the evidence of the statistics. Repeatedly reviewing the parts already written, Xenophon would have eliminated by successive corrections any stylistic features peculiar to an earlier stage of composition. Sordi consequently reasons thus: since the first part would not have escaped these revisions, the stylistic differences between it and the other works of Xenophon do not indicate anything about the relative order of composition. The differences are therefore attributable to the caprice of the author's style.[368] Besides, there is the circumstance that in the early part Xenophon is consciously imitating Thucydides; words, such as μήν, not frequently employed by that author are here avoided also by Xenophon.[369]

In conclusion, Sordi finds Xenophon at Scillus after 386 writing his memoirs of the previous fifteen years. He closed the *Anabasis* at the point where that episode connected with the Asian expedition of Thibron, Dercyllidas, and Agesilaus, but he continued to record his experiences down to the end of the Corinthian War. Later,[370] when he was engaged in writing his continuation of Thucydides' history, he employed much of the earlier material for the later account.[371]

These are the essential points of the thesis proposed by De Sanctis and Sordi to account for the nature and origin of the

[368] *Ibid.*, pp. 38-40.
[369] *Ibid.*, pp. 48-49.
[370] After 369; see above pp. 69ff.
[371] Sordi, *Athenaeum*, XXVIII, 50-53.

Hellenica. The peculiarities of Books Three and Four are their starting point: the composition of this section is identified with that of the *Anabasis* both in its spirit and in the time of its writing. It was intended originally as a record of the author's personal experiences; De Sanctis has it grow into a history imperceptibly during its composition, whereas Sordi reserves this conversion for a later date, when upon becoming acquainted with Thucydides' history, Xenophon deliberately transformed his memoirs by adaptation and addition into a general history. Let us now proceed to an evaluation of the hypothesis offered by these two students of the problems of Xenophon's *Hellenica*.

Enough has been said in the preceding chapter in refutation of De Sanctis' reasoning for the priority of the middle books of the *Hellenica* as based on a comparison with the *Agesilaus*. To these proofs, however, he also added some internal indications found within the pertinent sections of the *Hellenica* itself, and these arguments remain to be dealt with. The strongest of them is based on what is in a way a celebrated passage and one of the few most controversial in the whole work. Several allusions have been made to it and it has long been claiming our attention. We turn, therefore, to the remark of Xenophon's found in *Hellenica* iv. 3. 16 on the Battle of Coronea: διηγήσομαι δὲ καὶ τὴν μάχην, καὶ πῶς ἐγένετο οἵα οὐκ ἄλλη τῶν γ' ἐφ' ἡμῶν. De Sanctis returns to this passage twice; in the first case it was to argue for the priority of the account of the *Hellenica* at this point over the corresponding passage in the *Agesilaus* (2. 7-9). In the present connection, however, his argument is that the Battle of Coronea could have been called the greatest of the day only before those of Leuctra and Mantinea. Two possibilities suggest themselves. "Like no other": does this mean in kind or in size? The natural way to take the statement would seem to be in the sense of size, since nearly everyone so understands it, even if one is not always able to offer a reason for one's interpretation. Besides, Hatzfeld,[372] who wants to construe the statement in the other meaning, can offer little evidence to support his position. He notes that Xenophon does not relate the numbers nor the effects of the battle so as to impress us with the contrast that it is supposed to form in these respects with the other battles of his day. But as to Coronea being qualitatively unique he simply calls attention to the general impressiveness and dramatic character of the encounter in support of his view.[373] De Sanctis retorts that he is quite ready to admit that Coronea was different in kind from every other battle, but he goes on to say that, since after all every battle is somehow unique, Hatzfeld's interpretaton is pointless, and Xenophon must therefore have been referring to the size.[374]

Other meanings have been proposed. Croiset[375] thinks that Xenophon is saying that Coronea was the most famous battle of his age; but this is meaningless unless we know in what respect Xenophon is saying that it was so noteworthy. Eduard Schwartz[376] believes that Xenophon is referring to the representative character of the battle more than to its size or to the manner in which it was fought, since practically all of the Greek states came together at Coronea, whereas Leuctra was a struggle between Sparta and Thebes alone. To be sure, he concedes, Mantinea saw a great number of states join together in battle, but that conflict was indecisive. Schwartz's interpretation in full, therefore, would be: Coronea stands alone as being the only battle of our time in which all Greek states took part and in which one side was victorious. These qualifications, however, are too artificial to be acceptable. Eduard Meyer[377] believes that Xenophon is referring to the results and the significance of the battle rather than to its size but

[372] *R de P*, IV, 122-23.

[373] *Ibid.*

[374] De Sanctis, *Annali di Pisa*, II, I, 21.

[375] Alfred Croiset, *Xénophon, son caractère et son talent* (Paris, 1873), p. 205.

[376] *Rheinisches Museum für Philologie* (hereafter cited as *RMP*), XLIV, 182.

[377] Eduard Meyer, *Geschichte des Alterthums* (Stuttgart, 1901-1902), V, 237.

that, because of the defeat Sparta suffered at Cnidus, which prevented the immediate restoration of Spartan ascendancy over Greece, Xenophon was in error in his evaluation of the effects of Coronea. But this is surely doubtful. Cnidus was an important battle, but it was not owing to Sparta's defeat there that the victory of Coronea was not of great military significance to her. Bury[378] more rightly observes:

But though the Battle of Coronea, like the Battle of Corinth, was a technical victory for the Spartans, history must here again offer her congratulations to the side which was, superficially, defeated. . . . When an aggressor cannot follow up his victory, the victory is equivalent to a repulse. Agesilaus immediately evacuated Boeotia—that was the result of Coronea.

Xenophon, accordingly, would have been wrong in attributing to Coronea any great importance for the Spartans even if they had won at Cnidus.

The usual construction of Xenophon's meaning, as has been said, is that he is referring to the size of the battle, to the number of the participants, but, since Coronea was not as momentous as Leuctra or Mantinea, it is likewise agreed, as we have also seen, that Xenophon erroneously allowed the evaluation to stand after Coronea was superseded by those later battles. But the error is not always attributed to the same cause. Some[379] hold that Xenophon knew that Coronea was inferior to those subsequent engagements but that he was indulging in exaggeration to glorify the achievements of his hero, Agesilaus. In the opinion of most of those who believe that Xenophon is referring to the magnitude of the battle, however, the presence of the statement in the final draft of the *Hellenica* is accountable to simple inadvertence on the part of the author.[380]

A number of serious objections can be made to the view that Xenophon could ever have thought that Coronea was the largest battle of his day. Schambach[381] undertakes to show that

[378] Pp. 544-45.
[379] MacLaren, *AJP*, LV, 251.
[380] See below, pp. 173-74.
[381] P. 23.

Coronea was larger than Leuctra. We shall leave it to others to evaluate the success of his attempt in other respects, but inasmuch as his thesis favors there being as great a number as possible at Coronea, we may look upon his calculation as high. He arrives at the figure of twenty-two thousand foot and horse present at Coronea. At the Battle of the Nemea, however, which took place a short time previously and to which Xenophon devotes a more detailed narrative than to Coronea —at that battle, according to Xenophon himself *(Hellenica* iv 2. 16-17), over forty thousand participants contested the field. Xenophon would not, therefore, in 394 or at any other time thereafter have described Coronea as the greatest battle of its time, since he stands himself as our most trustworthy witness that it was not—the figures of Diodorus for the Battle of the Nemea are even higher.

If Coronea was not the greatest battle of Xenophon's age, then, he did not say that it was, and we are thus compelled to construe his words in the qualitative sense proposed by Hatzfeld, even if we are unable to determine for certain just which feature it was to which Xenophon was alluding in distinguishing the battle as unique. The argument, however, is negative and it rests on the circumstance that no acceptable explanation can be offered for the contrary view. But even so it avails to deprive the passage of any value for those who would see in it an indication of the date of its composition, and in that respect we might regard the matter as closed. Yet there is more: there is positive evidence, too, and it has been provided for us by Xenophon himself.

The attention that has heretofore been directed to the problem of Xenophon's appraisal of the Battle of Coronea has been concentrated on the expression, οἷα οὐκ ἄλλη, as our review of the arguments has shown. The corresponding passage in the *Agesilaus* (2. 9) reads: διηγήσομαι δὲ καὶ τὴν μάχην· καὶ γὰρ ἐγένετο οἷαπερ οὐκ ἄλλη τῶν ἐφ' ἡμῶν. Here we can take ἐγένετο to mean "was," rather than "became"; and since καὶ γὰρ is as much as to say, "And it was well worth narrating (seeing that it was like no other battle of our time)," the version of the *Agesilaus* can be interpreted as presenting Coronea as the greatest battle of the age. In any event, the reading of the *Agesilaus* has been to no little degree responsible for the notion that in the *Hellenica* Xenophon speaks of Coronea as the largest battle of his time. Plutarch was already making the shift: he quotes Xenophon as saying that Coronea was a battle οἵα οὐκ ἄλλη τῶν πώποτε.[382] And by our own time at least one writer, Wilhelm Meyer, believed that scholars should no longer hesitate to acknowledge the true provenience of their interpretation: he quotes the version of the *Agesilaus* and smartly gives as the reference, *Hellenica* iv. 3. 16.[383] Not without due acknowledgement, of course, of the numerous advantages such a solution would afford, let us for purposes of the present discussion abandon this playful misconstruction and confront the problem presented by the *Agesilaus* on its own merits alone, for even if we assume, rightly or no, that Xenophon is indeed saying in the *Agesilaus* that Coronea was the greatest battle of his age, is the version of the *Agesilaus* decisive in interpreting the *Hellenica*? Not at all, for whereas Xenophon quite understandably permits himself certain liberties with the truth in the encomium, the account is always set aright in the *Hellenica*.[384] And it is of course agreeable to the purpose of the encomium that this glorious climax of Agesilaus' career should be made to appear the most momentous encounter of an entire era. This is

---

[382] Plutarch *Agesilaus,* 18.

[383] W. Meyer, p. 32.

[384] See above, pp. 118-19; also compare, for example, a passage like *Ages.* 1. 37 with its match, *Hell.* iv. 2, 3ff. In the eulogy the Greeks of Asia show that their fondness for Agesilaus was undesigned (οὐ πλαστὴν τὴν φιλίαν) by following him voluntarily to meet the foes of Sparta on the mainland. In the *Hellenica,* however, we learn what this affectionate obsequiousness was all about: a bargain had been made whereby, in return for assistance against the mainland Greeks, the Spartan promised to return to Asia and continue the fight against the barbarian. Moreover, there was a great aversion among the soldiery for lending support to the Spartan cause against their fellow Greeks (cf. iv. 3. 13-14), and special measures had to be taken to insure that unwilling troops were not brought along. In the *Agesilaus* (1. 37) the king is extolled for his benign sway over harmonious subjects in Asia; in the *Hellenica* Xenophon tells us that, just the same, the departing ruler was careful to leave a strong garrison behind to insure the "safety" of his subjects.

flattery. For history we turn to the *Hellenica*, and what do we
find? The expected alteration. Here Xenophon wrote: . .
τὴν μάχην, καὶ πῶς ἐγένετο οἷα οὐκ ἄλλη . . . . Obviously
this "how" cannot refer to the size of the forces, for he has
already described the contingents that took part. In fact he
distinctly separates this matter from the battle itself as
though it were an independent consideration: ἡ μὲν δὴ δύνα
μις αὕτη ἀμφοτέρων· διηγήσομαι δὲ καὶ τὴν μάχην, καὶ
πῶς ἐγένετο οἷα οὐκ ἄλλη τῶν γ' ἐφ' ἡμῶν.   The phrase
"like no other," then, does not refer to the size of the armies
but refers to something to come. Finally, there is the word
ἐγένετο, which to be sure in the *Agesilaus* can be translated
"was," in view of the absence of "how." But in the *Hellenica*
γίγνομαι is elsewhere used of battles and often can mean
only "develop."[385] In fine, there is no impediment to our
rendering Xenophon's thought in some such form as: "Now
this was the strength of both contestants; I shall also relate
the course of the battle and how it unfolded in a manner
distinguished among battles of our day."

With that we may consider the matter closed and conclude
that *Hellenica* iv. 3. 16 contains no indications as to the date
of its composition, except that it could not have been written
before 394. The peculiar character of the battle derives from
the manner in which it was fought, even though we might not
exactly know to what Xenophon was alluding in terming
the engagement unique. It would be challenging, however,
to make an attempt to learn. The most inviting place to begin
is the account of the Theban retreat. Xenophon separates it
from the rest of the fighting and sets off this episode as the
climax of the battle. It is the scene for which he reserves his
most poetic moment of description in the whole of the *Agesilaus*,[386] and it was probably not unworthy of his eloquence

---

[385] As in iv. 3. 10: ᾧ τρόπῳ ἡ ναυμαχία ἐγένετο. εἶναι μὲν γὰρ περὶ
Κνίδον τὸν ἐπίπλουν. Note that in the mere reference to the fact that
the encounter took place (when the reference is made to it only to establish
its location), εἶναι suffices; when it is the development of the battle that
is in question, ἐγένετο is used. Cf. iv. 2. 23: καὶ αὕτη μὲν ἡ μάχη οὕτω
ἐγένετο.

[386] See above, p. 128, n. 325.

Hatzfeld singles it out thus: "It is the succession of these unforseen and dramatic events, it is the unexpectedness of the initial Theban success, the dreadful counterattack of Agesilaus, and the clash of the two best infantries of Greece, which, in the eyes of Xenophon, rendered Coronea unique among battles of his time."[387] The general awe and magnificence, then, of the fray; and this, indeed, may be the proper explanation. But in order to justify it Hatzfeld was obliged to add, "in the eyes of Xenophon." In what respect, however, could this episode be considered unique without reference to the impressionability of the observer? Could it perhaps differ in kind among military manoeuvres and not just in intensity? If so, it must be the decision of Agesilaus to meet the retreating Thebans head-on that is the tactic that is here so unusual. It may have been a frequent occurrence that a body of soldiers made their way through opposing ranks only to find themselves isolated and compelled to withdraw, owing to the failure of their allies to achieve a commensurate success and keep abreast of them. Such a retreat would give the enemy an enviable advantage; he could hang on the rear of the retreating force and worry it from the flank without exposing himself to danger. Indeed, there would be no point in doing so; his opponent is already defeated: the retreat itself is evidence of that. Moreover—and this gives special point to Coronea—the mighty massed corps of the Thebans was irresistible. They had developed the tactic of organizing their force in great depth and exposing but a small front to the long, thin line of their opponent. Pagondas had employed this disposition at Delium, where the Thebans, though alone victorious of their allies, alone caused the defeat of the enemy.[388] Xenophon carefully explains the philosophy of the tactic in connection with Epaminondas' brilliant execution of it in the Battle of Mantinea in 362.[389] And of course it was the same organization that served Pelopidas so effectively at Leuctra.[390] The

[387] Hatzfeld, *R de P*, IV, 123.
[388] Thuc. iv. 93. 4, 96. 3-7.
[389] *Hell*. vii. 5. 23; cf. also iv. 2. 13, 18-19.
[390] *Hell*. vi. 4. 12.

Battle of the Nemea, however, serves as a more fitting comparison with Coronea since it was in these two that the Thebans, though themselves victorious, were on the losing side and were compelled to return through enemy lines. We are not specifically told that the Lacedaemonians did not openly confront the retreating Thebans, but only that they killed many of them. The tactics that the victor employed against them, however, are indicated by his dealing with the Argives, who likewise had been victorious over their opponents and were now withdrawing.

But the Lacedaemonians did come upon the Argives as they were returning from the pursuit, and when the first polemarch was about to attack them in front, it is said that someone shouted out to let their front ranks pass by. When this had been done, they struck them on their unprotected sides as they ran past, and killed many of them.[391]

This was the sensible course and must certainly have been the usual one. Directly to oppose a force, undefeated and still in good organization, unnecessarily, would be a dangerous and foolish deed in any circumstances, but it would be particularly so in the case of withstanding the Thebans, with their deeply massed phalanx in good order and coming on with great momentum. "Agesilaus was certainly brave, but he did not choose the safest course." This is sometimes looked upon as a compliment Xenophon is paying Agesilaus for the courage he here displayed, but it is more likely that the force of the remark is disapproving. It is the stricture of a soldier who is condemning reckless tactics that violate customary and sensible military usage, although Xenophon fully acknowledges the impressiveness of the exploit:

For while he might have let the men pass by who were trying to break through and then have followed them and overcome those in the rear, he did not do this, but crashed against the Thebans front to front; and setting shield against shield they shoved, fought, killed and were killed.[392]

But we have been long away from our task. We have seen that De Sanctis and Sordi associate Books Three and Four

---

[391] Brownson's translation of *Hell*. iv. 2. 22.
[392] *Ibid.*, iv. 3. 19.

with the *Anabasis*. This identification is suggested by the fact that the narrative of this part begins virtually at the place where the *Anabasis* comes to a close, and it would seem natural, they contend, that the author should have written the two accounts consecutively and in the same spirit and style. This is simply not true. The coincidence of the two works is of no significance, and the contrast between them is about as strong as that between any two that Xenophon ever composed. The difference in extent alone is enormous. The *Anabasis*, which narrates the events of two years, is written over two hundred and forty-three (Oxford) pages. To the memoirs[393] of eleven years, only fifty-five (Oxford) pages are given; yet the same proportion would require more than one thousand three hundred pages. It will be objected that extent is not the same as treatment, but it will also be apparent to anyone that it is impossible to maintain the same treatment—let one define that word as he will—in one twenty-fifth of the original compass. We might as well ask Aeschylus to re-write his *Eumenides* in the space of forty-two lines and yet preserve the same spirit and treatment. Let us examine the treatment of the two works, however. The latter portions of the *Anabasis* contain many speeches; in the memoirs there is not even one. And certainly no student of ancient history could propose that the orations are not an integral part of historical writing and that they can be omitted without altering the author's conception of his work. It is precisely the fact that the *Anabasis* contains many of Xenophon's own speeches, moreover, that sets it off distinctly from *Hellenica* iii and iv. The *Anabasis* is in large measure autobiographical; the memoirs are the record of the experiences of others. We refer to "Xenophon's *Memoirs of Socrates*," and in that way of speaking the memoirs in the *Hellenica* are those of Dercyllidas and Agesilaus, written by Xenophon. But the memoirs in the *Anabasis* are in large measure the memoirs—the thoughts, the re-

---

[393] Excepting those passages, of course, that were supposedly added later and that have nothing to do with Agesilaus, Xenophon, or the Asian expedition (iii. 2. 21-23, 5. 1-25, iv. 2. 9-23); and stopping with Sordi at iv. 7. 7.

flections, and the actions—of Xenophon himself. And this cannot be dismissed as merely owing to the coincidence that Xenophon had to write about himself because he and no one else happened to be the leader of the Cyreans. Xenophon was not the leader of the Asian expedition in the years after 399, and yet as he disappears from view there go with him as well the fine characterizations, the spirited interviews, the robust interest in life and activity so noticeable in especially the final parts of the *Anabasis*. There is no counterpart in what follows to the portrayal of brawling, drunken Seuthes,[394] of shifty, designing Heraclides,[395] or of Arystas, the voracious Arcadian;[396] no more evenings of warm entertainment[397] and roaring barbarian banquets;[398] no more informative digressions on peasant customs,[399] tradition,[400] or topography.[401] And, finally, if it should be objected that this character of the story had to be sacrificed to the greatly reduced proportion, then we have returned full circle; for we began by saying that treatment is affected by extent.

There is no denying, of course, that in the memoirs there are similarities with the *Anabasis*. Indeed, there are similarities there with a number of Xenophon's works. In the part dominated by Agesilaus in fact, the work brought to mind is not the *Anabasis* but the *Cyropaedia,* where we meet with the same ponderous display of sentiment and archaic virtue, the same extravagant protestations of eternal fidelity so much in evidence in just this part of the *Hellenica*. Xenophon is here trying to write in the style of Herodotus; but, as he lacks the sincerity and simplicity of that master for this type of composition, the attempt turns out bathetic: the naivete is contrived and the artless expression of great ideals is here wooden and stilted. When Xenophon turns his hand to a scene of the

---

[394] *Anabasis* vii. 3. 33-34.
[395] *Ibid.*, vii. 3. 15-20, vii. 5. 5-11.
[396] *Ibid.*, vii. 3. 23-25.
[397] *Ibid.*, vi. 1. 5-13.
[398] *Ibid.*, vii. 3. 21-34.
[399] *Ibid.*, vii. 4. 3-4.
[400] *Ibid.*, vii. 2. 22.
[401] *Ibid.*, vi. 4. 1-6, vii. 5. 12-13.

style of "Croesus and his son," it can only turn out melo-
dramatic:

"And the beautiful dwellings and parks, full of trees and wild animals, which
my father left me, in which I took delight,—all these parks I see cut down,
all the dwellings burned to the ground. If it is I that do not understand either
what is righteous or what is just, do you teach me how these are the deeds
of men who know how to repay favours."

Thus he spoke. And all the thirty Spartiatae were filled with shame before
him and fell silent; but Agesilaus at length said: "I think you know, Pharnabazus, that in the Greek states, also, men become guest-friends of one
another. But these men, when their states come to war, fight with their
fatherlands even against their former friends, and, if it so chance, sometimes
even kill one another. . . . Being free is worth, in my opinion, as much as
all manner of possessions. . . . And if, being free you should at the same
time become rich, what would you lack of being altogether happy?" . . .
"O that you, noble sir, a man of such a spirit may come to be my friend. But
at least," he said, "be assured of one thing, that now I am going away from
your land as speedily as I can, and in the future, even if war continues, we
shall withhold our hands from you and yours so long as we can turn our
attack against another."

With these words he broke up the meeting. And Pharnabazus mounted
his horse and rode away, but his son by Parapita, who was still in the bloom
of youth, remaining behind, ran up to Agesilaus and said to him: "Agesilaus,
I make you my guest-friend." "And I accept your friendship." "Remember,
then," he said. And immediately he gave his javelin—it was a beautiful one—
to Agesilaus. And he, accepting it, took off and gave the boy in return a
splendid trapping which Idaeus, his secretary, had round his horse's neck.[402]

This was the scene, by the way, that Theopompus of Chios
liked so well that he lifted it whole out of Xenophon for his
own *Hellenica*.[403]

Now there is also an interview between the leader of the
Greeks and a barbarian recorded in the *Anabasis*. The topic
is again a proposed entente between the two parties; the
advantages that will accrue to the barbarian are also recited,
just as in the other scene, and the Greeks likewise pledge
their faith.

Gnesippus, an Athenian, got up and said: "It was a good old custom, and
a fine one too, that those who had, should give to the king for honour's
sake, but to those who had not, the king should give; whereby, my lord,"
he added, "I too may one day have the wherewithal to give thee gifts and
honour." Xenophon all the while was racking his brains what he was to

[402] *Hell.* iv. 1. 33-39 (Brownson).
[403] Eusebius *Praep. evang.*, p. 465.

do; he was not happier because he was seated in the seat next to Seuthes as a mark of honour; and Heracleides bade the cupbearer hand him the bowl. The wine had perhaps a little mounted to his head; he rose, manfully seized the cup, and spoke: "I also, Seuthes, have to present you with myself and these my dear comrades to be your trusty friends, and not one of them against his will. They are more ready, one and all, still more than I, to be your friends. Here they are; they ask nothing of you in return, rather they are forward to labour in your behalf; it will be their pleasure to bear the brunt of battle in voluntary service. With them, God willing, you will gain vast territory; you will recover what was once your forefathers'; you will win for yourself new lands; and not lands only, but horses many, and of men a multitude, and many a fair dame besides. You will not need to seize upon them in robber fashion; it is your friends here who, of their own accord, shall take and bring them to you, they shall lay them at your feet as gifts." Up got Seuthes and drained with him the cup, and with him sprinkled the last drops fraternally.

At this stage entered the musicians blowing upon horns such as they use for signal calls, and trumpeting on trumpets, made of raw oxhide, tunes and airs, like the music of the double-octave harp. Seuthes himself got up and shouted, trolling forth a war song; then he sprang from his place and leapt about as though he would guard himself against a missile, in right nimble style. Then came in a set of clowns and jesters. . . .[404]

There is no room here for the objection that the strong contrast between the two depictions is merely due to a difference in setting; the difference is one of style of writing, of literary genre, and of conception. The sentiments themselves are about the same, and they must have been expressed in much the same informal manner: in the *Hellenica* the two men were seated alone on a blanket on the ground. In the one case, however, the two parties are satified if they can only die wearing Honor, Piety, Nobility, and Virtue; in the other, the ideals are even more lofty yet: Horses, Money, Slaves, and Women. In the one scene, the bombast of talking statues; in the other, the earthy realism of living men. Or, even allowing that the difference in setting brought with it the profound difference in treatment, why do we not find Agesilaus portrayed—at least once—in the *Hellenica* in one of these human settings in which the *Anabasis* so abounds? The reason is that Xenophon was writing these parts of the *Hellenica* for those young boys he seems always to have been carrying about with him in his head. In these scenes in the *Anabasis*,

[404] *Anabasis* vii. 3. 28-33 (Dakyns).

however, there is nothing useful for moral instruction or the inculcation of virtue. The bracing stuff here is for their later years.

Theopompus likewise might well have borrowed the scene of the massacre during the Euclean Festival at Corinth in 392, for it is full of just the sort of turgid rant that he made peculiarly his own.[405] It is a kind of little epic in prose:

In the first place, they devised the most sacrilegious of all schemes;[406] for other people, even if a man is condemned by process of law, do not put him to death during a religious festival; but these men chose the last day of the Euclea; . . . they drew their swords and struck men down. . . . Now when the situation became known, the better classes immediately fled, in part to the statues of the gods in the marketplace, in part to the altars; then the conspirators, utterly sacrilegious and without so much as a single thought for civilized usage, both those who gave the orders and those who obeyed, kept up the slaughter even at the holy places, so that some even among those who were not victims of the attack, being rightminded men, were dismayed in their hearts at beholding such impiety. . . . And at first they retired beyond the territory of Corinth with the intention of going into exile; but when their friends and mothers and sisters kept coming to them and trying to dissuade them, . . . some of them returned home. They saw, however, that those who were in power were ruling like tyrants, and perceived that their state was being put out of existence. . . . Some of them, accordingly, came to the belief that life under such conditions was not endurable; but if they endeavoured to make their fatherland Corinth again, even as it had been from the beginning, and to make it free, and not only pure of the stain of the murderers, but blest with an orderly government, they thought it a worthy deed, if they could accomplish these things, to become saviours of their fatherland, but if they could not do so, to meet a most praiseworthy death in striving after the fairest and greatest blessings.[407]

So they steal away to the Lacedaemonians and Agesilaus. Sordi[408] also refers to the delicate interlude where little Archidamus compassionately implores of Agesilaus the acquittal of his playmate's father, Sphodrias, and she used it as

[405] At least according to the usual interpretation of the manner of that historian. See, for example, G. Busolt, "Der Neue Historiker und Xenophon," *Hermes*, XLIII (1908), 283-85.

[406] Hideous atrocity! Actually, the Greek of the day would have yawned. Massacres at festivals had formed part of good Greek practice from the days of Harmodious and Aristogiton on down. In fact Aeneas Tacticus (17ff.) recommends choosing a festival day if one is going to commit a massacre, and he advises the magistrates always to march fully armed in religious processions.

[407] *Hell.* iv. 4. 2ff. (Brownson).

[408] *Athenaeum*, XXVIII, 17, n. 1 and 35, n. 1.

possible documentation for her thesis that the memoirs are written in the spirit of the *Anabasis*. Xenophon nowhere wrote a passage more effusive with maudlin honor and high piety, so languishing in bitter tears:

Now when Archidamus saw Cleonymus weeping, he wept with him as he stood by his side; and when he heard his request, he replied: "Cleonymus, be assured that I cannot even look my father in the face, but if I wish to accomplish some object in the state, I petition everyone else rather than my father; yet nevertheless, since you so bid me, believe that I will use every effort to accomplish this for you." At that time, accordingly, he went from the public mess-room to his home and retired to rest; then he arose at dawn and kept watch, so that his father should not leave the house without his notice. But when he saw him going out, in the first place, if anyone among the citizens was present, he gave way to allow them to converse with Agesilaus, and again, if it was a stranger, he did the same, and again he even made way for anyone of his attendants who wished to address him. Finally when Agesilaus came back from the Eurotas, and entered his house, Archidamus went away without even having approached him. On the next day also he acted in the very same way. And Agesilaus, while he suspected for what reason he kept going to and fro with him, nevertheless asked no question, but let him alone. But Archidamus, on the other hand, was eager, naturally enough, to see Cleonymus; still, he did not know how he could go to him without first having talked with his father about the request that Cleonymus had made. . . . Afterwards, however, . . . he went to Agesilaus and said: "Father, I know that if Sphodrias had done no wrong, you would have acquitted him; but as it is, if he has done something wrong, let him for our sakes obtain pardon at your hands." And Agesilaus said: "Well, if this should be honourable for us, it shall be so." Upon hearing these words Archidamus went away in great despondency. . . . "Agesilaus . . . says to all with whom he has conversed the same thing,—that it is impossible that Sphodrias is not guilty of wrong-doing; but that, when, as a child, boy, and young man, one has continually performed all the duties of a Spartan, it is a hard thing to put such a man to death; for Sparta has need of such soldiers." The man, then, upon hearing this, reported it to Cleonymus. And he, filled with joy, went at once to Archidamus and said: "We know now that you have a care for us; and be well assured, Archidamus, that we in our turn shall strive to take care that you may never have cause to be ashamed on account of our friendship." And he did not prove false to his words, for not only did he act in all ways as it is deemed honourable for a citizen of Sparta to act while he lived, . . . [but,] while his death caused extreme grief to Archidamus, still, as he promised, he did not bring shame upon him, but rather honour. It was in this way, then, that Sphodrias was acquitted.[409]

Where is all this tender drivel in the *Anabasis*? The virile sophistication of that work has here given way to an in-

[409] *Hell.* v. 4. 27ff. (Brownson).

effectual high style designed to provide a setting for the mock-heroic deeds of Agesilaus.

Sordi includes in the memoirs *Hellenica* iii. 3. the section in which the contested election to the throne is related. It also contains the story of Cinadon and his abortive conspiracy. Strictly speaking, these are not memoirs, for Xenophon was not present when the occurrences took place. But perhaps we can assume that, since Agesilaus became the leading figure in the memoirs, Xenophon later thought it fitting to provide the story of Agesilaus' reign with an introduction, so that we might be willing to allow the episode to be included in the memoirs on account of its indirect connection with the events there related, even though it does not actually form a part of Xenophon's own experiences. But what of the conspiracy of Cinadon? Can we rightfully argue that this also has claim to be considered an exception and to be included in memoirs of which it has no part? There is of course a relation between this occurrence and the career of Agesilaus. At the very outset we are given an ominous token of the moral degeneration that was proving to be the downfall of Sparta and that during Agesilaus' own reign was to bring her low and reduce her to impotence. But even if we were to concede that the episode should be included in the memoirs on the strength of this very indirect connection, we should be embarrassed by the futher consideration that Sparta's decline, occurring to be sure during Agesilaus' reign, does not even begin until well after the King's Peace—a point Xenophon makes himself.[410] Yet according to De Sanctis that event is the extreme possible limit of the memoirs, while Sordi brings them to a close even earlier.[411] So that not only does the story of Cinadon's conspiracy, unlike that of the royal election, have no direct connection with the memoirs, it does not even bear an indirect relation to them.

[410] *Ibid.,* v. 1. 36 and v. 3. 27. It is interesting to read on from this latter point.
[411] At *Hell.* iv. 7. 7; thus 388.

We shall in time consider certain other passages as well that, although found in Books Three and Four, contradict Sordi's criteria for the memoirs. She asks that these passages be removed from the memoirs, we shall see, and justifies their removal on the grounds that Xenophon did not witness the events related in them. By like token, however, we would also expect the removal of the campaign into Elis, the election to the throne, and the conspiracy of Cinadon. Yet these cannot be removed—certainly not the last-mentioned incident, since it answers Sordi's requirements for the memoirs more than does any other passage. With its great reliance on dialogue, which amounts almost to stychomythia, and with its long spoken passages that are turned into indirect discourse, it should be at the center of the episodes that constitute the memoirs. Yet to justify its inclusion would justify the inclusion of all those other passages just as loosely connected with "Xenophon's Memoirs of Agesilaus."

Sordi likewise includes Agis' campaigns in Elis in 399-97 in the memoirs. On what possible pretext? Agesilaus has not yet appeared on the scene. The campaigns have no connection with the affairs in Asia. Agis never again returns in the memoirs. And Xenophon himself, of course, was far off in Ephesus at the time of these undertakings. The campaigns in Elis, therefore, like the affair of Cinadon, have no proper place in the memoirs.

Why, then, were these events included by Xenophon in the *Hellenica*? Because they have a place there as *history*. In his account of the Corinthian War, when the other Greek states attacked Sparta, Xenophon dwells at length on the outbreak of that conflict. He distinguishes the superficial from the profound causes, and he inserts a long speech in which the grievances of the Spartan allies are sympathetically explained.[412] In the case of the Lacedaemonian campaigns against Elis, however, no such treatment is given. Nothing is said about the significance of the war, and in place of the careful analysis of the true causes, Xenophon gives undue

---

[412] *Hell*. iii. 5. 1-15.

prominence to some trivial pretexts that one would think undeserving of the historian's attention. As to the serious interpretation of the campaigns, however, nothing is said, and the reader comes away from the account dissatisfied. Only when he reaches v. 3. 27-4. 1, however, does it become clear that Xenophon was not omitting to explain the meaning of those events but was only delaying his explanation of them. In this passage and in vi. 3. 7-9, which corresponds to it, the historian finally records his interpretation of the many aggressions committed by Sparta during the period of her ascendancy over the other states of Greece after the Peloponnesian War. By the King's Peace Sparta had become the protector of the independence of all the Greek states by accepting the leadership in the enforcement of a contract whereby all powers had sworn not to interfere in the autonomy of other states. Yet Sparta herself, the executrix of the treaty, was the very power that violated the autonomy of independent states most often and most flagrantly, and in emphasizing the triviality of the pretexts for Spartan actions, Xenophon is pointing up Sparta's haughty contempt for the rights of her victims. The most sensational incident, of course, is the very one with respect to which Xenophon later imparts to us openly his impressions about Spartan imperialism: the seizure of the Cadmea. After putting themselves in possession of the citadel, the Spartans sent the Theban patriot, Ismenias, off to Sparta to be tried for his alleged crimes.[413] Xenophon's treatment of the incident is masterly. As in the case of the aggression against Elis or that against Mantinea,[414] he does not spoil the exposition by baldly explaining the true character of the Spartan actions, but resorting to suggestion, he dwells heavily on the flimsiness of the charges that the arrogant Spartans urged against their hapless captive.

But perhaps we have been led too far in pressing our point, which was, after all, only that episodes such as the conspiracy of Cinadon and the expedition against Elis have no part in

---

[413] *Ibid.*, v. 2. 35-36.
[414] *Ibid.*, v. 2. 1-2.

Xenophon's personal memoirs of the Asian campaign but are significant only insofar as the *Hellenica* is a historical account of the entire age. It is a critical issue, however, for, in order to show that the greater part of Books Three and Four was written for a different purpose and at an earlier time than the remainder of the *Hellenica,* it was necessary for De Sanctis and Sordi to say that these books were written as a continuation of the *Anabasis,* and thus their identity with that work in style and characterization as memoirs is basic to this interpretation of the peculiarities in these two books. That we have no justification in connecting the style of these books with that of the *Anabasis* has already been sufficiently established; and the present demonstration, it is hoped, makes it clear that there are certain episodes in them that unquestionably exhibit "memoir" peculiarities but that cannot conceivably be included in the memoirs.

Just as De Sanctis and Sordi rely heavily on the differences that the memoirs of Books Three and Four show over against the other books, so, too, it behooves them to emphasize the unity that the other parts of the *Hellenica* present in contrast with the character of the memoirs. To the extent to which the memoirs constitute the only exception to the unity of style and conception of the *Hellenica,* the argument that they were written much earlier and for a different purpose than the rest gains credence. The argument loses its force, however, if we should find among remaining parts of the *Hellenica* differences of style and conception comparable to those that distinguish these parts in turn from the memoirs. Do any such differences exist? Sordi speaks of "a profound continuity of style, of tone, of method" between the first two books and the last three.[415] This is a pretentious claim. There is a number of points that require explanation in view of it, but we shall consider only the most demanding of them.

Enough has already been said about the stark differences between the first two books, or the greater part of them, and the remainder of the *Hellenica.* De Sanctis himself in fact

[415] Sordi, *Athenaeum,* XXVIII, 24.

characterizes this opening part as no more than a spare, hasty, and imprecise outline of facts,[416] and since practically all other students of the *Hellenica* have observed the peculiar nature of the opening part, De Sanctis' statement has the support of many critics whose judgment concurs with his own. But De Sanctis is embarrassed about the support of another witness to the truth of his observation that the opening part presents differences in confrontation with the remainder of the *Hellenica*. It brings strong but unwanted confirmation. It is the witness of the "statistics." For, however much they serve to establish a great difference in character between the first and the following parts, they also constitute strong evidence that the composition of i-ii. 3. 10 antedates that of all that follows by many years. We have seen that all of De Sanctis' conclusions stand in great contradiction to any such arrangement as this, and the evidence of these stylistic studies, therefore, becomes a critical issue for the success of his theory. Sordi, we remember, admits that, although some of the conclusions of these studies could be explained away, there remain points too strong for her theory to deal with. But De Sanctis believes no such thing, and he denies that it is necessary to concede anything to those like Hatzfeld who hold that the first two books were written long before the others.

Now this is a major issue. It has come to be accepted that the stylistic studies have conclusively established that the first part of the *Hellenica* is written in a manner peculiar to itself and markedly different from the style of the remaining ones. Accordingly, if one were successfully to impugn the findings of these investigations, one's work would have a profound effect on the study of the composition of the *Hellenica*. De Sanctis takes up the issue of the "statistics" in his refutation of the position of Hatzfeld,[417] and we have already noted[418] that De Sanctis, after quoting that scholar's conclusion, pronounced it "hardly very decisive in itself." Perhaps the reader was puzzled to learn that a position such as Hatz-

[416] *RF*, n. s. XVI, 71.
[417] De Sanctis, *Annali di Pisa*, II, I, 30-31.
[418] See above, pp. 137-38.

feld's could be argued so strongly when dependent on conclusions as weak as De Sanctis' statement of them indicates. Was De Sanctis misrepresenting Hatzfeld's conclusions? Not outright; it is only that the statements De Sanctis quotes do not pertain to the matter in question.

De Sanctis approaches the matter of the stylistic differences between the first two books (actually, of course, only up to ii. 3. 9 or 10) by observing that as far as he knows he is the first who has even considered whether Part One of the *Hellenica* might not have been the first composed.[419] (Mac-Laren[420] takes the trouble to point out to him at least five others who have already discussed this possibility.) Then he mentions the work of Dittenberger,[421] who first investigated Xenophon's use of certain adverbs and particles, and finally he approaches Hatzfeld's statement of the latest findings of this method. But, passing over Hatzfeld's discussion of the differences between i-ii. 3. 9 and the rest of the *Hellenica,* De Sanctis quotes the statement which applies, not to the differences in question (those between the first and the successive parts) at all, but refers exclusively to the differences that occur within the remaining books of the *Hellenica.*[422] It is necessary, therefore, that we relieve Hatzfeld's conclusions of this misconstruction and note carefully the full statement that he has made as a result of his own and others' studies of Xenophon's style in the first part of the *Hellenica.* They find "une solution de continuité très nette" between the narrative of the Peloponnesian War and that of the events after the capitulation of Athens. And this of course constitutes a major objection to De Sanctis' theory that this first part was written at the same time as the history of the Thirty, which shows a very different style and treatment, and the last

---

[419] He compares the critics of Xenophon to the critics, "if such they can be called," of Thucydides, who considered the opening books of Thucydides the first ones written.

[420] *AJP,* LV, 260.

[421] *Hermes,* XVI, 330ff.

[422] Hatzfeld, *R de P,* IV, 220-21.

three books, which represent the most mature style of the *Hellenica*.[423]

Thus De Sanctis rejects the statistics. Besides, he claims to have proven by his "synonym" argument that the *Hellenica* underwent revisions, and these revisions could have affected words other than ἕπεσθαι and ἀμφί. Hence it is not known to what extent the present stylistic condition of the *Hellenica* is due to a natural development of the author's style and to what extent to later revision.[424] We have already challenged the evidence on the basis of which De Sanctis and Sordi, who follows him, argue that Xenophon subjected his text to a considerable number of revisions, but there is

---

[423] De Sanctis meets the formidable problem of the "solution très nette" head-on only once—in a footnote to p. 30 (*Annali di Pisa*, II, I). We shall accord his comment a commensurate dignity. He there says that the stylistic studies of Roquette lead us to the same conclusion as those of Hatzfeld (a conclusion which De Sanctis nowhere states). Then he proffers two reasons to account "in part" for the stylistic revolution at ii. 3. 10: that in the first part Xenophon was following an "annalistic" exposition; and that he took no interest in the events he there narrates. I am as puzzled as MacLaren (*AJP*, LV, 251) as to how an annalistic method of arranging the events could regulate one's use of particles. Be that as it may, Sordi as we are presently to see, points out that Xenophon tends to return to this annalistic exposition in the last books; yet these are the very books that represent Xenophon's most developed style, where it shows the greatest use of particles. As to the other matter, it has already been pointed out that the "problem" of the first part would be much simpler but for the unevenness of the treatment there found. If it were true that the entire section showed the same carelessness, incoherence, brevity, and lack of interest throughout, De Sanctis might have a point. But there are also passages there in which Xenophon takes the greatest interest, as Hermocrates' farewell, the Battle of the Arginusae, and the trial of the generals. Yet for all of that, μήν, occurring more than fifty times in the last part, never appears here even once; μέντοι there one-hundred and ten times, here twice, etc., etc. All of which serves to emphasize again that the problem of the first part of the *Hellenica* is not just the poverty of the exposition, but rather the *intermittent* poverty of that exposition.

[424] *Annali di Pisa*, II, I, 31. Note that De Sanctis does not reject the statistical method itself, but because of the revisions impugns the significance of the results. We shall attempt to reconstruct tabularly a process of composition which involves the two variables of stylistic development and revision and which would produce the aspect of stylistic variation presented by our copy of the *Hellenica*. The letters "A" to "H" represent the successive stages of the development of the author's style with time ("A" representing his earliest style, "H" his last and most mature style);

still another particular to be mentioned that was not touched on in our discussion. According to Hatzfeld's table (De Sanctis calls it accurate) ἕπεσϑαι is used six times in the first two

the first column ("Initial Composition") indicates the stage of style in which the various parts ("I" to "IV") of the *Hellenica* were written (the stage, that is, that his style had reached at the moment of their initial composition), and the columns to the right of it show whatever subsequent revisions the parts may have undergone during which they were re-written, in whole or in part, in a later style.

Hell.	Initial Composition	1st Rev.	2nd Rev.	3rd Rev.	4th Rev.	5th Rev.	6th Rev.	7th Rev.	Final Aspect
Pt. I	B								B
Pt. II	B	C	D	E					E
Pt. III	A	B	C	D	E	F			F
Pt. IV	C	D	E	F	G				G
Ages.	A	B	C	D	E	F	G	H	H

Notes:
Hell., Pt. III: iii-v. 1. 36. It is not necessary to suppose that each Part underwent all intermediate revisions, but only that it was originally written in the style of the first column and was finally left in the state indicated by the last column. As De Sanctis and Sordi have Pt. III written considerably earlier than the others, its initial draft has been assigned to period "A."

Thus we arrive at a condition wherein there is a "solution très nette" between the first two Parts and only a "légère progression" thereafter. The arrangement advocated by Hatzfeld *et al* achieves the same result in the following way:

Hell.	Initial Composition and Final Aspect
Pt. I	A
Pt. II	D
Pt. III	E
Pt. IV	F
Ages.	G

It would have been simpler for De Sanctis to deny, with Schwartz, Hartman, and others, that there was any regular progression in Xenophon's use of stylistic phenomena and thus to challenge the statistical method

books, ἀκολουθεῖν only once. De Sanctis[425] says that these
two books were written between 375 and 368. Sordi[426] puts
them "in the years after 369." Thus the memoirs of iii and
iv were supposedly written in the style favoring ἕπεσθαι
exclusively and these parts were revised in subsequent years
enough to convert the ἕπεσθαι's to their later equivalents.
But Xenophon's style, it now appears, was still in the stage
almost exclusively favoring the earlier form as late as the
period 370-365, when he wrote i and ii. And then, as we saw
above, by 360, when the *Agesilaus* was written, the author's
style was still in that same stage, only to suffer a violent
reversal by the time of the composition of the last books
a few years later. In those remaining years so much revision of the memoirs was to set in as to change all the
ἕπεσθαι's of the *Agesilaus* to the ἀκολουθεῖν's of the *Hellenica.*
In contrast to such an implausible arrangement, let us consider
the orderly development indicated by the statistics that De
Sanctis rejects in favor of his "revision" argument:[427]

Books	ἕπεσθαι	ἀκολουθεῖν	No. of Pages
i	0	0	32
ii. 1-3. 9	3	0	12
ii. 3. 10-end	3	1	21
iii	4	6	37
iv-v. 1. 36	3	12	57
v. 1. 36-end.	3	14	35
vi.	0	15	44
vii	0	14	44

Between the two possible explanations here presented, the
reader will probably have little difficulty in making his choice.
Sordi notes that the system employed for the arrangement

itself, but this would of course have made it impossible for him to use
the "synonym" argument, which posits such a progression.

[425] *Annali di Pisa*, II, I, 34.
[426] *Athenaeum*, XXVIII, 50.
[427] Hatzfeld, *R de P*, IV 220.

of events in iii and iv differs from that used in the remainder of the *Hellenica*. In this center section the events are grouped according to their development, the author pursuing a sequence through several years before returning to events in another quarter, whereas elsewhere the chronological or annalistic exposition is used. We shall not here challenge the accuracy of this statement but shall only remark that such a procedure seems contradictory to Sordi's own thesis. For according to her Xenophon wrote the first two and last three books at the same time that he was assimilating the memoirs of Books Three and Four to the general history into which he was incorporating them. Why did he not, then, change the order of narration in iii and iv and adapt it to the method of exposition that he was following in the other parts? Are we to be told that this would have been too difficult at so late a stage of composition, after the memoirs had been revised and highly perfected? Sordi seems to hint at some such thing. She notes that Xenophon could not have conducted an original criticism of the events of the early years of the century as late as 365 or so, when he was composing the history, and accordingly he merely copied out the memoirs that he had written long before.[428] Yet we are of course not expecting Xenophon to have conducted a new inquiry or to have subjected his original version to another investigation, but simply to have rearranged his exposition in accordance with the rest of the history of which it was to form a part. In one other place[429] Sordi touches on this question, where she is speaking of Xenophon's insertion of the events of the naval war of 394-389, which is narrated in iv. 8ff. She notes that the exposition here, where the events are contemporary with those of the memoirs, is consecutive and not annalistic, since Xenophon, she says, "felt constrained" to adopt this method rather than to integrate this series of events with the contemporary ones of the memoirs. But why? Sordi does not say. But whatever reason she might offer seems to be refuted in

---

[428] Sordi, *Athenaeum*, XXVIII, 25.
[429] *Ibid.*, p. 34.

advance by a statement she makes elsewhere to account for the fact that the place where the original memoirs end in our *Hellenica* is not very apparent, for in dealing with this problem she calls attention to the fact that we have no way of knowing but that the memoirs, at the time of their adaptation, were in the form of a "sketch."[430] We shall assume, therefore, that Xenophon was at liberty to insert the new material in the memoirs at its proper place, just as he was freely combining separate accounts in the annalistic fashion in other parts of the history. And the fact that he did not so incorporate the new material of course makes it all the more doubtful whether the procedure Sordi proposes is that to which we owe the present form of the *Hellenica*.[431]

We have seen that, in support of his argument that the first two books were written considerably later than the following two, De Sanctis calls attention to a difference in the author's prejudice toward the democracy at Athens in each of these parts. In iii. 1 Xenophon is hostile to the democracy, and he notes how the Athenians, as though ridding themselves of a nuisance, willingly dispatch to Thibron three hundred knights who had served under the Thirty. In ii. 4. 43, however, the history of the Thirty is brought to a close on an elevated note of reconciliation, and the democracy is commended for its toleration toward those who were associated with the regime of the Tyrants. Yet how could Xenophon have failed to record "that most glorious accomplishment of the Athenian democracy," the foundation of the Second Athenian Confederacy, if at the time of that event he had been on the good

---

[430] *Ibid.*, p. 35.

[431] We may anticipate one final objection. Lest it should be thought that, since the events in Asia form a continuous series of several campaigns, Xenophon would have felt it improper to interrupt the succession with foreign material, we note that Xenophon felt no such compunction elsewhere. He does not hestitate, for example, to interrupt the account of the Olynthian expedition of 382-379 with the narrative of affairs at Phlius (v. 3. 10-18) in 381, in order to preserve an annalistic arrangement. And even if this were Xenophon's reason for adopting the sequential exposition for the Asian expedition, he could just as well have decided on such an arrangement in composing the whole at one time as in adapting memoirs written earlier.

terms with his countrymen that his fine tribute to Thrasybulus indicates?[432]

Sordi is in agreement with this interpretation. The memoirs of Books Two and Three were written under the influence of a "profound" pro-Spartan prejudice. During this period Xenophon pictured Sparta as the gracious benefactress of Greece, and he saw her every intention as inspired by the noblest motives. In other parts of the *Hellenica,* however, we find Sparta treated in a different spirit, since these passages were written after Xenophon had become undeceived of his earlier impressions. The speech of the Theban ambassador (iii. 5. 8-15), for example, wherein Sparta's "benign" hegemony is exposed as oppressive tyranny, must have been written long after the naive passages of the memoirs in which it was inserted.

But what of the theory of revisions? If the text of the *Hellenica* underwent all the revisions that this theory predicates,[433] how is it that so many glaring contradictions[434] could have survived these repeated reviews? Let us consider, for example, the question of the supposed changes in Xenophon's prejudices with regard to the Athenian democracy or the Spartan hegemony. After Xenophon had become convinced that his former interpretation of the deeds of these institutions was misconceived, why did he not, as he was so often returning to the passages in which he had commemorated these erroneous impressions, set the account aright, rather than knowingly perpetuate historical inaccuracies? This is, of course, no small matter. It is equivalent, shall we say, to our supposing that a certain scientist makes a discovery but before he publishes his work his subsequent investigation

---

[432] De Sanctis, *RF,* n. s. XVI, 71.

[433] These supposed revisions, moreover, must have been rather thorough. After reminding us that they were responsible for the substitution of ἀκολουθεῖν in every case where ἕπεσθαι appears in iii and iv of our *Hellenica,* De Sanctis adds, "Di tali ritocchi possono, anzi debbono esservi stati assai più di quelli che noi possiamo constatare confrontando l'Ag. e le Hell." (*Annali di Pisa,* II, I, 30).

[434] Sordi, *Athenaeum,* XXVIII, 29: "all'improvviso e bruscamente il rovescio della medaglia."

hows that his previous findings were wrong, as he has in the meantime come upon the true solution to his problem; but that he nevertheless publishes the original discovery, which he knows to be erroneous. Or perhaps one conceives Xenophon deliberately falsifying history to ingratiate himself with the Athenian democracy at a time when he had prospects of returning from exile.[435] The problem still remains; for what would the pretence of attachment in one part avail Xenophon, when an open affront in another part would belie the sincerity of the profession? However we may care to consider the problem, it is clear that if Xenophon had revised his work, he would have removed these contradictions; or, if these contradictions do not exist, the theory which they support must fall.

The greatest objection to the revision theory, however, still lies before us. We have seen that one of the main arguments adduced by De Sanctis and Sordi to show that the second part of the *Hellenica* was written much earlier than the other parts was the statement in iv. 3. 16, where Xenophon supposedly declares Coronea to be the largest battle of his time. For the revision theory, however, this argument presents difficulties. When the attempt is made to apply Dittenberger's method to establish the relative chronology of the parts of the *Hellenica,* the objection is raised that according to the "synonym" proof Xenophon repeatedly revised the parts of the *Hellenica* after their initial composition. Again, when the argument that the second part was the first written is shaken by the testimony of Hatzfeld's inscription, which showed a late date for a passage[436] said to be written early, we are told that the text underwent many revisions during which the information in question would have been inserted. But when we wonder why the same fate did not therefore overtake the celebrated appraisal in iv. 3. 16, we are carefully reminded of the proviso that, although to be sure extensive,[437] the revisions were not always systematic and did not take place in

---

[435] De Sanctis seems to suggest some such thing (*Annali di Pisa,* II, I, 35).
[436] *Hell.* iii. 5. 25.
[437] See above, pp. 131, 136.

the same measure everywhere.[438] And when for all that we nevertheless impatiently begin to doubt whether, even if the statement could have been overlooked by so many revisions, it would actually have been copied in the *Agesilaus* as well, then we are simply asked not to be so intolerant of a little mistake.[439]

Now the Mistake as a scholarly device would make an interesting subject for investigation. Errors of carelessness and misunderstanding of course occur and, as they have undoubtedly affected the composition of the works of ancient authors to some extent, we are justified in making allowance for the possibility that certain difficulties in these writings are due to mistakes committed by their authors. But, as we do not trouble to distinguish which type of error it is that is likely to occur and which we are therefore authorized to make allowance for in reconstructing the reasoning of an author, the notion openly obtains that we are permitted to make indiscriminate use of the "erroneous" argument, frequently even before all reasonable ones have failed. Instead of a legitimate philological technique, then, this argument has become a tricky expedient, a kind of *deus ex machina* improvised *ad hoc* and let down to rescue hypotheses inextricably fouled in contradiction. In the case of our present theory, the dilemma is an understandable one. In order to show that the middle section of the *Hellenica* was written much earlier than the remaining ones, the statement about Coronea was adduced. This was said necessarily to have been written before Leuctra and Mantinea, thus dating the middle part, where the judgment is passed, before those later battles. As the priority of the center section, however, is refuted by the stylistic investigations, the revisions were called up to explain away this op-

---

[438] De Sanctis, *Annali di Pisa*, II, I, 24-25.
[439] Cf. Leopold Freese, *Ueber den Plan, welchen Xenophon im zweiten Theile seiner hellenischen Geschichte verfolgt* (Stralsund, 1865), p. 11: "ein Versehen"; Nitsche, p. 41: "gedankenlos"; De Sanctis, *Annali di Pisa*, II, I, 20: "sbatamente."

osition. But the revisions would also have corrected the statement about Coronea. So: "Mistake."[440]

Let us now examine our present passage to see how likely t is that Xenophon would have overlooked this error. In the course of the supposed retouchings and reviews undertaken in a casual spirit and ones, therefore, that may not have included every passage, was the episode of the Battle of Coronea included? Indeed it was, for in this very place we find that there was an ἀμφί in the original memoirs *(Agesilaus* 2. 11) that was changed to περί *(Hellenica* iv. 3. 17) during the revisions, and a ἕπομαι (2. 12) that became ἀκολουθεῖν (iv. 3. 19). And the replacement of these words by their synonyms is supposed to be conclusive evidence of revision, so that one cannot object that Xenophon never reviewed his account of Coronea and thus did not notice this striking anachronism. But if the change of synonyms is only certain evidence, there is another circumstance that constitutes outright proof that Xenophon reviewed the passage that we are discussing. For we recall that Xenophon copied the *Agesilaus* out of what became our text of the *Hellenica.* This occurred no earlier than 360 (when Agesilaus died) and thus after Leuctra and Mantinea; and yet Xenophon reiterates his original appraisal of the battle. "But it could have been copied out inattentively." It was not. We recall that De Sanctis has Xenophon

---

[440] Is it likely that one could re-read his own words, even repeatedly, and not notice erroneous statements? Aside from remote implications, we must distinguish between thoughts and the expression of thoughts. We often express a thought in an illogical form and we often re-read the record of our thought incoherently written, but owing to our familiarity with the ideas we miss the illogicality of the form in which the thought is expressed, even though we may fully perceive the meaning. For example, let us suppose one were to write the following statement: "The size of the armies that fought in the Spanish-American War were greater than in any conflict of our time." Now he might conceivably re-read his sentence several times over without seeing that he has given a plural verb to a subject in the singular or without noticing that he should strictly have said, "in any other conflict," since otherwise the comparison includes the S. A. War itself, which he did not mean it to do. These errors of expression, or form, then, we allow. But we cannot possibly allow that he could later have re-read his statement after World War One and World War Two without then perceiving the error of *fact.*

insert in the *Agesilaus* a discussion not found in the *Hellenica*.
This addition had disturbed the sense, De Sanctis goes on to
say, so that Xenophon was obliged to alter the wording in the
new version to restore coherence of thought. Rather than any
inadvertent transcription, therefore, we find that the passage
underwent a very careful scrutiny when the account of the
Agesilaus was taken from it. But exactly which words of the
passage was it that, being affected by the insertion, were so
closely inspected and so carefully revised? "And now I shall
relate the battle and how it was like no other of our day."

We have now to treat of what is perhaps the strongest
argument adduced by Sordi as evidence for her belief that the
middle section of the *Hellenica* is the result of an adaptation
of memoirs to the character of a general history. We have
said enough about how this assimilation was effected, and we
have made frequent reference to the passages that were inserted to broaden the outlook of an account originally confined in scope to Xenophon's personal experience. If these additions were introduced into a pre-existing account written
for a different purpose and possessing a unity of its own,
Sordi asks whether it would have been an easy matter to incorporate the foreign elements without disrupting the exposition to such an extent that no evidence of the combination
would remain. In short, can we find traces of these insertions?
Sordi points to three passages that are open to this possibility.
The last, iii. 2. 21-31, is that for which, she says, the evidence
is the least convincing. It is the account of the campaigns in
Elis that were conducted by King Agis in 399-97. We have
seen above that Sordi allows that this episode could have been
part of the original memoirs, and besides, she adds, owing
to those frequent revisions with which we are now only too
familiar, practically all evidence has in this case been apparently removed. Nevertheless, the account of this episode is
introduced and concluded by those characteristic phrases that
Sordi has elsewhere found to be evidence of adaptation. With
iv. 3. 1, however, the case is different. Agesilaus is hurrying

from Asia to meet the forces of the coalition at Coronea. Between the time of his departure from Asia and his arrival at Amphipolis, the encounter at the Nemea had taken place. At Amphipolis Agesilaus is informed of the event and of its successful issue for the Lacedaemonians. Dercyllidas bears the tidings, and his message is reported in indirect discourse and constitutes a summary of the battle. But the summary is unnecessary, for Xenophon (in iv. 2. 23) has just concluded a detailed account of the battle that is here being recapitulated in brief. Sordi accordingly believes that we have to do here with a notice that stood as the only reference to the battle in the original memoirs.

Let us now inspect the statement in question:

Meanwhile Agesilaus was hurrying from Asia to the rescue; and when he was at Amphipolis, Dercyllidas brought him word that this time the Lacedaemonians were victorious, and that only eight of them had been killed, but of the enemy a vast number; he made it known to him, however, that not a few of the allies of the Lacedaemonians had also fallen.[441]

Now this is a strange statement to be taken "to represent as much of the battle that was narrated in the original account."[442] We would reasonably expect the notice of a battle to tell which battle it was that was fought, and where it took place, and who were the participants, and under what conditions the encounter occurred. But the notice in question provides us with so little information about whatever battle it is supposed to be designating that we even count ourselves fortunate to learn that the Lacedaemonians themselves took part. From the fact that military terminology is employed we might tend to suspect that the event was a battle rather than, let us say, a horse race. Yet no sensible author would identify an event in this way, with a reference that is no reference. We are informed of a small particular of an occurrence, without being apprised of what occurrence it is of which our information constitutes that small particular. The author must have assumed, therefore, that the reader was already informed about the event to which allusion is here being made. All the evi-

[441] *Hell.* iv. 3. 1 (Brownson).
[442] *Athenaeum*, XXVIII, 30.

dence points in that direction. "This time" as opposed to what time? The reference is of course to the Battle of Haliartus, where the Lacedaemonians had just been defeated, rather than victorious as they were at the Nemea. Yet the account of the Battle of Haliartus formed one of the sections that Sordi says were added later and did not appear in the original memoirs, nor has there been any allusion to that battle in the meantime (i.e., iv. 1. 1-2. 9) to which the present notice could refer.

Sordi tries to find a parallel to this report of Dercyllidas in the narrative of the Battle of Cnidus (iv. 3. 10-12), which is also reported indirectly. But this account refutes, not confirms, her contention. Here practically all that we normally expect from brief summaries is given. First of all, the author takes the trouble to name the event he is relating and to give its location: a sea battle fought off Cnidus. We are told the identity of the participants and of the commanders on each side. The contingents of each fleet and their disposition in the line are described, and, finally, we are informed of the course of the battle and of its outcome. More surprising still is the fact that this engagement is much less related to the memoirs in a formal sense than is the Battle of the Nemea. Cnidus only affected Agesilaus' fortunes in a general way. In consequence of the lack of success in Asian waters, the Lacedaemonian cause in Greece could not fully prosper, and even if Pisander had come off the victor at Cnidus it is still rather probable, as we have seen, that Agesilaus would have enjoyed no more success at Corinth than he did. The Battle of the Nemea, however, affected Agesilaus much more directly. The armies that had opposed his countrymen in that conflict were the same ones that he was presently to face at Coronea. In fact the failure of the Lacedaemonians to achieve complete victory over the alliance at the Nemea was the very reason that Agesilaus was obliged to attack the enemy at Coronea. The Battle of the Nemea, then, the encounter that was in the direct succession of events that occasioned the recall of Agesilaus to Greece and the operations at Coronea and Corinth—this is dismissed in the memoirs in a contemptuous hint; whereas the more remotely related Battle of Cnidus is there accorded a satisfying review.

There is little likelihood, therefore, that we have to do here with separate stages of composition, and we are under no obligation to recognize the findings of Sordi and discern the vestiges of a later addition at this point. Sordi partially owns the weakness of the evidence in this instance, however, and it is clear that it is in our final passage that she vests the greatest confidence in her quest for traces of insertion. Our consideration of the evidence begins with the examination of the notice in *Hellenica* iii. 5. 1-2, where Xenophon turns away from the account of Agesilaus' activities to mention the measures taken by the satrap Tithraustes to draw off the Spartan from Asia and to embroil him in difficulties in mainland Greece. Timocrates of Rhodes, the agent of Tithraustes, sets about distributing Persian gold among political leaders in the largest states with a view to promoting an alliance hostile to Lacedaemon:

Then those who had taken the money set to work in their own states to defame the Lacedaemonians; and when they had brought their people to a feeling of hatred toward them, they undertook, further, to unite the largest states with one another.[443]

With iii. 5. 3 we leave the Asian scene altogether and begin an episode that was to terminate in the Battle of Haliartus (to the end of iii). With the beginning of iv we are back with Agesilaus in Asia, and there is no suggestion that Tithraustes' plan had borne any fruit until iv. 2. 1, where we learn that Agesilaus is recalled:

But the Lacedaemonians at home, when they found out definitely that the money had come to Greece, and that the largest states had united for war against them, believed that their state was in danger, and thought that it was necessary to undertake a campaign. And while themselves making preparations for this, they also immediately sent Epicydidas to fetch Agesilaus.

Agesilaus thereupon begins his homeward march, and his progress is described up to his passage of the Hellespont. At this point (iv. 2. 9), however, the scene again changes. We are back in Greece to witness the council of the allies that

---

[443] Brownson's translation.

have formed together against Lacedaemon, the preparation for battle, and, at last, the engagement at the brook Nemea (to iv. 2. 23). After resuming the account of the journey at Amphipolis, the activities of Agesilaus are kept in view without interruption until iv. 7. 7, where according to Sordi the memoirs cease.

The question Sordi asks is this: how is it that Xenophon in iii. 5. 1-2 gives a summary of events that in the sections immediately following he narrates in detail? The formation of the Greek coalition, the border dispute between Phocis and Locris, the entrance of the Athenians into the league against Sparta, and the Battle of Haliartus are all comprehended in the brief allusions made in the two sections that immediately precede this detailed exposition. And when in iv. 2. 1-2 Xenophon has occasion to explain the recall of Agesilaus, he returns to the same wording that he employed in iii. 5. 1-2, as we have seen, just as though he were taking no notice of that full narration of the events occasioning the recall. The passage does not represent an advancement of the narrative but only a circumstantial presentation of matters already related in brief; yet it is not presented as an expansion of a previous summary but is introduced into its setting without its relation to the context being made clear. Surely, then, Sordi continues, we have to do here with an insertion introduced to extend the scope of the pre-existing account by devoting greater interest to matters in Greece. For Xenophon to repeat in iv. 2. 1-2 what has been already related so fully only serves to confuse the reader and impair the continuity of the exposition. When we remove the insertion, however, clarity is restored, and if the account is again reduced to modest limits it proceeds consistently within them.

It requires a good deal more imagination than one is normally expected to possess to see in the statement of iii. 5. 1-2 all the meaning that Sordi maintains it carries. However it is taken to read (we shall return to this), it is certain that it cannot refer to "the formation of the Greek coalition" and "the entrance of Athens into the league against Sparta," since at that time those events had not yet occurred. The very opening of the passage (iii. 5. 3ff.) that describes the developments leading up to the Battle of Haliartus makes this clear: "But the leading men in Thebes, aware that unless someone began the war the Lacedaemonians would not break the peace with their allies. . . ." Here the order is that of outbreak of war first and severance of relations afterward. From iv. 2. 1-2 we learned that the reason for Agesilaus' recall was "that the largest states had united" against the Spartans, who "believed that their state was in danger"; but where is any of this in the "insertion"? There (iii. 5. 5) we read, "They also reasoned that it was a favourable time to lead forth an army against the Thebans and put a stop to their insolent behaviour toward them; for matters in Asia were in an excellent condition for them, Agesilaus being victorious, and in Greece there was no other war to hinder them."[444] Accordingly, there was no necessity at this time for the Spartans to recall Agesilaus, as they were confident that Pausanias and Lysander would dispatch the Thebans without great difficulty, and as there was great reluctance, besides, to withdraw Agesilaus from the sanguine prospects that lay before him.[445] Then, too, if there had been an alliance already formed against the Lacedaemonians, why did it not come to the support of its member, Thebes, who had begun the trouble for the very purpose of broaching hostilities? Pausanias (sec. 17) arrives "with the troops from home and those from Peloponnesus except the Corinthians, who refused to accompany them." Is this the proper way to refer to the existence of a hostile alliance? "Except the Corinthians," moreover, implies that Argos was represented; yet how could this have been possible if Argos had already become a member of an alliance against Sparta? In the speech of the Theban ambassador at Athens there is no mention of an alliance under way, and the Athenians are merely being requested to aid the Thebans against the impending attack of the Lacedaemonians. The Corinthians and Argives are mentioned only as resentful, and the ambassador

[444] Brownson's translation.
[445] Cf. *Hell.* iv. 1. 41.

exhorts the Athenians: "If we and you are found in arms together against Lacedaemonians, be well assured that those who hate them will appear in full numbers."[446]

The account of Diodorus is in full agreement. He first narrates what he calls the Boeotian War, ending with Haliartus (xiv. 81. 2-3); then the formation of the Corinthian Alliance (xiv. 82. 1ff.); and the Lacedaemonians thereupon summoning Agesilaus (xiv. 83. 1).[447]

If the Corinthian Alliance is not mentioned in the "insertion," then, how is it that in the preceding section (iii. 5. 2) as well as in the later passage (iv. 2. 1-2) that harks back to it this alliance is referred to? Let us examine these passages more closely. In the second one the reasons are given that led the Ephors to summon Agesilaus from Asia. They took cognizance of the Persian encouragement and support of the dissenting states, and of the alliance that had been formed for the purpose of war against Sparta. But there is no reference here to the conflict with Thebes alone, for at this point the alliance had already come into being and the Peloponnesian allies were in open hostility to Sparta. This is, accordingly, a wholly different situation from that which existed just prior to Haliartus. The description of affairs found in this passage, therefore, accords perfectly with all that has taken place up to the point where the statement is found. This passage, however, is supposed to be a repetition of the former one (iii. 5. 2), where reference is said to be made to these same events. Yet that former passage falls before the narrative of the Boeotian War, which as we have insisted was prior to the formation of the Corinthian Alliance.

The difficulty is resolved upon close examination of the

---

[446] *Hell.* iii. 5. 11 (Brownson).

[447] For the concurrence of modern authorities consult Grote, VII, 456 (no alliance before Haliartus), 467 (death of Lysander, the occasion for formation of the alliance), 469 (the alliance is that which causes Agesilaus' recall); Beloch, III, I, 68 ("Mit den Boeotern hoffte man ohne grosse Schwierigkeit fertig zu werden."), 70 (the alliance is the result of Haliartus), 72 (Agesilaus now recalled); Bury, pp. 540-42, 844; Marchant & Underhill, pp. lxxxvi-lxxxvii.

wording of iii. 5. 2, which is taken as referring to the Corinthian Alliance. The passage reads:

οἱ μὲν δεξάμενοι τὰ χρήματα εἰς τὰς οἰκείας πόλεις διέβαλλον τοὺς Λακεδαιμονίους· ἐπεὶ δὲ ταύτας εἰς μῖσος αὐτῶν προήγαγον, συνίστασαν καὶ τὰς μεγίστας πόλεις πρὸς ἀλλήλας. Whereas the verb, συνεστηκυίας, which is found in the later passage, rightly denotes that the alliance had already come into being, the same cannot be said for the corresponding verb, συνίστασαν, of the present passage. The tense here is not aorist but imperfect, and it denotes that the action was beginning and was still short of fulfillment at the moment in question. We may compare διέβαλλον in the preceding clause, which suggests a comparable stage of action being described. We should render these verbs therefore in some such form as, "began to calumniate," and "set about organizing." At this point, therefore, Xenophon does not yet know of the existence of any alliance, and there is, accordingly, no evidence here of an anticipation of what is to be related in the passage that follows or any one beyond it.

There is a final objection, however, that must be considered. Sordi notes that in iv. 2. 1-2 we have a repetition of a number of events that she believes to have already been related: the Corinthian Alliance, the Battle of Haliartus, the expedition of Pausanias and Lysander. We have seen that, except for the first of these, there is really no mention here of the events to which she refers. Supposing that there were such a repetition, however, and that "Xenophon relates anew in brief that which he had already narrated extensively" in the inserted passage, does it likewise follow that a brief reference to events previously narrated in full would constitute "a useless repetition, one even harmful to the sense because it is illogical and apt to disorient the reader"? No more than it does when it occurs elsewhere in the *Hellenica*. There are several instances but none that makes so neat a parallel with iv. 2. 1-2 as that of iv. 8. 12. In iv. 8. 1 we learn that the islands and the coastal cities are defecting from the Lacedaemonians to Conon; in iv. 8. 3 Conon receives a fleet from Pharnabazus; and in iv. 8. 10 the walls at Athens are being rebuilt with Conon's support. Then Xenophon inserts a discussion of naval matters, enumerating the succession of navarchs that led up to the appointment of Teleutias and relating how the Lacedaemonians came into possession of Rhium. The next topic for discussion is the mission of Antalcidas to the Persian satrap Tithraustes; but before Xenophon can relate the mission he must tell of the motives that led to it, and so he reviews the situation, which he had described some sections earlier, from the viewpoint of Sparta:

Now the Lacedaemonians, upon hearing that Conon was not only rebuilding their wall for the Athenians out of the King's money, but was also, while maintaining his fleet from the latter's funds, engaged in winning over the islands and coast cities on the mainland to the Athenians, conceived the idea. . . .[448]

Here the circumstances that had previously been narrated in full are reviewed to provide the setting for actions about to be described. Now let us compare our passage in iv. 2. 1:

But the Lacedaemonians at home, when they found out definitely that the money had come to Greece, and that the largest states had united for war against them, and that their state was in danger, thought that. . . .

In the latter example no more than in the first is there any "useless repetition" or impairment of the sense due to the brief recapitulation of events already treated profusely. Actually, if either of the two instances is to be taken as evidence of redundance owing to an insertion, it is that of iv. 8 rather than the notice giving the reasons for Agesilaus' recall; for there are only one and one-half sections of the text separating the last event included in the summary of iv. 8. 12 from the summary itself, whereas the last previous reference to any events that are summarized in iv. 2. 1 occurs forty-one sections before their restatement as the cause for Agesilaus' return. The reader, accordingly, could not be expected to retain in memory the full impression of a narrative from which his attention has been distracted for so great an interval, and we should find Xenophon at fault if he had chosen to omit the retrospect that Sordi finds so useless and misleading.

[448] *Hell.* iv. 8. 12 (Brownson).

Is it not, moreover, difficult to conceive that Xenophon would have committed this stark blunder of which Sordi holds him guilty in his repeating an episode already referred to? The example in question is the more striking in that it is found immediately after the statement it is taken as duplicating. If our supposed insertion (iii. 5. 3-25) appeared in some other part of the narrative, it would be easier to believe that an error of the sort that we have to do with here could have been made by the author in effecting his later adaptation. But from its present location it is clear that the passage was introduced deliberately into the position it occupies. Xenophon, therefore, must have cast about for the place in the narrative where incidents related in the insertion would appropriately fit into the general development of events, and what position was supposedly chosen? The one immediately following the passage in which the matters about to be related in the insertion have just been detailed. Can we really imagine that Xenophon would have selected the statement saying that the alliance for war on Sparta had already come into existence, as the very point in the narrative at which to insert an account of events that occurred prior to the alliance?

Finally, we have seen that the stylistic variations observable in Books Three and Four were also used to support the contention that there are two evident stages of composition in those parts. That the dissimilarities in treatment exist is beyond question; that they indicate different periods of composition is simply a conjecture. The same judgment that could have included two so greatly differing manners of treatment in the same work in close juxtaposition would have been just as inclined to compose that same work concurrently in those two different styles. If Xenophon were so little solicitous of the consistency of treatment in his history as is evident from the great inconsistency that it in fact possesses, he would have been just as capable of putting the two contrasting styles together originally as of putting them together later on. But is it not incumbent on one who asserts this to account for that difference in treatment? Not at all. Whatever explanation is offered for the difference by those who hold that the two series of (Asian and Greek) events were composed long apart will suffice for one thinking them to have been written simultaneously. Those who account for the disparity in treatment by positing two widely separated periods of composition do not understand that they are equally obliged to account for the appearance of those two different, even conflicting, styles side by side in the same work, particularly if we are to think of it as possessing a unified and well-defined organization: a comprehensive history of Greek affairs conceived according to the principles of Thucydides.[449]

One will certainly argue that Xenophon was careless and that, shrinking from the labor of re-writing the earlier account, out of convenience he simply transcribed it to serve as the exposition of the events it embraced.[450] Such an objection, when raised, must be immediately put down. It is difficult, in the first place, to believe that Xenophon would not have rewritten the memoirs in the style of the greater part of the work of which they were to form so integral a part. It would have cost him but little trouble to do so. But there is in addition evidence that it was not through indolence that Xenophon chose to employ the earlier account, in view of the fact that there is much in the memoirs that is unsuited for inclusion in a general history. Seeing that Xenophon, nevertheless, did not avoid the trouble of transcribing this matter into its new setting when he would have done better to omit it, we must conclude that he did not regard the presence of these episodes, so different in interest and importance from those around them, as untoward or inappropriate. And yet many of these chatty little scenes could have fallen away with advantage:

Then Meidias, not knowing what to do, said: "Well as for me," said he, "I will go away to prepare hospitality for you." And Dercylidas replied: "No, by Zeus, for it would be shameful for me, who have just sacrificed to be entertained by you instead of entertaining you. Stay, therefore, with us, and

[449] Sordi, *Athenaeum*, XXVIII, 25, 53.
[450] Sordi seems to suggest something of this sort: Xenophon probably did not "feel the necessity" of conducting a new critique of these events. *Ibid.*, p. 25.

while the dinner is preparing you and I will think out what is fair toward one another and act accordingly." When they were seated Dercylidas began asking questions: "Tell me, Meidias, did your father leave you master of his property?" "Yes, indeed," he said. "And how many houses had you? How many farms? How many pastures?" As Meidias began to make a list, the Scepsians who were present said, "He is deceiving you Dercylidas." "Now don't you," said he, "be too petty about the details." When the list of the inheritance of Meidias had been made Dercylidas said: "Tell me, to whom did Mania belong?" They all said that she belonged to Pharnabazus. "Then," said he, "do not her possessions belong to Pharnabazus too?" "Yes, indeed," they said. "Then they must be ours," he said, "since we are victorious; for Pharnabazus is our enemy. Let some one, then," said he, "lead the way to the place where the possessions of Mania—or rather of Pharnabazus— are stored.[451]

Occasionally entire episodes could have been unceremoniously lopped away, and none offers itself more distinctly in this regard than the tender little passion play on the acquittal of Sphodrias (v. 4. 25-33), which we have discussed above.[452] It is found deep in the "historical" part of the *Hellenica* long after the memoirs proper have expired, so that the remarkable contrast that it forms with what we are accustomed to find in general histories in not softened by the fellowship that similar matter would have afforded it. But perhaps Sordi herself has provided the best statement of the case for the elimination of this episode from a history of Greece in stating that in the "historical" parts of the *Hellenica* "the descriptive element is present . . . only in the episode of Sphodrias. . . .The episode is in fact isolated from its context. . . .We have to do here with an exception, and it is, moreover, not truly an integral part of the events."[453] Its inclusion, therefore, which was not only unnecessary but undesirable as well, makes it clear that it did not spare but rather cost Xenophon effort to insert the incongruous scene, and that, accordingly, one who would not be offended by this evident incompatibility could with equal likelihood have purposely written just such a scene for inclusion in a general history. The "memoir" parts of the *Hel-*

[451] *Hell.* iii. 1. 23-26 (Brownson).
[452] See pp. 159-60.
[453] *Athenaeum*, XXVIII, 17, nn. 1 and 2.

lenica, in fine, could just as well have been written during as after or before the "historical" parts with which they stand in so noticeable contrast. All possibilities are inviting; there is evidence against none.[454]

[454] I cannot let this chapter finally close without appending at least a word of valediction to Miss Sordi, from whose work I have greatly benefited. The reader has seen that I have had to disagree with her on many points, but let him not infer that I have for that any less respect for her endeavors. Her two articles are in point of accuracy and conscientiousness exemplary, and in calling attention to many hitherto unobserved features of Xenophon's style she has made a worthy contribution. Moreover, her work is marked by a plain show of honesty that is quite disarming. She seems to have set herself the task, for one thing, of actually reading her author to see what he says, itself a remarkable instance of humility for one dealing in these matters. I particularly remember too my reaction to her somewhere frankly stating that an opposing thesis contained some points she could not argue away. It made me quite forget that I was reading a work of scholarship, and I actually regretted that I had to go on to dissent from any of her conclusions. Her genuine interest in detecting every trait of her authors style unfairly works against her, for if there is ever any inconsistency in her conclusions, it can be detected right from the replete data she herself offers. In all, we need less of the vanity of the mere theoreticians and more of the method she has followed—σὺν τῷ ἀληθεῖ μᾶλλον ἥπερ σὺν ὑπερηφανίᾳ.

EPILOGUE

EPILOGUE

For history has a certain affinity with poetry.—Quintilian (*Institutes* x. 1. 31)

Any observations made at this point on the composition of the *Hellenica* would only be provisional, since not all of the theories which have been proposed as solutions to that problem were considered; but if those that have been examined do not therefore fully represent the present state of knowledge, they nevertheless sufficiently indicate the approach to which attempts at solutions have characteristically been confined. The singular disappointment which has attended these endeavors is not owing to lack of effort expended, for indeed the greatest interest has been taken in the problem for well over a century, and often too by students of no mean qualifications. That so little progress has been made in studying Xenophon's method of composition is therefore something of a paradox, in view of the fact that for all his qualities he does not enjoy the reputation of being as profound a thinker as certain other writers, like Homer or Aeschylus, in analyzing whose works our efforts have met with some measure of success. Xenophon, as he is revealed in his writing, is straightforward and undissembling, and therefore less capable of disguising his feelings or concealing his motives from us. This is the beginning of error. His unaffected manner is too often deceptive and easily leads us to conclude that because it is simple it is also transparent or because it is candid it is uncontrived. We have vested too much confidence in our insight into Xenophon's manner of exposition and passing over this as a problem have permitted ourselves to proceed immediately to drawing inferences based on assumptions about his style that have not, therefore, been carefully established. We are fond of beginning studies of his composition by noting the unfortunate circumstance that he suffers from what might be described as being a greater philosopher than

191

Thucydides, a greater historian than Plato, and by regretting in a patronizing way that he had to suffer comparison with those illustrious figures; and when at length we feel that by these and like observations we have made a strong enough case for regarding his nature as patently simple, we openly set about taking any liberty we care to in discovering his motives or revealing his method. In fact, in these constant repetitions of the condescending theme, that although superficial Xenophon is yet sincere, one can usually sense an attempt to prepare the way for some hypothesis which is to presume heavily on his ignorance or his carelessness or his credulity.

But have the qualities of the author's narrative been accurately established? It is, after all, whether in the case of Xenophon or any Greek historian, the narrative itself on which our reasonings about historiography are based, and it is with it that we should logically begin in studying the composition. But, heedless of this obligation, we begin directly with our combinations, inferences, and interpretations, using as the substance for these deductions matter that is so inaccurate and ill-defined that erroneous statements made about these histories are astonishing in number and degree. The hypotheses erected on these conclusions are also astonishing.

To state the case plainly: whereas the greatest attention has been given to interpretive analysis of histories, descriptive analysis, the necessary preliminary to that study, has been left aside. Nor is it difficult to discover why. It is a pedestrian task, unavailing in itself and of use only as it provides the substance for its exciting counterpart, interpretation; and in the case of Xenophon it seems unnecessary besides, seeing how it is generally agreed that all his attitudes and sentiments are so readily apparent as not to require investigation. But all this is wrong, and before any progress can be expected in interpreting the *Hellenica* or any history like it, the narrative must be subjected to an analysis as fully systematic as that made in determining the method, order, and purpose of its composition.

By descriptive analysis is not meant examination of the

contents as facts of history, but rather the author's subjective approach to those facts as revealed in his treatment of them. In the case of ancient poets or dramatists we think it altogether natural to consider matters like the handling of scenes, manipulation of plot, treatment of character and action, but it would never seem appropriate to examine a history in such a light. Yet how can we otherwise discover the author's emotional interest in the events he is relating, an interest which deeply affects his historiography? For it is necessary to realize that the study of history for its own sake is a modern pursuit unknown to the classical Greek, for whom history was a form of literature—an attitude not to be confused with our own expectation that a history consist of a narrative of facts meaningfully arranged and written in a pleasing style, for such is only literature in a superficial sense. History is literature when an artist perceives the genius of an age and reveals it through the facts of history. The first approach to history is therefore aesthetic.

But perhaps it will be objected that investigations of the *Hellenica*, in the sense here meant, have in fact been made, and perhaps it may be allowed that to a certain extent this is true. What has been the nature of these investigations? And can it be denied that the serious attention the narrative of the *Hellenica* has received from scholars has been rewarded with fruitful and stimulating results? To pursue our discussion further and along the lines indicated by this interesting question, it might be well to resort to examples, to actual cases in point, since it is difficult to understand topics such as the present one when discussion only consists in abstract definitions, however carefully worded these may be. Our object, of course, will not be to deal with problems, or arrive at results, for their own sake at all, but rather to view each passage as an exercise in criticism, as an illustration, that is, of the considerations involved in the descriptive analysis of a literary work. Let us therefore consider, as a convenient method of selection, three representative examples: one taken from the beginning of the *Hellenica*, another from the end, and a third applying directly to no one scene but in fact affecting them all.

We begin with the account that Xenophon has left us of the trial of the generals who took part in the Battle of the Arginusae (i. 7). It is one of the few circumstantial passages in the first part of the *Hellenica,* and it is largely free of the problems consequent to the brief and disconnected character which habitually distinguishes the narrative of those first two books. Yet it is not without its difficulties, and as these have been the object of considerable attention it could surely be argued that here if anywhere a scene of the *Hellenica* has been subjected to searching analysis. Perhaps the problem which has proved most troubling of all is that of Xenophon's treatment of Socrates in this scene. Although Xenophon does not, to be sure, neglect here to mention Socrates' firm adherence to justice, beyond this passing reference nothing is said of the actions or speech of the great philosopher throughout the whole affair. Indeed, this one remark constitutes the very sum and substance of reference to Socrates in the entire *Hellenica*—the very Socrates who was the teacher and friend of Xenophon. Certainly then, the conclusion is reached, this part of the *Hellenica* must have been written while Xenophon was yet a very young man, before his attachment to Socrates was very strong, and surely before Socrates had given the great meaning to the principles he advocated by persevering in his convictions even unto death. We are not yet dealing, therefore, with the Socrates of the *Memorabilia,* in which account Xenophon finally returns to do justice to the personality of his master and realizes at last the profound significance of his life. In the *Hellenica,* as we have seen, Xenophon does not even trouble to distinguish Socrates as *epistates* of the Prytany, but negligently allows us to assume that he was an ordinary Prytanis. So little notice is taken of Socrates here, in fact, that when Xenophon at last mentions him, he identifies him as "the son of Sophroniscus," as though the reader would not otherwise be expected to recognize which Socrates was meant.

We are now ready to test the value of these observations by reviewing the account of the trial from the standpoint of the author's own interest. The scene opens quietly enough.

We are not told the reason why two of the generals who took part in the battle did not return to Athens with their colleagues. It may have been because they sensed danger, to be sure, but as no motive is assigned to their action we cannot be certain. Perhaps, however, they were chosen to remain in charge of the fleet in Asia until the successors—two in number—of the eight deposed generals had arrived to take command. Besides, the very fact that the six did return to Athens is sufficient indication that there were no dreadful consequences to be expected as a result of their conduct in the battle (cf. i. 6. 35). In any event, the dissatisfaction of the people is soon made evident; the six are taken into custody and Theramenes comes forth as their accuser. When the generals are permitted to make their defense, however, their justification both appears reasonable to the reader and is presented as having been convincing to the Assembly as well: "With such arguments they were on the point of persuading the Assembly, and many of the citizens rose and wanted to give bail for them; it was decided, however, that the matter should be postponed to another meeting of the Assembly (for by that time it was late in the day and they could not have distinguished the hands in the voting). . . ."

The hopeful prospects that Xenophon allows to prevail at this point serve a peculiarly effective purpose in the evolution of the action. For a moment the uneasy foreboding of the initial events is relieved, and the acquittal of the generals seems assured. But psychologically this fleeting respite acts as a foil for a series of events that beginning at this point proceeds in steady development to a surprising climax. First Theramenes' deceitful subterfuges: the false mourners and the corruption of Callixinus; and then the illegal proposition with its terrible demand. The proposals are read and placed before the people. How would they act, being thus confronted with these sudden and drastic measures? Everything now turned on their response; some desperate and ingenious device was necessary at once to resolve all perplexity and drive them to precipitate and utter compliance. "And there came a man before the Assembly who said that he had been saved by floating upon a meal-tub, and that those who were perishing charged him to report to the people, if he were saved, that the generals did not pick up the men who had proved themselves most brave in the service of their country." "I venture to say," comments the great historian Grote, "that there is nothing in the whole compass of ancient oratory more full of genuine pathos and more profoundly impressive than this simple incident and speech," and so too must it have affected its hearers. The case of the generals is now becoming critical as the sentiment of the Assembly is clearly moving over to the side of the prosecution. Refuge is taken in legality: Euryptolemus, acting on behalf of the accused, dares to raise the question of constitutionality, but it is too late. "Some of the people applauded this act, but the greater number cried out that it was monstrous if the people were to be prevented from doing whatever they wished."

With this clear statement of the disposition of the Assembly we enter at this point upon the final stage of action. The outcome is evident, but the manner in which it came about remains to be described; yet, the dramatic effect of the entire scene is accomplished in this description. It is arranged in a series of stages, each represented by an opposition to the will of the Assembly. The resistance with which the successive challenges are met increases in violence, and the resolution and number of the opponents to the popular will noticeably decline with each defeat. A mounting effect is felt throughout in the progressively greater vehemence of the people expressing their impatience with those who dare oppose them, in the increasing contempt for legality and the thinness of the legal pretences employed, and in the steady falling away of those intimidated by the threats of the raging mob until at last all opposition has vanished.

After those who are inclined in favor of the motion of Euryptolemus encounter the fury of the majority, we hear no more of any resistance from them. This test of strength successfully met, the party of Theramenes is now emboldened to make a still more arrogant move: "When Lysiscus thereupon proposed that these men also should be judged by the very same vote as the generals, unless they withdrew the summons, the mob broke out again with shouts of approval, and they were compelled to withdraw the summons." All resistance from the floor thus removed, the issue now lay solely with those who were presiding, whose opposition alone remained to be dealt with. "When some of the Prytanes refused to put the question to the vote in violation of the law, Callixinus again mounted the platform and urged the same charge against them." Thus, with the demagogues abandoning all pretence at legality and openly resorting to coercion, and with the wrath of the mob grown to an ungovernable magnitude as its passion is enflamed by the submission of all opponents to its blind will, we are now effectively prepared for the climax at last: "The crowd cried out to summon to court those who refused. So the Prytanes, stricken with fear, agreed to put the question,—all of them except Socrates, the son of Sophroniscus, who said that in no case would he act except in accordance with the law!"

Now the development of this entire scene was obviously contrived with no other object in view than to set off the adamant refusal of the great philosopher in the face of overwhelming constraint. All objections that Xenophon in according Socrates only this one line is slighting him or that he does not recognize the meaning of his life are intolerable and can only arise from a profound misconception of the artistry of the description. So far from neglecting to mention the presence of Socrates, Xenophon is rather resisting the temptation to mention him or even to intimate his association in any way whatever with the proceedings, but carefully guarding his secret until the moment for which he has so long been preparing, he then at last suddenly acquaints us with the presence of Socrates at the very crisis which alone was sufficiently grand to give meaning to his act. And just as Xenophon is careful not to prejudice the effect through untimely anticipation, he does not dissipate it by ponderously dwelling on the morality of Socrates' deed after it has been mentioned or try by words to increase an impression already rendered supreme.

We have remarked that Xenophon has depicted this scene
with skill and, although it is indeed unmistakable that great
care has gone into its making, it is nevertheless, in one respect
at least, not altogether perfect. It contains an artistic flaw.
Much of the effect Xenophon gains by imposing upon himself
a judicious restraint and refusing to dispel an effect so skil-
fully conveyed is lost by his failure to separate carefully the
scene in question from the action which follows, and as a
result the development which culminates in Socrates seems
to continue and merge evenly with the activity which succeeds it. The latter is the speech of Euryptolemus which,
coming where it does, poses a difficult problem. Out of de-
votion to Socrates we would like to believe that, so profound
was the influence that the great philosopher exerted by his
firm resistance, the anger of the people subsided to the point
that Euryptolemus was able to command their attention. Some
such thing as this may in fact have happened. What is presently in question, however, is Xenophon's description of what
happened, and this version—let us make bold to declare—is
simply impossible. No amount of philosophic defiance conceivable would have been able in a short time to quell the
raging passion of the crowd Xenophon here presents Euryptolemus as addressing. This is the same Euryptolemus, moreover, who, as Xenophon gives us to believe, but a few minutes
before had been so intimidated by a virtual threat of death
that he withdrew his support and abandoned the hapless generals to their fate. In the speech, however, he expresses an
opinion and urges a course of action in full contradiction to
the outrageous demands before which minutes earlier he had
shrunk in trepidation. His address is extended, reasoned, un-
impassioned; there is nothing to indicate that it was interrupted or indeed that it was not heard out by a patient and,
to judge by its tone, even sympathetic audience. The literary
critic would say at this point that the action was poorly
motivated and unconvincing. In short, art has somewhere in-
tervened, and Xenophon has taken liberties with his matter.
Either the address of Euryptolemus did not, as Xenophon
leads us to believe, immediately follow the scene which

culminates in Socrates' refusal, but occurred much later, many hours or even days; or the fury of the assembly has been deliberately exaggerated to point up the effect of Socrates' defiance. And Xenophon's neglect to set off distinctly the account of the tumult from that of Euryptolemus' address is partly the reason why the effect that Xenophon so earnestly tried to achieve in this scene has nevertheless gone unobserved.

Finally, we have to deal with the opinion that at the time he wrote this account Xenophon had not yet recognized the significance of Socrates which he came to appreciate only by the time of the *Memorabilia,* wherein, in contrast to the *Hellenica,* Xenophon accords the deeds and sayings of his master a satisfactory treatment. But we need only recall the full impression of the scene that Xenophon has just presented to our imagination: the furious rabble maddened at the show of resistance to its arbitrary will, the demagogues encompassing by lawless threats the submission of all opponents, and finally Socrates set over against it all alone, unmindful of the tumult and unterrified by the threat of death—in this we have the proper reply to all charges of neglect, unfamiliarity, or want of appreciation by Xenophon of his great teacher; the effective rejoinder to all idle considerations about Socrates' precise relation to the other Prytanes, his being designated with or without his patronymic, and his deeds being allotted this one brief notice rather than the sympathy and appreciation supposedly indicated by the detailed version of the *Memorabilia.* And just the same is to be said of the objection that no account is given in the *Hellenica* of Socrates' trial and his death. This can of course be accounted for on other grounds, but with regard to the present argument it is only necessary to ask what purpose would be served by such a report. It would have furnished us with interesting information about the proceedings of his trial, but it could have added nothing to our interpretation of Socrates' *character.* The circumstances of a formal arraignment, besides, permitted him to meditate at length beforehand on his deportment and his defence to the jurors, but his behavior before the Assembly was perforce

a spontaneous and instinctive reaction to the supreme challenge to the sincerity of his life. "But the *Memorabilia!*"
Yes, the pleasant, moral, garrulous *Memorabilia:* it must
surely have been written at a time when Xenophon knew
Socrates well, but did not yet understand him; when he was
surprised by his character, but not astonished at it; and at a
time when he regarded him as an outstanding figure of his
day, but did not yet recognize him as one of the few great
individuals of all time.

The second example will differ somewhat from that with
which we have just dealt and the one we are later to examine.
Those other two concern interpretations of the versions Xenophon has written of certain historical incidents; in the present
case, however, we shall consider a version of history he *failed*
to write.

The final narrative of the *Hellenica* (vii. 5) describes the
operations preliminary to the Battle of Mantinea and concludes with the account of the battle itself. This section
primarily concerns the activities of two leading figures in the
history of Greek affairs, Agesilaus and Epaminondas. For
the moment we shall say nothing of the former, but it will
not be possible to proceed without first considering Xenophon's presentation of the great Boeotarch. The ordinary
interpretation of Epaminondas is that, as the representative
of the Theban ascendancy, he offends against Xenophon's
partiality to Sparta, so that Xenophon is reluctant to show
him in a commendable light. He cannot bring himself, for
example, to mention the presence of Epaminondas at the
Battle of Leuctra, and indeed he keeps the Theban leader and
his achievements generally out of sight throughout the account of the Theban incursions into the Peloponnesus. When
at length, however, Epaminondas' part in the affairs of Greece
becomes so prominent that it can no longer be supressed, the
historian is forced "to give the devil his due, as it were," and
"from the unwilling pen of Xenophon" at last the belated
distinction is conferred.

We must have no patience with this view. Whatever we

may think of Xenophon's disposition toward Sparta, his
neglect, if so it be, of Epaminondas cannot be attributed to
any feelings of hostility, since the tribute Epaminondas finally
draws, so far from being that due the devil, is much more
worthy of a saint. No other figure in the entire *Hellenica*, one
might venture to say, does Xenophon hold up to our admiration in higher terms of honest praise than the great Theban
leader, and if the commendation Xenophon bestows on him
was grudingly elicited from an unwilling pen, then the historian is simply to be trusted in nothing he says. In fact,
the section—τὰ Ἐπαμεινωνδιακὰ it could almost be called
—in which the exploits of the Theban general are described
(vii. 5. 8-end) is less a narrative written for the sake of the
events themselves than a disquisition on the resourcefulness
of Epaminondas in his final campaign. The history itself in
this remarkable passage serves as little more than a back-
ground for the study of Epaminondas' tactics, and in fact so
little notice is taken of other events, which are usually mentioned at all only when they are incidental to Theban activities, that a number of particulars important to our understanding of the enemy's movements are omitted altogether from
the account. Attention throughout is fixed on Epaminondas:
great significance is attached to his every act, however in-
conspicuous; his failures are turned off as successes; and even
his great moral fault of aspiring to the domination of Greece
is extenuated in such a way as to cast doubt on the sincerity
of Xenophon's most fundamental convictions on that subject.

But the manner in which Epaminondas is treated in this
passage is also surprising in view of what is usually regarded
as the first axiom of Xenophon's historiography. It is not that
he actually fabricates history outright, say the many exponents
of this view; his method consists rather in distortion, suppression, and exaggeration; in minimizing or omitting the achievements of those who represent ideals contrary to his own and
in exaggerating the importance of events that suit his own
moral and political interests. His presentation at this point of
Epaminondas, the enemy of Agesilaus, the support of demo-
cracies and the bane of Sparta and her allies, is disturbing

enough for the soundness of this commonly held thesis, but it is in his treatment of Agesilaus that its validity is actually decided. Many examinations have been made of the way in which Xenophon wrote this closing section of the *Hellenica,* but a more promising approach would be to observe the way he *refrained* from writing it. For it is remarkable that the nature of these events is such as to lend itself with the greatest facility to suppression, omission, and distortion for producing an impression precisely the contrary of that which Xenophon chose herein to give.

Perhaps no more inviting opportunity for convincing exaggeration presents itself anywhere in the *Hellenica* than the episode of the defence of Sparta. Agesilaus, Xenophon's great hero, ineffective and all but forgotten for many pages, returns at last (vii. 5. 10-13) for a final appearance, and his actions at this moment were among the finest of his splendid career. To have attempted to defend the unwalled city with a small number of soldiers against a full army, to have sent less than a hundred men attacking uphill against an overwhelming number of opponents, and to have gained the desperate victory in that attack constitutes one of the most glorious achievements in all of Spartan history. Xenophon does not discredit these performances; his account, in fact, gives us just enough evidence for thinking that they were capable of a much more favorable treatment. For if he does not minimize them, neither does he magnify them, and although the description is somewhat dramatic it is much too brief. Thus Xenophon forgoes this unparalleled opportunity to end his history extolling the achievements of his great hero, Agesilaus, and hastens instead to return to the activities of Epaminondas, with whom he seems thoroughly preoccupied.

Yet just how important were these activities? Perhaps one will object that, however much Xenophon would have liked to enlarge on Agesilaus' brilliant defence of his city and to make that the last major event of the *Hellenica,* his sense of historical accuracy forbade him to take this liberty and required that due attention be given to Epaminondas' part in the events of major significance that followed. But is this really so? And what did Epaminondas actually accomplish? Xenophon begins the narrative of his operations by defending himself for devoting great attention to manoeuvres which, however interesting to the study of military tactics, had no influence on the course of history. And the Battle of Mantinea, which Xenophon is in such a hurry to get to, was so meaningless and ineffecutal that he is left with its lack of results rather than its results to dwell on after it is over. Nevertheless, if of no importance to the outcome of history, the encounter affords an excellent occasion for observing the bold though inconsequential activities of Epaminondas, whom Xenophon enormously admired.

It is in no way here being maintained, however, that the passage Xenophon wrote as an ending to his history is at all inappropriate, for in fact the tenor of the concluding remarks alone probably tells us as much about the spirit of Greek history in the fourth century as can be inferred from the contents of the preceding five books, and it is an ending which for the purpose it was calculated to serve is stylistically very effective. But the passage is also one of the most effective for testing the thesis that the author made use of suppression, exaggeration, and concealment to present certain parties in a favorable light and to humiliate their enemies.

Xenophon's history of the fourth century begins with the campaigns of Agesilaus, and it is the activities of that figure which more than those of any other dominate the course of events throughout the remainder of the work. There was every incentive, therefore, whether from considerations of style and organization, or of the author's partiality, to encourage him to bring his history to a close in a memorable scene devoted to his great ideal, whose heroic defence of Sparta, if Xenophon's own account can be trusted, must have been a notable and stirring achievement. But instead he relinquishes all the possibilities of a situation so favorable that one might almost think it especially devised for treatment by a writer employing the method Xenophon is accused of using, for if exaggeration and suppression are in evidence they have been used to effect the impression opposite to that called for by the conventional interpretation of Xenophon's historiography. He chooses instead to conclude his history by dramatizing the Battle of Mantinea, which in view of its brief and indecisive character could easily have been turned off as little more than a skirmish and could have been handled as an epilogue to the defence of Sparta, and by glorifying some tactical evolutions of Sparta's great enemy, which could have been omitted altogether.

In fine: if, as is generally agreed, Xenophon used distortion to magnify aristocracy, Sparta, and her leaders, in whose favor, as is also generally agreed, he was strongly prejudiced, why did he not employ his dubious skills on this very critical and yet most opportune occasion? To say that he was unable to do so is only to make him out as incompetent at his chosen art, for the situation is such that it lies easily within the powers of any writer, and particularly a dishonest one, to make of it what he please; and yet, in order to say that Xenophon did not want to do so, we must question the authority of a well-established principle of his method.

The final problem remaining to be discussed is one about which so much confusion reigns and which has been treated of in such a discouraging and irresponsible manner that it might understandably appear put off until last if not avoided altogether. It is the matter of Xenophon's prejudice. Its highly subjective nature renders it at once the easiest and the most difficult of all the problems of the composition of the *Hellenica,* since evidence of prejudice is the easiest to establish because it is impossible to refute. Unfortunately, scholars were not long in recognizing the singular possibilities held out by a subject of such an elusive character, and one despairs of putting before the reader an adequate impression of the disorder into which discussion of the topic has consequently fallen. No attempt to define prejudice; no recognition of the prodigious difficulties presented by problems of its kind; no signs of caution in the face of matter so fugitive as emotional dispositions and attitudes of the mind; no indication whatsoever, in a word, that the topic required anything but simple observation of whatever one looking for prejudice might care to take for its manifestations. When investigation of a literary work consists in reckoning the number of one's subjective reactions to an issue, computing totals for and against it, and simply letting the higher figure decide the inclination of an author's partiality, there is no telling what might emerge as the results of such a procedure, except that in the case of the *Hellenica* they would of course be expected to support the thesis that Xenophon was prejudiced in favor of Sparta and against Thebes, but a recent study has provided an instructive demonstration of the fatuousness of this arithmetic approach, though to have done so was the least intention of its author. With no apparent appreciation of the enormous complexities of its subject, this inquiry like others before it simply sets about counting sensations in the approved manner, only to find in the end that it has made a strong case for the opposition. Since it is guilty of employing the same crude methods in its turn, this study is naturally of as little value as those it happens to contradict, but it effectively illustrates the futility of expecting useful results when a matter better meant for their consideration as philosophers is taken in hand by scholars acting as clerks.

Yet Xenophon favored Sparta and disliked Thebes—this fact is undeniable. And once the premise, the existence of prejudice, has been established, there would remain only the process of detecting the particular instances of prejudice according to one's own subjective judgment and private criteria, and there is no controlling matters when they have reached this stage. We are therefore thrown back on the premise itself as the only area in which any hope remains of dealing with the problem; and yet how could one possibly hold that Xenophon does not show partiality in treating of, not to mention lesser matters, Sparta and Thebes? Nevertheless, there is no other way out than actually to challenge whether in some very important respect it has in fact been established that Xenophon was prejudiced toward these states. It is an ambitious task and perhaps futile besides; the probability of finding agreement is small and the opposition can be expected to be almost universal. But as this is the most important problem of Xenophon's historiography it cannot be honestly evaded.

We must begin by conceding a great deal. Xenophon admired Sparta. He viewed her in a grand light, and her name and memory are invested in his pages with an aura of sanctity and lofty feeling. He describes her deeds and her heroes in a noble manner and can find a dignity even in her disgrace. Thebes on the other hand merits no such reverential treatment. Her motives are regarded with a reserve that suggests suspicion, and there is evident at times, even in the narrative of her splendid achievements, a kind of courteous brevity by which Xenophon seems to convey his contempt.

Now making such a declaration would seem to end the matter at the outset and leave no reason for continuing to discuss such a question as, to begin with, that of Xenophon's prejudice toward Thebes; but in fact it settles very little until we first determine whether his want of esteem for that state arose from prejudice or—a question never raised—whether Thebes was in fact deserving of his affection. Let us begin by considering the role Thebes played in the history of the fourth century and the issue she represented to the Greeks of that age. Thebes was not a small state; had she been one, Xenophon's view of her might have been notably different. But it was more important that Thebes was not exactly a large state, either; she was of the second rank, just below but not equal with Athens and Sparta, the two great leaders of Greece. Yet Thebes had much to commend her. Her mythological origins and her traditions, for example, were inferior to none, and, although she could boast of no great number of distinguished literary figures, the few she had produced were accounted among the best. And as a military power her reputation was excellent. But Thebes also suffered under grave disadvantages. No one had quite forgotten, for one thing, that she had fought with Mardonius at Plataea, nor had she herself been permitted to forget that she had been humiliated in that conflict by her proud Athenian neighbors. But the circumstance that weighed most heavily against Theban ambition was a conviction which had long taken firm possession of the Greek mind and against which any aspirations of Thebes or of any power like her to rise above her traditional station were bound to offend, for it had come to be regarded as part of the settled order of Greek affairs that the general political leadership, or hegemony, of the Greek states was to be shared alone by Athens, who would lead by sea, and Sparta, who would lead by land. Such a policy had both received the support of tradition, on the one hand, and was so strongly recommended by the Greek sense of order and balance, besides, that the emulation of another for equality would have appeared intolerable—yet just this was the ambition of Thebes. In addition, there is no reason to believe that the principle of equilibrium which so strongly prevailed in the thinking of the rest of Greece was not also shared by the Thebans themselves. Nor is this refuted by the fact that the Thebans were the very ones who aspired to ascendancy, since confirmed and enduring conviction is not the same as a momentary feeling, and the latter, especially when incited by encouraging prospects, often prevails; and we may therefore imagine that the Thebans did little to conciliate the outraged sentiments of their fellow Greeks in displaying before them that overweening behavior which inevitably accompanies a quickly conceived ambition conscious to itself of the insecurity of its claims. Had Thebes been content to requite the arrogance she had suffered at the hands of the Spartans and chastise them severely, she might have merited the respect of Greece. But Thebes was an upstart, and upstarts do not observe such limitations. "The Thebans were continually planning how they might obtain the hegemony of Greece" *(Hellenica* vii. 1. 33).

Therefore, if we choose to reproach Xenophon for viewing the ambition of the Thebans with disrespect, we must first establish the likelihood that Theban intentions were worthy of respect, and before we can charge him with prejudice, in the proper sense of that word, in his treatment of Theban actions, we must be prepared to show that his conception of those actions was one peculiar to himself and was not a conviction generally shared by his contemporaries.

But perhaps there are many who would not be too unwilling to accept in itself some such construction of Xenophon's attitude toward Thebes, if only his feelings toward Sparta were equally as objective. Our judgment of Xenophon's treatment of Thebes must be modified by his treatment of Sparta, for it is difficult to believe that he could look upon Sparta with adulation and nevertheless be objective toward her enemy, Thebes, since the tendency toward excessive admiration of a party has as its negative manifestation and natural correlative the disdain of that party's opponents. It is also unmistakable that Xenophon viewed Sparta in a special light and treated her differently from the other states of Greece, and this would hardly seem fair. Sparta's crime after all—and Xenophon is here our best witness—was the same as Thebes' in that each aspired to empire, to which neither was entitled. Perhaps some difference lies in the fact that, whereas Thebes went beyond her rightful sphere and sought to exercise a control to which she had no claim, Sparta's offence consisted more in abusing a leadership which was acknowledged by the other states of Greece. But this is a pedantic distinction, and it certainly would do little to exonerate Xenophon from the generally accepted charge of being philo-Laconian. Nevertheless, although it is true that Sparta's having a traditional claim to leadership in Greece should not have made her transgressions appear any more venial than similar ones of ordinary states, could there somehow be any significance in the very fact itself that Sparta, after all, had won general recognition of her superior status? Yet how could even this consideration bear on the universally acknowledged charge levelled against Xenophon of being philo-Laconian?

We should be making a great mistake in thinking that the influence exerted by Sparta on the rest of Greece proceeded from no other cause than a superiority in size and power. Sparta was more than a state; to Greece she was an institution. To the Greek mind, the ancient ideals of the Hellenic race had been preserved in the constitution and the traditions of Lacedaemon. The qualities that recommended her to her contemporaries of classical times were not, to be sure, the splendid virtues of Athens. Sparta could boast no intellectual accomplishments. She was no restless center of innovation and emprise, no spectacle of physical magnificence, not the Ionic purveyor of change and ideas that was Athens. The excellence of Sparta consisted rather in having retained something old and honored than in having devised something new. If Athens was admired, Sparta was revered. The sophistication and enlightenment which distinguished the classical Greeks had not so far removed them from their former condition that their conception of virtue had ceased to be dominated by the severe and simple ideals of primitive military society, and it was in Sparta that these ideals were thought to have survived. As a soldier alone, the Spartan was looked upon by his fellow Greeks with a reverence that was wonderful, and considering the renown of that nation as the best soldiers of their day if not of all antiquity, such an estimation, made not by those who beheld the Spartan from afar but who on many disastrous occasions had met him in the field, cannot lightly be set aside. Whatever may be said of the differences that had come to pass by the fourth century between Sparta's reputation for virtue and the realities of its fulfillment, the great respect she commanded from her fellow Greeks even in her decline cannot merely be set down to unrealistic adulation of an expired ideal. However much she was generally agreed to have merited the punishment that was visited upon her, the fall of Sparta must have been an event the Greek beheld with painful eyes. For Sparta had stood as a testimony to the superiority of the Hellenic race. The issue of her permanence was one which far exceeded that of the decline of one of the states of Greece; as Sparta fell, the rest of Greece, to the extent to which it was identified with her, fell too. Sparta had supplied that need for the Greeks which all people feel of having available a model of virtue with which they stand in some close relation and of which they can vicariously partake, admiring safely from afar; to whose exalted condition, however, they make no pretention themselves, if indeed they would not actually eschew it. When the Greek derived satisfaction from the differences which separated him from the rest of the world, he was in large measure secretly comparing the barbarian's dissolution and excess with the austere discipline and continence of Sparta. The Greek's faith in Sparta was almost equivalent to faith in himself. Every Greek was philo-Laconian.

In conclusion: we are not yet ready to interpret ancient histories, like the *Hellenica*. Before determining how, why, when, and where the ancients wrote, we must first discover what they wrote.

BIBLIOGRAPHY

Standard histories and works of reference (Busolt's *Gr. Gesch.*, the *C. A. H.*, the *F. Gr. Hist.*, etc) have not been included.

Banderet, Albert. *Untersuchungen zu Xenophons Hellenika*. Basel 1919.

Breitenbach, Ludwig. *Xenophons Hellenika*. Vol. I. 2nd ed. Berlin, 1884.

Bruns, Ivo. *Das literarische Porträt der Griechen*. Berlin, 1896.

Büchsenschütz, B. *Xenophons Griechische Geschichte*. Vol. I. 7th ed. Leipzig (Teubner), 1908.

————. "Xenophons Hellenika Buch I," *Rheinisches Museum*, XXVII (1889), 497-519.

Bury, John B. *The Ancient Greek Historians*. London, 1909.

————. *A History of Greece*. 3rd ed. rev. by R. Meiggs. London, 1951.

Busolt, Georg. "Zur Chronologie Xenophons," *Hermes*, XXXIII (1898), 661-64.

Campe, J. Ch. F. "Die Kämpfe der Athener und der Peloponnesier im Hellespont (411-409)," *Jahrbücher für classische Philologie*, CV (1872), 701-22.

Clinton, Henry Fynes. *Fasti Hellenici*. Vol. II. Oxford, 1834.

Colin, Gaston. *Xénophon Historien d'après le livre II des Helléniques*. Paris, 1933.

Croiset, Alfred. *Xénophon, son caractère et son talent*, Paris, 1873.

Dakyns, H. G. *The Works of Xenophon*. Vol. I, London, 1890. Vol. II, London, 1892.

Delebecque, Édouard, *Essai sur la vie de Xénophon*. Paris, 1957.

De Sanctis, Gaetano. "La genesi delle Elleniche di Senofonte," *Annali della R. Scuola Normale Superiore di Pisa: Lettere, Storia e Filosofia*, Serie II, I (1932), 15-35.

————. Review of *Xénophon: Helléniques*, Vol. I, by J. Hatzfeld, *Rivista di Filologia*, n. s. XVI (1938), 69-78.

Dindorf, L. "Ueber die Ueberschrift der griech. Geschichte des Xenophon," *Neue Jahrbücher für Philologie und Paedagogik* (known after 1856 as *Jahrbücher für classische Philologie*), IV (1832), 254-56. Translated into English with a valuable note not in the original, in the *Classical Museum*, II (1833) 241-43.

Dittenberger, W. "Sprachliche Kriterien für die Chronologie der Platonischen Dialoge," *Hermes*, XVI (1881), 321-45.

Freese, Leopold. *Ueber den Plan, welchen Xenophon im zweiten Theile seiner hellenischen Geschichte verfolgt*. Stralsund, 1865.

Fricke, Wilhelm. *Untersuchungen über die Quellen des Plutarchos im Nikias und Alkibiades*. Leipzig, 1869.

Friedrich, Gustav. "Zum Panegyrikos des Isokrates," *Jahrbücher für classische Philologie*, CXLVII (1893), 1-24.

————. "Zu Xenophons Hellenika und Agesilaos," *Jahrbücher für classische Philologie*, CLIII (1896), 289-99.

Gigante, Marcello, *Le Elleniche di Ossirinco*. Rome, 1949.

Gomme, Arnold W. *A Historical Commentary on Thucydides*. Vol. I. Oxford, 1945.

Grenfell, Bernard P. and Hunt, Arthur S. *The Oxyrhynchus Papyri.* Part VI. London, 1908.

Grosser, Richard. *Zur Characteristik der Epitome von Xenophon's Hellenika.* Barmen, 1873.

Hartman, J. J. *Analecta Xenophontea.* Leipzig, 1887.

Hatzfeld, Jean. "Le début des 'Helléniques,' " *Mélanges Desrousseaux.* Paris, 1937.

————. "Notes sur la composition des Helléniques," *Revue de Philologie,* IV (1930), 113-27, 209-26.

————. *Xénophon: Helléniques.* Vol. I. Série Budé. Paris, 1936.

Herbst, L. F. *Die Schlacht bei den Arginusen.* Hamburg, 1855.

Jungclaussen, W. Th. *De Campio et Büchsenschützio Xenophontis Hellenicorum interpretibus.* Meldorf, 1862.

Krüger, Karl Wilhelm. *De Xenophontis vita: quaestiones criticae.* Halle, 1882.

————. "Prüfung der Niebuhrschen Ansicht über Xenophons Hellenika," *Historisch-philologische Studien,* I. Berlin, 1836.

————. *Untersuchungen über das Leben des Thukydides.* Berlin, 1832.

Lipsius, A. *Ueber den einheitlichen Charakter der Hellenika des Xenophon.* Luckau, 1857.

Ludwig, Alfred. "Ueber den Anfang von Xenophons Hellenika," *Jahrbücher für classische Philologie,* XCV (1867), 151-57.

MacLaren, Malcolm, Jr. "On the Composition of Xenophon's Hellenica," *The American Journal of Philology,* LV (1934), 121-39, 249-62.

Marchant, E. C. and Underhill, G. E. *Xenophon: Hellenica.* Oxford, 1906.

Meyer, Wilhelm. *De Xenophontis Hellenicorum auctoris in rebus scribendis fide et usu.* Halle, 1867.

Müller, E. H. O. *De Xenophontis Historiae Graecae parte priori.* Leipzig, 1856.

Müller, Rudolf. *Quaestionum Xenophontearum capita duo.* Halle, 1907.

Nitsche, Wilhelm. *Ueber die Abfassung von Xenophons Hellenika.* Berlin, 1871.

Opitz, Alfonsus. "Quaestiones Xenophonteae: de Hellenicorum atque Agesilai necessitudine," *Breslauer Philologische Abhandlungen,* XLVI (1913), 1-88.

Rapaport, Arthurus. "Xenophontea," *Eos.* XXVII (1924), 19-27.

Rausch, Alfred. *Quaestiones Xenophonteae.* Halle, 1881.

Reiske, Io. Iac. *Dionysii Halicarnassensis opera.* Vol. V. Leipzig. 1775. Vol. VI, Leipzig, 1777.

Richards, Herbert. "The Hellenics of Xenophon," *The Classical Review,* XV (1901), 197-203.

Riemann, O. *Qua rei criticae tractandae ratione Hellenicon Xenophontis textus constituendus sit.* Paris, 1879.

Roquette, Adalbertus, *De Xenophontis Vita.* Königsberg, 1884.

Rosenstiel, Fredericus. *De Xenophontis Historiae Graecae parte bis edita.* Jena, 1882.

Sauppe, Gustav. *Xenophontis Historia Graeca.* Leipzig, 1886.

Schambach, Otfried. *Untersuchungen über Xenophon's Hellenika.* Jena, 1871.

Schwartz, Eduard. "Quellenuntersuchungen zur griechischen Geschichte," *Rheinisches Museum für Philologie,* XLIV (1889), 104-26, 161-93.

Seyffert, Gualtherus. *De Xenophontis Agesilao quaestiones.* Göttingen, 1909.

Sievers, G. R. *Commentationes historicae de Xenophontis Hellenicis.* Vol. I. Berlin, 1833.

Sordi, Marta. 'I caratteri dell'opera storiografica di Senofonte nelle Elleniche," Part I, *Athenaeum*, n.s. XXVIII (1950), 3-53; Part II, XXIX (1951), 273-384.

Spiller, Josephus. *Quaestionum de Xenophontis historia Graeca specimen.* Breslau, 1843.

Stahl, J. M. Review of *De Xenophontis Vita*, by A. Roquette, *Philologischer Anzeiger*, XVI, (1886), 34-43.

Volckmar, C. H. *De Xenophontis Hellenicis commentatio.* Göttingen, 1837.

Vorrenhagen, Elizabeth. *De orationibus quae sunt in Xenophontis Hellenicis.* Elberfeld, 1926.

Treves, Piero. "Per la cronologie di Senofonte," *Mélanges Desrousseaux.* Paris, 1937.

von Fritz, Kurt and Kapp, Ernst. *Aristotle's Constitution of Athens and Related Texts.* New York, 1950.

Watson, J. S. and Dale, Henry. *The Cyropaedia and the Hellenics.* London, 1861.

Weber, Philipp. *Entwickelungsgeschichte der Absichtssätze*, II, Part II of the *Beiträge zur historischen Syntax der griechischen Sprache*, edited by M. Schanz. Würzburg, 1885.

INDEX OF SUBJECTS

(Numbers in Parenthesis Indicate Footnotes)

214

INDEX OF AUTHORS

DATE DUE

OCT 6　'70			
OCT 2 8 '70			
MR 1 5 '79			
AP 5　'79			
NO 1 9 /9			
DE 10'84			
GAYLORD			PRINTED IN U.S.A.